KNOCKSHINNOCH

THE GREATEST MINES RESCUE IN HISTORY

IAN MCMURDO

THE AUTHOR

Ian McMurdo is a retired education professional who has become an author. He is the son of the late John McMurdo, one of the survivors of the Knockshinnoch Castle Colliery disaster.

From the day his mother, Jean, handed sixteen-year-old Ian a copy of the British Government's formal inquiry into the causes of the disaster, he became captivated by the fearsome drama that was Knockshinnoch. The subject was never discussed in the family home, never at any time. As Jean later put it, 'we didn't ever speak about it, we just pretended that it had never happened and life went on'.

However, Ian had already made up his mind. One day, he promised himself, I'm going to lift the lid on the Knockshinnoch disaster and write a book telling the full story, warts and all.

This is that book.

Other books by Ian McMurdo:

A Life Worth Living
Dogmanese for Daydreamers
The Juniors – the Story of Cumnock Juniors Football Club

KNOCKSHINNOCH

THE GREATEST MINES RESCUE
IN HISTORY

IAN MCMURDO

CARN PUBLISHING

© Ian McMurdo, 2015.
First Published in Great Britain, 2015.

ISBN - 978 1 9110430 1 0

Published by Carn Publishing,
Lochnoran House,
Auchinleck, Ayrshire, KA18 3JW.

www.carnpublishing.com

Printed by Bell & Bain Ltd,
Glasgow, G46 7UQ.

Contents

This book is dedicated to the memory
of my father, John McMurdo

Acknowledgements

I would wish to extend my sincere gratitude to the following people, for their unswerving and ever-dependable support in the face of my outrageous demands on their time during the writing of this book.

My brother-in-law, Dr Bill Turner, for performing the role of 'critical friend' throughout the entirety of this project. I am indebted to Bill for his determination to challenge my interpretation of research statistics, his meticulous attention to detail, and his uncanny ability to translate complex medical jargon into words that mere laypersons like I can actually understand.

My trusty old pal, Dan Park, for having the courage to allow himself to resurrect his own personal and painful mental imagery of the disaster scenario. Dan's amazing capacity to bring these events back to life, together with the dramatic testimonies of numerous eye-witnesses, were critically important in enabling me to 'feel' my own way through the unrelenting drama of that fateful weekend in September 1950.

Professor Paul Younger, Rankine Chair of Engineering and Professor of Energy Engineering, Glasgow University, for his willing and ongoing support. A recognised world authority on mining, Paul's advice on the highly technical and often sinister world of underground working was of great assistance to me.

Douglas Skelton, who provided an experienced 'author's eye view' as the text developed.

Andrew Watson, Commercial and Operations Director, British Mines Rescue Service, for his technical advice all along. New Cumnock born-and-bred, Andrew's intimate knowledge of mines rescue procedures in general, and of the Knockshinnoch disaster scenario in particular, were invaluable to me.

I would also like to thank the following organisations and individuals for their advice and support throughout the project.

The Coal Authority, Mansfield; The Burns' Centre, Kilmarnock; The Scottish Mining Institute, Newtongrange; The Mining Museum, Edinburgh; The National Library Association; Bank Pit Miners' Reunion Group; BBC Scotland; The Cumnock Chronicle; South Ayrshire Council; East Ayrshire Council; The Ayrshire Post; Trinity Mirror; George Sanderson; Molly Sanderson; Dan Stillie; James 'Dick' Armour; May Robertson; Molly Robertson; Billy McMichael; Jim Cameron; Ian Purdie; Jimmy Cairns; Charlie Husband; Bill Ritchie; Tom Smith; Ronnie Storey; Dan Jess; Catherine Gemmell; Margaret Benson; Sammy Brown; Jimmy McCreadie; Matt Burns; Isobel Walker; Jenny Carballo (Walker); Anna Copland; George McConnell; Bob Dickson; 'Jessie'; Maureen Webb; May Miller; Eddie Smith; Billy Harrison; Christine McGilly; Roddy McVake; Willie Lopez; Jessie Lopez (Lee); John Mills; Sam McCracken; Matt Brown; Andrew McDicken; Jean McMurdo; George Harvey; Alastair Wilson; Billy Turnbull; Robert 'Rab' Cockburn; James 'Jas' Ferguson; Graham Guest; Ellie Swinbank; Elaine Clayton.

Introduction

My father was John McMurdo, the son of a coalminer of the same name.

Born in 1920, he left school in 1934 to go 'down the pit', just as his own father had done before him. He did so because in those days there was very little option. As soon as a New Cumnock lad hit his fourteenth birthday, he dumped his schoolbag and he went down the pit, plain and simple. Anything bordering on academic or professional ambition was the domain of the privileged few.

My father was a very clever lad at school, top of his class in fact. One afternoon in the late 'sixties when I was studying for my own 'Higher' exams in preparation for the life of academia that he could only ever have dreamt about, my mother showed me some of the books he had won for his sterling school achievements. One of them was called *Tom Brown's Schooldays*, written by Thomas Hughes. The book was a bit tattered in appearance and it had been signed by his headmaster, whose name now escapes me. Apparently it is an English classic, but you could have fooled me. I found it about as interesting as ditch water. However, my father had won that book for being first in his class, which was all that mattered to me.

Another one of the 'books' which my mother showed me that afternoon was the report of the official inquiry into the Knockshinnoch Castle Colliery Disaster of September 1950, which I found considerably more interesting than Master Brown's decidedly dreich schooldays. I also found it very sad. You see, my father was one of the 129 coalminers who had found themselves buried half-a-mile below the earth in the most high-profile mining disaster in history, while his frantic 24-year-old wife and 16-month-old baby son were left helpless up above on terra firma.

Try as I might, I never did manage to purge the unspeakable horror of his three-day-long entombment from my mind. A total of thirteen men perished beneath the farming fields of New Cumnock that fateful weekend, leaving behind their distraught wives and children, mothers and fathers, brothers and sisters. My own father survived along with the others, but according to my mother he was never the same again, and the whole hellish experience changed him for ever.

Not once since the disaster did the man known to his friends as 'Big Jock' ever mention what happened during that awful weekend, not even to his own wife or children. However, I have always wanted to tell his story.

The real story of Knockshinnoch. The miners' story.

PROLOGUE

A Walk in the Hills

The village of New Cumnock is situated on the south-eastern extremity of the delightful county of Ayrshire, the very last outpost before entering neighbouring Dumfriesshire. Immortalised in song by Scotland's national bard, Robert Burns, the famous Afton Water 'flows gently' in a perfect south-to-north direction all the way from the Afton Reservoir in the shadow of Blackcraig mountain, to New Cumnock itself, where it finally bids farewell to the village before joining the River Nith on its meandering journey to the Solway Firth.

In the hope-laden years following the Second World War, a magnificent new state-of-the-art colliery sat proudly beside the west bank of the Afton. It was called Knockshinnoch Castle, and it was by far the largest of over a dozen collieries located in what was known as the New Cumnock Coalfield. The next largest was the Bank Auld Pit, located one mile further west behind the miners' rows in the tiny village of Connel Park. Between them, the two collieries provided employment for over one thousand men.

'Coal was King', the thumping heartbeat of this proud little community.

And then during one fateful weekend in September 1950, its relentless pursuit finally led to disaster. A disaster of such magnitude and horror that it would hit the front pages of major newspapers all across the planet.

Today, the surface terrain between the sites of the neighbouring collieries is hopelessly overgrown. It is essentially a long and desolate stretch of rugged old roadways and boggy moorland, as my two mud-loving Labrador Retrievers discovered to their huge delight when we made the journey on foot one glorious summer's afternoon. That day, our chaperone was 'weel-kent' New Cumnock-born worthy, Knockshinnoch veteran Dan Park.

I really ought to have known better. Within minutes of our arrival at the site of the former Knockshinnoch pit-head, Dan had become visibly shaken by the eerie silence of the whole thing. After all, vivid memories of the colliery's perpetual hustle-and-bustle were still reverberating in his well-worn ears. That sultry afternoon, though, the silence hit Dan in the guts like a sledgehammer.

It was a deep, intense silence that wept wordlessly of great days turned sour, and screamed of tragedy.

'I just cannae get my bearings at all, Ian,' he muttered in head-shaking frustration as we stood at the top of Castle Hill, the old concrete roadway that leads to a large flat area, a hundred yards or so above Knockshinnoch farm. This was the area of land which once housed the enormous pit-head operation that was Knockshinnoch Castle Colliery itself.

As Dan spoke, he couldn't have been more uncomfortable than if a rabid fox had just run up his trouser leg.

'There's something no' quite right here, Ian. It's just no' right at all.'

Try as he might, Dan simply couldn't piece the jigsaw together. He instinctively remembered many of the old pit-head's main features, but their precise juxtaposition was proving impossible for him to figure out. The pit canteen was the first building you came to, he assured me, situated on the left at the top of Castle Hill, but there was something wrong with the hill's trajectory. The engineer's shop was over there at about eleven-o'clock, but where exactly? This meant that the boiler house must have been over yonder. But no, that couldn't be right, because the washers were housed away over there in the other direction. The only thing he knew for sure was that the magazine (explosives) store was up that hill in front, where those three bovine beasts now grazed in blissful ignorance of frustrated human nostalgia.

As Dan leapt over a succession of fences in his 82nd year, a pair of fine big chestnut-coloured horses stared at him in bemusement, before returning to munch on the lush green grass.

'So Ian, if the boiler house was here, and the washers were over there, then the pit shaft must have been round about here, in fact just where we're standing right now.'

Then he stroked his chin for the one thousandth time. 'But no, that cannae be right. Och, it just disnae make sense, nae sense at all.'

And so it went on, Dan straddling assorted drystane dykes and wooden fences on a determined mission, as my dogs and I skipped after him like impressionable rats trailing in the footsteps of their pied piper. We made our way down the gentle hillside in a south-easterly direction. It took us towards the Afton Cemetery, which lies peacefully above Danny's Brig on the banks of the magnificent Afton Water.

That afternoon, Dan Park wasn't the only one to be overcome by a huge wave of nostalgia. How vividly I remembered my own grandmother taking me as a toddler along the banks of the famous river and across Danny's Brig, to return via Afton Road to her home in New Cumnock's bustling town centre, The Castle. New Cumnock was a very special place for me as a child, and it will always have a very special place in my heart. The sun shone from dawn till dusk, and my granny's kitchen always smelled of freshly-baked girdle scones.

'Wait a wee minute!' Dan suddenly exclaimed, grabbing my shoulder and snapping me out of my wistful daydream.

'It's coming back to me now, as if it was yesterday!' he announced excitedly. 'We had been working on the pit-head on the Friday, the morning after the disaster. "Right boys, take your piece-break now," we were told. Everybody was running all over the place, trying to do anything they could to help. It was chaos, pure chaos, and hardly a word was spoken. We were all in shock, I suppose. As I was drinking my tea, my dad came up to me and told me to go down and see it for myself. The disaster scene, I mean.'

Dan paused momentarily, as if to compose himself in his resurrection of a memory so vividly intense that it had probably lain buried away in his sub-consciousness for the past 65 years.

'So Toe Melvin an' me walked down the hill. And I'll tell you this, Ian, I'd never seen anything like it in my life. It had stopped raining for the first time in several days, and the sun was shining onto the big field below the Laight farm over there. And that's when we saw it.'

Dan swallowed deeply.

'The hole, Ian, that's when we saw the hole. The big field that had been there … there forever … was gone. It was just gone … gone completely.'

Dan paused to clear his throat, before continuing. His voice was shaking.

'And there was this hole … this great hole in the ground, an enormous black hole. The crater, Ian, that's what they called it, the crater. And the sun just seemed to light it up like a great big torch. It would be impossible to describe the feeling in my guts when I saw it. It shook me to the core, Ian, it really did. The sight of the crater, the sheer enormity of the whole thing. It looked … it just looked … evil. It must have been the size of a fitba' field, maybe even bigger. And it had sunk 40, 50 or even 60 feet down below. It was black, and slimy … and stinkin', really stinkin'. There were at least a hundred men down there, most of them good pals of mine. A hundred men, Ian … a hundred men.'

As Dan and I stood there staring into the huge hollow which is now securely fenced off from its natural cover of leafy foliage and decorated by hundreds of big boulders that uncannily resemble ancient Neolithic headstones, not another word was spoken for a good couple of minutes. Even the dogs sat obediently by the memorial cairn that now stands silently as the sole testimony to a mining disaster that once gripped the world's attention like a giant malevolent vice.

It was Dan who eventually broke the silence. By now, there were tears in his eyes.

'I can still remember watching a pair of farm horses trying to haul some stuff through the fields towards the crater. They were up to their guts in muck. I'll never forget how sorry I felt for them, poor buggers.'

Suddenly, Dan let out a big hearty laugh, one clearly designed to cut through the horror of the indescribably dark images that had been flashing through his mind. I looked at him, seriously puzzled. The dogs reciprocated, tilting their heads first one way then the other.

'When Toe an' me were walking back up towards the pit-head that morning, a Daily Record reporter shouted over to us,' Dan recalled, with a forced laugh. 'The guy pointed to a great big puddle, and asked if we would mind jumping into it, so that he could take our photograph. Toe just looked at me, then glowered at the reporter and grunted, "away an' take a f - - - tae yoursel'!"'

The whole thing had simply been too much for Dan. He had just been transported over six decades back in time to revisit a scene that no eighteen-year-old should ever have had to witness. Now this quite remarkable and thoroughly engaging elderly gent was back in control of his emotions again, as he very skilfully shifted the focus from the sheer hopelessness of the blackest day in the village of New Cumnock's history to the irrepressible spirit and sharpness of wit that defined its incredibly courageous coalmining community.

'Right Ian, let's head for the Bank Pit!' Two hyperactive dogs barked in eager compliance.

We climbed back up the slope to the former site of the Knockshinnoch Castle pit-head, Dan still shaking his head in geographical bewilderment, and descended Castle Hill once more towards the farm. Turning one last time to look up the old access road, he made one final pronouncement which made me catch my breath.

'Your dad cycled up that road to his work every day, Ian. And he would have done exactly that the day the pit fell in.'

I felt a sickening jab in my stomach. Suddenly, it was all starting to become very real for me too. I thought of my own father picking up his 'pit-piece' that fateful afternoon, and kissing his young wife and baby son goodbye as he headed off to work on what was supposed to have been just another day, another ordinary day. He would then have cycled the one-mile trip to the Leggate district on the western boundary of New Cumnock, before turning left into Knockshinnoch Road, to the very spot where Dan and I were now standing. From there, he would have had to pedal like blazes up the final thirty-odd yards of Castle Hill's steep incline, before parking his bike outside the canteen and collecting metal token number 57 from timekeeper Sammy Brown. Finally, he would have walked into the engine room with his workmates – or 'neebors' as they were more affectionately dubbed - and found himself in a giant metal cage plummeting down into the bowels of the earth.

Try as I might, though, my cack-handed efforts at incident scene reconstruction stopped there and then, and for one very good reason. It is not a particularly good idea to force oneself to imagine the unimaginable.

'So Dan, where does that track over there lead?' I asked my expert guide, pointing up the moorland hill to our right, but somehow already knowing the answer that was coming.

'To the Bank Auld Pit,' Dan replied, 'so let's get going.'

Less than 30 minutes later, we had walked up the length of the old overgrown track and then down the long slope on the other side. We waded through a huge puddle of surface water at the foot of the valley, then straddled an old wooden gate before trudging up the shorter hill to a big white building which was surrounded by high-security fencing.

'This is the Bank sub-station, Ian.' Dan announced, clearly still very proud of his long association with the coalmining industry. 'In the old days, it supplied the electricity that powered the Bank Pit, as well as providing auxiliary power to operate the huge machines at Knockshinnoch. The power lines ran right above the route we've just followed over the hills. Even today, the sub-station still feeds the national grid.'

He then pointed to a spot about twenty yards away and slightly downhill from the modern-day sub-station.

'See right about there, Ian? That's where the entrance to Bank Number Six Mine was.'

A shiver ran up my spine. I just stood and stared in silent contemplation of past events that I had never witnessed, yet had somehow managed to import into a very secret compartment of my sub-consciousness. I was aware that Dan was watching me intently. He then turned, and with his forefinger, drew an imaginary circle on the grassy banking behind us.

'And that's where your mum would have been standing that night. Standing in the rain for hours on end, just praying that your dad might eventually get out alive.'

I walked up the banking and stood on the very spot that Dan had circled, trying to imagine the myriad of hellish emotions that must have been assaulting my mother's hopelessly confused mind on that bitter-cold Saturday night all those years ago, and those of other frantic loved ones in exactly the same boat.

The initial disbelief. The dawning realisation. The gut-wrenching horror. The sheer helplessness. The embryonic hope. The rising expectation. And of course, the indescribable terror that faint hope might collapse into desperate tragedy at any moment.

'I've got to tell this story, Dan,' I said. 'I've simply got to tell it.'

Dan just nodded, and smiled.

'I know you do, Ian,' he replied earnestly.

When he then narrowed his eyes and stared straight into my own with all the intensity of a laser beam, I just knew that his next words would be well worth heeding.

'But if you're going to tell the story of the Knockshinnoch disaster, first you need to meet the real people. Meet those who actually lived through every hour, minute and second of that whole weekend. Listen very carefully to what they have to say. Only then will you be able to tell your story. The real story of Knockshinnoch.'

PART 1:
OLD KING COAL

The Collier's Symphony

The year was 1938, and the venue was a little coalmining hamlet called Connel Park, situated half-a-mile to the west of the much larger village of New Cumnock.

It wasn't the gently-swaying beech trees in the foreground that captured the mood around these parts. Nor indeed was it the splendour of the gently rolling hills in the background. Instead, it was the dramatic backdrop of the Bank Auld Pit's 'three lums' that dominated the skyline above the famous miners' rows, those towering brick-built chimneys clearly visible from a distance of some five miles or more.

The first lum sprang skywards from the mighty boiler house, whose job it was to generate the vast quantities of high-pressure steam that powered the enormous wheels of the winding gear, much better known as 'the horrals'. The horrals' task was to haul the coalminers up Bank Number One shaft in a mechanical cage, all the way from the ebony blackness of the bowels of the earth below to the blinding light of the surface above.

The second lum belonged to the Auld Pit's very own power station, also coal-fired of course, which generated the high-voltage electricity needed to operate the pit's vast and elaborate inventory of heavy machinery.

The third lum adorned the adjacent brickworks, in which the abundant local reserves of claystone were mercilessly crushed to powder by a giant cylindrical steel grinder, then fashioned into rectangular grey blobs, before being fired in the searing hot kilns, from which by some scientific miracle they finally emerged as reddish-orange building bricks. The very bricks, of course, which had been used to build the three lums themselves, famously spawning Connel Park's most enduring conundrum:

Whit came first, the bricks that made the lums, or the lums that made the bricks?

And then there were the huge cooling towers, the screening plant, the woodshed, the wagon repair shed, the engineers' and electricians' workshops, the joiners' shop and the daddy-of-them-all, the giant blacksmiths' building more affectionately known as the 'smiddy'. Factor in the pit baths, the lamp cabin, the ammunition store and the pit offices, and you will soon appreciate that the Bank Auld Pit was no tuppence-ha'penny little business. It was a huge, complex industrial operation which provided many thousands of tons of coal to power the national grid, and much needed employment for many hundreds of men from the locale to support their families.

The men themselves had very little leeway in their choice of vocation. However, they would always be able to get a job down the pit, meaning that their precious bairns would never starve. That was the upside. The downside was that the miner's lot would forever be an unforgivably backbreaking and extremely perilous one. They all knew it themselves, and their families knew it too, but nobody ever spoke about it. Never, ever.

Adjacent to the cavernous shaft of Bank Number One Pit was Bank Number Six Mine, access to which was provided not by a mechanical cage in a vertical shaft, but by a 'man-riding haulage' being fed down a perilously steep slope called a 'dook'. The man-riding-haulage, more commonly known as 'the rake' was the more technically polite term for eight big metal hutches – or 'bogies' – being yanked up and down the dook by over half-a-mile of thick steel rope wound around an enormous metal drum on the pit head, itself also powered by a coal-fired steam engine.

And then there was the noise. The rhythmic thump-thump-thumping of the donkey engine in the boiler house as it battled to keep the water levels constant, while the blazing coal fires converted water to the hissing steam required to power the various engines. The successive roars from the exhausts of the mighty steam winders at Bank Number One and Bank Number Six. The ear-jangling clank-clank-clanking of the coal-laden hutches clattering along the gangway on their never-ending race towards the screening plant and picking tables, before emerging empty-handed once more to commence yet another return journey down into the gloomy depths below. The screaming of the industrial saws in the woodshed. The constant high-frequency whines of the three enormous electricity generators in the power station.

All of those uniquely definitive sounds, and countless others, made up the incredible cacophony that defined the aural character of the Bank Auld Pit complex. To the unsuspecting visitor, the ear-splitting mayhem created by this incredible matrix of utterly relentless sounds assaulted the eardrums like some kind of enormously confused, tuneless and malevolent industrial din, each of its component sources belting out a quite different form of garish white noise.

However, to the indigenous miners, it was akin to a glorious heavenly choir. They called it 'The Collier's Symphony'.

Whistle While You Work

At precisely 6.00 a.m. on the chilly spring morning of Wednesday, 20 April 1938, young James Armour tumbled wearily as usual from the warmth of his cosy bed.

As dawn was battling to break through the gloomy skies above Craigbank, a little mining hamlet about half-a-mile to the west of Connel Park, the seventeen-year-old rubbed his bleary eyes and high-tailed it out the back door of his terraced one-bedroom home towards the 'lavvie' in the corner of the yard. After a quick pee and an even quicker splash of near-freezing water over his still half-slumbering adolescent face, James bolted back into the 'scullery' and rubbed his hands together vigorously above the big stove.

'Help yoursel', James,' his sister Rose said. 'That stuff'll stick tae your ribs!'

James willingly shovelled a man-sized pile of sticky porridge into his bowl, grabbed a spoon from the kitchen drawer and sat down at the big wooden table, while Rose poured the milk over his breakfast.

'Get that doon you,' she smiled, the pride radiating from her generous eyes. 'That'll put a good linin' on your belly, while you're graftin' doon that pit.'

James gratefully scoffed his oats, then grabbed his pit-bag from the kitchen table, together with his tin flask of steaming-hot tea which would, of course, be stone-cold by the time the pit horn had signalled piece-time. However, it would still be his big sister's tea, and to James that was all that mattered. The big sister who had looked after him ever since his beloved mum had passed away in his early childhood.

'Whit's in ma pit-piece the day, Rose?' he enquired with his customary impudent grin.

'Strawberry jam, as weel you ken!' she laughed. 'But I've made you twae slices on cheese as well, tae put a big smile on that cheeky wee face o' yours!'

And off went young James Armour on his mile-long trek to the dayshift at the Bank Auld Pit, on what was just another day, another ordinary day. As he strode along the tarmac road in the half-light, he began humming the catchy little tune that he had heard on the 'wireless' the previous evening. It was

'Whistle While You Work' from the new Walt Disney film, *Snow White and the Seven Dwarves.*

What James could never have known, though, was that today would be anything but ordinary. Today would be the stuff of recurring nightmares.

Today would be the day from hell.

The Runaway Train

'You're there, Dick!' shouted Jock Sanderson. 'Your big sister wiped your erse this mornin' as usual, has she?'

James Armour let out a big hearty laugh, both at the crass insensitivity of Jock's typically brash remark, and at the very mention of his own brand-new nickname. Everyone who started at the Bank Auld Pit was immediately given a nickname, never of their own choosing of course, and they just had to like it or lump it. However, James could have done an awful lot worse than 'Dick', and he knew it. Dick Armour it was then, and for the rest of his mortal life Dick Armour it would always be, even today at the ripe old age of 94.

He pushed open the lamp-shed door and collected his personally-numbered cap-lamp as usual, then made his way towards the brick-built entrance to Bank Six Mine. There the eight bogies of the rake sat waiting patiently like an intrepid Eskimo's team of obedient Huskies, by which time daylight had broken through to reveal an ominously watery-looking sky.

A few minutes later, the only light to split the jet-blackness of the pit bottom would be the one attempting valiantly to beam from his own cap-lamp, as he began trudging in the humid subterranean heat up, down and along the various unlit roads, until he had to crawl the remainder of the way on his hands-and-knees to the coal-face itself. There for the next eight hours, Dick's job would be to hack away with his pick-axe at the vast seam of coal that glistened like diamond in the diffuse light of his cap-lamp.

This was the famous 'eight-foot seam', the much-revered seam of 'main coal' that stretched an incredible thirty-odd miles underground all the way from the village of Dalmellington to the west, through the New Cumnock Coalfield itself and almost as far as the market town of Sanquhar in the more southerly county of Dumfriesshire.

However, young Dick had no time to ponder the economic riches that were sure to come the way of the fortunate shareholders who owned New Cumnock Collieries Limited. His job was a very simple one. Hack out as much of the black stuff as humanly possible, and get it chucked into the waiting hutches as quickly as his developing biceps could manage, before the pit horn sounded the end of his shift. Like everyone else in Bank Six, Dick's take-home pay would depend on one thing and one thing only, and that was the number of hutches he managed to fill before sending them on their way to the pit-head.

At 2.30 p.m. precisely, the glorious sound of the pit horn signalled the end of the dayshift, at which point the miners all began their long and exhausting return treks from the complex web of underground roads that led from their individual coal-face locations to the foot of the main Bank Six dook. There the rake again lay loyally in wait to take them back into the blinding daylight of the surface above, normally about 30 at a time.

The men piled into each of the first seven bogies, two in the front and two in the back as usual, Dick Armour finding himself in the third bogie from the head of the rake. As always, they sat on the cold metal floors with the backs of their heads pointing towards the pit head. The rule was simple, and enforced assiduously. When you went down the mine you faced the pit bottom, and when you came up the mine you still faced the pit bottom. No argument.

The only exception was the 'rake runner', the inimitable Biker Watson, who always sat in the top bogie. He too faced the pit bottom on the way down, but he and only he alone was permitted to face the surface on the way up. Biker's job was to keep his beady eyes out for any possible obstacles that might have fallen onto the dook's rail-track, at which point he would simply short-circuit the two parallel overhead power cables with his metal file to ring the bell that would alert the operator on the surface, who would then bring the rake to an abrupt halt until the debris was cleared off the track.

The eighth bogey? That was used to carry the 'graith' – the machinery, the equipment and the miners' toolbags – and no one was ever allowed to climb into the eighth bogey, under penalty of being sacked on the spot, plain and simple.

Once all the men's backsides had hit the floors of the bogies that afternoon, Biker gave his familiar call.

'Yous a' in, boys?'

'Aye, Biker!' came the near-synchronised reply, and the man-riding haulage commenced its laborious climb stealthily up towards the pit head, the enormous wire rope still attempting to glisten ever-so-faintly at the head of the rake in the weakening glow of the miners' near-spent lamps, as it began to take the strain.

'An' get a move on, Biker. Oor Jessie's got my mutton stew on the stove!'

As the rake reached to within the last few hundred yards of the surface, Dick Armour could already make out that the sky awaiting the miners' return was considerably brighter than the one that had shrouded them in gloom some eight-and-a-half hours earlier. For the merest moment, he purred at the delightful prospect of striding back along the Craigbank road in the spring sunshine, in the general direction of the big plate of mince-and-tatties that his sister Rose would have waiting for him on the kitchen table. Glory be!

Suddenly and without any warning, the rake came to a juddering halt, and the men were thrown abruptly forward, before recoiling backwards again. Then, as if by magic, the bogies began tilting upwards from the rear, as the 'jock' sprang into action in a commendably valiant attempt to do its job. The jock, a rather crude safety device, took the form of a big metal spike which would immediately drop downwards and impale itself into the earth between the wooden sleepers of the rail-track, on the occasion of the rake coming to an unexpected halt, holding it in place. At least, that was the theory.

In that instant, not a word was spoken, not a single word. A couple of seconds later, there was a blood-curdling creak as the jock attempted desperately to take the weight of seven metal hutches laden with 28 burly coalminers, before it eventually gave way under the enormous strain. Down onto the rail track with a tremendous thump went the eighth hutch and its cargo of graith, followed in rapid succession by seven other similar thumps. And in that single moment, the whole man-riding-haulage began to slide backwards down the dook.

'Oh my God!' shouted Biker Watson, shining his torch upwards in the direction of where the steel rope ought to have been, but no longer was. 'The f - - - in' rope's broken!'

As the rake's bewildered occupants froze in terror, Rab Ferrans was the first to react. With no time to think about what he was doing, he leapt upwards in the darkness and somehow managed to grab the overhead girder, hauling his flailing legs towards his chest as the rake began its involuntary journey downwards in the general direction of the pit bottom. Jim Brown did likewise, but completely missed the girder. As he was falling back down towards what he knew was certain serious injury at best, his hands came into contact with the bell-wires, which he gratefully grabbed, pulling his legs upwards as the rake gathered speed.

The runaway train rapidly accelerated out of all control, as it began plunging down the one-in-three slope of the dook in almost total darkness. Within a

26

matter of seconds, ten miles-per-hour became twenty, then thirty, then sixty. Two of the men attempted to get to their feet as the others clung onto the sides of the bogies for dear life. In that instant, their heads were smashed to pulp by the protruding flanges of the water pipes that lined the full length of the pit walls, their cranial blood splattering over their horrified neebors like a thundery cloudburst on a warm summer's evening.

A third miner called Sam McKnight had also intended to attempt a daring escape from his own bogie, only to receive an almighty kick in the teeth from another miner's flailing pit boot. It was a kick that would save Sam's life, since he too would surely have had his head smashed asunder by those same pipes, as the rake sped past at enormous velocity.

To this day, Dick Armour remembers nothing else about that hellish journey, not even the terrific impact when the rake finally exploded into the buffers at over 80-miles-per-hour, catapulting its remaining petrified occupants in all directions like exploding pellets from the barrel of a shotgun. Maybe it was the severe concussion on impact that wiped that awful event from Dick's recollection. There again, perhaps it was just nature's way of eradicating an indescribably horrific memory for eternity.

When Dick did eventually regain some form of consciousness in the pitch blackness of the pit bottom, he soon realised that he had sustained a terrible head wound and seriously injured his back. Completely oblivious to the death and destruction that lay all around him, the young lad's only thought was of 'gettin' oot o' there, and back up tae the pit-heid as quick as my legs could cairry me.' Other, that is, than a very hazy memory of scrambling back up the dook with one hand clasped around the small of his aching back, while the other attempted to stem the flow of blood from his swollen forehead.

Once at the pit head, his superficial examination by a doctor lasted no more than a few seconds, after which a nurse quickly wrapped a big white bandage around his head and fastened it with one of those little safety pins that young mums routinely deployed to secure their babies' towelling nappies in place. Dick was then instructed to go home and get straight to bed, at which point a passing Good Samaritan gave him a lift to Craigbank on the back of his motorbike.

By the time Dick Armour was fit to return to work at Bank Number Six Mine, three awful months had elapsed and five of his closest friends had been buried in New Cumnock cemetery on the banks of the Afton Water, one of whom was a mere fourteen-year-old lad who had just started his first-ever job only a few days before the tragedy. Meanwhile, the others like Dick himself were still trying to come to terms with the long-term effects of their terrible physical injuries, and the dreadful emotional scars that they would carry with them for the rest of their mortal lives.

When Dick eventually plucked up the courage to climb back into the rake on the day of his return to work, his whole body began to shake so violently that he could actually hear his teeth chattering above the howls of the big steam engine. However, there was nothing else for it, and his choice was a simple one. Either get his backside back down the same mine that had almost killed him, or spend the rest of his days idle and unable to support his family.

Bank Number Six Mine had just been the scene of the worst mining disaster ever to befall the county of Ayrshire. However, in only twelve years' time, that same old mine would contrive to play centre stage to the greatest mining rescue in world history.

The Mighty Knockshinnoch

By the time the Second World War had broken out in 1939, the demand for coal became so enormous that literally no stone was left unturned in the nation's relentless quest to get hold of the stuff.

It was coal that heated every single abode in Great Britain, from the humble council houses in Glasgow's Gorbals and New Cumnock's Dalhanna Drive to the majestic opulence of Windsor Castle and Buckingham Palace. It was coal that fired every school canteen's stoves all the way from John o' Groats to Land's End. And it was coal that fuelled the nation's factories, printing presses and steel forges the length and breadth of the country.

'Coal was King', and George VI would just have to deal with it.

Just before the outbreak of hostilities, it was the then local pit owners William Baird & Co. who had instructed their senior engineers to devise the daring plan that would sink a cavernous new shaft to the east of Old Knockshinnoch pit, situated between Connel Park and New Cumnock. The old pit's coal reserves were by then near-exhausted, and the new shaft's purpose was to facilitate access to the vast reserves of rich coal that the surveyors were now certain lay at a far greater depth than Old Knockshinnoch could ever hope to reach. And thus, when the deepest shaft in the New Cumnock Coalfield was duly sunk to a depth of 120 fathoms (720 feet), Knockshinnoch Castle Colliery was born, or 'The Castle' as it would forever be more affectionately known around these parts.

So up went the outbuildings on the pit-head, their roofs camouflaged to conceal them from the ruthless firepower of the German Air Force's much-feared *Luftwaffe*, as was the practice at the time for every industrial unit across the British Isles. Absolutely no expense was spared in the development of one of the most modern pits in the entire country. From the huge electric power hammer in the smiddy, to the brand-new milling machines, grinders and lathes in the engineers' shop, to the state-of-the-art steam engines that operated the pit's enormous winding gear, the pit-head at The Castle had it all.

Meanwhile down below, a British record was already being set, as a pioneering team of planners, engineers, miners and their assorted stone-cutting machinery drove an underground road to a remarkable distance of 1,100 yards to the west of the pit bottom. There, in what would become known as the 'West Mine' district of the pit, they had already reached the copious supplies of precious coal that would keep many hundreds of local men in employment and feed the national grid for donkeys' years.

Then some two years after the cessation of the war in 1947, the country's new Labour government under the leadership of Prime Minister Clement Attlee, decided to nationalise the coal industry and place it in the hands of the National Coal Board (NCB). Before much longer, the organisation more commonly dubbed as the 'Coal Board' would have become the largest employer in the world. Yes that's right, the biggest company on Planet Earth.

And that was when the Americans arrived, together with their huge wads of dollar notes and their enormous fancy machinery. Within a matter of months, the joy loaders, the shuttle cars, the arc wall coal-cutters and the electric and diesel locomotive trains would all be thundering around underneath the New Cumnock fields, busily ripping out and hauling enormous quantities of coal to the pit bottom, for triumphant transportation to the surface.

However, first of all, their various component parts would have to be fed down the shaft piece-by-piece in the giant steel cages, to await assembly by squads of feverishly-excited, glassy-eyed engineers who had never seen anything quite like it. An extensive network of belt conveyors was then constructed, linking the cages from the pit bottom to the working coal faces. The smaller belts that did the coal runs in the lesser three-to-five-foot coal seams were called the 'Little Davids', while the much larger ones that took the 'main coal' away to the waiting hutches were, of course, the mighty 'Goliaths'.

Back up on the pit head, the engine room was like something out of a particularly far-fetched sci-fi movie, boasting some of the most modern machinery ever assembled. Those in charge of the engine room would have guarded it with their lives. The huge engine's mighty piston rods and slides were kept polished to such perfection that the men could make out the chin stubble in their own reflection. The young apprentice whose job it was thrice-daily to replenish the supplies of cylinder oil and liquid graphite required by the lubricators was made to wear a pair of immaculately clean carpet slippers whilst he did so, on the instruction of the wonderfully officious lady who kept the terracotta tiles on the floor so pristine that you could have eaten your dinner off them. However, it was perhaps the plant pots full of geraniums and fuchsias lining the window sills that contrived to define the near-sterilised ambiance of The Castle's magnificent engine room, in which a clinical appendectomy could probably have been carried out without the slightest fear of infection.

The adjoining boiler house was a veritable hive of frenetic activity, the separate shifts of burly, youthful stokers having the unenviable task of keeping the three huge Lancashire boilers fed continuously, in order to produce the requisite quantities of pressurised steam needed to keep the engines thumping away at full capacity. Meanwhile, the older men on the shift were deployed in slightly less onerous tasks, such as those requiring attention in the wood-yard. There they would stack and load the wooden bogies, before despatching them underground to the various pre-determined locations chalked on their sides, names like Garrowscairn, Lanemark, South Boig and Golden Stairs adorning them, the latter steeply-stepped area of the pit called after the famous New Cumnock drapery store of the same name.

Pride of place on the pit-head's 'Colliery Square' was afforded to the engineers' shop, with its 40-plus workforce, the mechanical side managed by Sanny Allardyce, while Geordie Paton supervised the electrical contingent. The occasional local lad found himself having the very good fortune to be selected as an apprentice in the engineers' shop, where he would be given a wonderful opportunity to learn not only one vocational discipline but two, courtesy of the craft and experience of many a seasoned tradesman. There he would be able to feel the glorious warmth of the three smiddy fires on his backside on a cold winter's morning, whilst marvelling at the metal pickaxes being fashioned and sharpened, and the white-hot steel chains being hammer-linked together. In the workshop, many an important life skill was learned by the young apprentices, but many a practical joke played on them too. Another team of local lads, some as young as fourteen years of age, would be found at the picking tables in the screening plant, separating stone from coal, and 'big coal' from 'wee coal', before the latter was sent on its way by conveyor to the washer plant.

The Castle really was the state-of-the-art colliery, a veritable prototype for the future of British coalmining, and the New Cumnock community was very, very proud of it. And while hard, unforgiving graft in exceptionally tough and dangerous conditions was the order of a long, laborious day, the spirit of teamwork and camaraderie within the workforce was simply exemplary. Each man's earnings and security of tenure depended on him doing his own job to the best of his ability. However, his very life depended not only on him doing his, but on his neebors doing theirs too. This was a work ethic and self-supporting culture of the very highest order, and the men would have walked the plank for each other.

Such was The Castle's phenomenal capacity, that towards the end of the 'forties a huge workforce of almost 800 men saw the pit winding around 1,500 hutches and producing an astonishing 1,000 tons of coal each day. The Castle really was the business, and the coalmining bigwigs from all over the country fairly flocked to see it in operation, before returning to their own primitive little collieries in awe-stricken envy.

One day soon, though, many would find themselves returning to the very same scene. Not this time green-eyed at the breath-taking efficiency of this magnificent colliery, but heavy-hearted at the desperate plight of the New Cumnock community in its time of greatest need.

All Eyes on the Prize

It was on New Year's Day 1947, forever afterwards to be remembered as 'vesting day', that the big blue 'NCB' flag was first hoisted majestically above Knockshinnoch Castle Colliery's enormous winding gear.

That flag, like so many others across the assorted coalfields of Great Britain, now conveyed its profoundly symbolic message to the New Cumnock community. The Castle was no longer being run by a handful of faceless company directors whose only interest was in lining their own silk pockets. From now onwards, it would be run 'by the people, for the people', and lifetime employment would be guaranteed for the miners of the locale.

Britain had won the war, Winston Churchill and his Tories had been summarily booted out of office, and the pits were under state ownership at last.

Moreover, the 'mighty Knockshinnoch' itself now belonged to the people of New Cumnock. The feelgood factor was back again, and nowhere was it more tangible. That day, the village's Ne'erday celebrations took on a whole new poignancy, and how the people rejoiced.

It was never all going to be plain sailing, though. To manage such a vast organisation and run it efficiently would now require an enormous national superstructure with responsibility for strategy, while an exceedingly complex web of divisional, regional and area headquarters would be needed to oversee all operational aspects. Before long, planning and surveying decisions that had previously been made in New Cumnock were being taken in hastily-constructed Coal Board offices in the villages of Dunaskin and Lugar, each located some ten miles away from The Castle itself.

The administrative set-up quickly expanded beyond all recognition. Very soon, teams of developers, planners, draughtsmen, surveyors, accountants, personnel officers, administrators, clerical staff and umpteen others with assorted fancy titles found their feet resting comfortably under the steadily-growing rows of wooden desks, while yet more squads of janitorial, catering and cleaning staff were moved in too. Before much longer, the number of administrators in the Coal Board actually began to rival those of the miners they had been appointed to support, their wages being paid by one thing and one thing only. Coal itself.

And thus began the era of productivity targets, which soon became the be-all and end-all for the Coal Board's top brass. Coal was still king, but achieving fiercer and fiercer productivity targets was now the sole means by which the king's tenure on the throne could be sustained. Very soon, every colliery across the land came under increasingly intense pressure to hit its productivity quotas, and none more so than the exceedingly lucrative Knockshinnoch Castle, with its mouth-watering eight-foot seam of rich main coal. Absolutely no effort was spared by the boffins to get their hands on the stuff, even if it meant that some risks might have to be taken now and again.

And some pretty big risks at that.

As the decision-making process gradually grew more and more faceless and involved the local miners less and less meaningfully, it was perhaps inevitable that the sense of 'ownership' began to diminish. Gradually, the workforce grew pretty scunnered with the way things were working out. Planning decisions by anonymous officers who had never even set foot in New Cumnock paid scant regard to the views of experienced managers and miners, and proved to be at odds with the topography and conditions of the Knockshinnoch terrain and strata. Vital repair and maintenance works were transferred from local to central workshops, with the inevitable result that the workforce was kept waiting for crucially important replacement parts that would previously have been delivered in jig-time by local engineers, electricians and joiners.

By September 1950, The Castle still employed around 600 men underground and 120 personnel on the pit-head, the colliery's coal output averaging close on 5,000 tons per week. This level of production was rendered all the more impressive by two stark factors. The relatively isolated geographical location of Knockshinnoch, and the complexity of the area's geological profile, the former residing at the extreme edge of the wider coalfield area, with the latter being defined by the Southern Uplands Fault, a large 'upthrow fault' on its southern extremity.

It was Knockshinnoch's main coal seam that would provide the lion's share of the colliery's output, and it was this seam's relentless pursuit that would entice the bigwigs to keep their eyes on the prize, when those same eyes ought to have been focused much more firmly on the ball. If the prize was the irresistible lure of very rich pickings, then the ball was surely the safety and welfare of the miners themselves.

Towards the south-eastern extremity of the pit, in what was known as the South Boig District, the reserves of high-quality coal were positively mouth-watering for the salivating beaks of the Coal Board's high command. The composition of the main coal seam was fairly consistent throughout, its roof consisting of the rather insecure calmstone, which meant that the 'head coal' was always left on for safety reasons. When the remainder of the seam was then worked and the 'breast coal' and 'bottom coal' extracted - first by firing rounds of high-explosive shots to separate it from the dirt and then by the miners hacking the stuff out with pickaxe and bare hands - this gave the men a working height of approximately seven feet. The coal was routinely hand-loaded onto the belt conveyors, then deposited into the hutches sent down from the pit-head. From there, the full hutches were duly transported by locomotive along the rail tracks to the pit bottom, where they would then be hauled up the shaft in the cages to the surface.

In truth, Knockshinnoch Castle Colliery really was a magnificently efficient production line.

The main heading in the South Boig District was called Number Five Heading, the new jewel in the crown. It had started out innocently enough at a gradient of only one-in-fourteen, but due to severe faulting as it approached the position of the Southern Upland Fault, the gradient had continued to increase until it eventually reached a gut-busting one-in-two, or thirty degrees. Incredibly by that time, the men, who had been instructed to 'chase the seam', had driven the heading to almost fifteen yards from the surface. Fifteen yards.

From the men-in-suits on high, down to the miners toiling away at the coal-face below, every single person employed in The Castle knew only too well that 'Number Five' was reaching perilously close to the surface. However, there was something else that none of them knew.

They didn't know what lay above.

PART 2:
THE ANATOMY OF A DISASTER

WEDNESDAY, 30 AUGUST 1950

7.45 a.m.

Fireman Dan Strachan carefully positioned his explosives into the boreholes that his team had fashioned with their 'hand-bore rickety drills', penetrating the breast coal at the face of Number Five Heading. He then stuffed the apertures with soft clay to ensure maximum internal impact, and immediately withdrew his men to the prescribed safe distance before firing the shot.

'Polar Ajax', the miners called the stuff, long cylindrical sticks of industrial dynamite, with a small detonator buried into the centre of each, from which trailed the electric wires that connected them to the battery-operated priming device. The incessant din of clattering pickaxes and shovels had ceased on Strachan's command, and now all that could be heard was the distant clunk-clunk-clunking of the belt conveyor as it continued on its mindless mission to transport the coal down the heading to the waiting tubs. Strachan surveyed the scene, and then began winding the handle rapidly in a clockwise direction in order to generate the electrical current.

A sharp flash of light, followed by a low-pitched 'boom'.

The resulting blast shocked none of the thirteen hardened miners in the heading, and provided not the faintest clue that this was anything other than a bog-standard, controlled underground explosion. Another ordinary explosion. Another ordinary day.

Strachan allowed the dust to settle for a few minutes, before signalling to his neebors that it was now safe to follow him back into today's working area. As far as the Coal Board was concerned, time was money and there was no time to lose. Strachan approached the area of the blast to inspect the condition of the dislodged coal, which for the first time since the Carboniferous Period some 300 million years ago would soon be making its way into the New Cumnock daylight.

Suddenly, the Fireman stopped in his tracks. Holding his right arm up above his head, he signalled to his men to stay put, while he inspected the blast-hole in the breast coal. It wasn't its two-and-a-half-foot diameter that immediately caught his attention, nor indeed was it the hole's five-foot depth. The thing that really put his antennae on full alert was what the blast had left behind. A bed of boulders and stones.

Suddenly, a jet of water burst out from the stone-bed. Strachan instinctively stepped back for a moment, then cupped his hands together to inspect the water. It was remarkably clear in colour and completely odourless, indeed not unlike the fresh, sweet nectar of the glorious Afton itself. The water began to cascade downwards. Several other boreholes had also been made in the coalface, but although none of those had actually been fired, water had now begun leaking from a couple of them as well. Strachan narrowed his eyes and stroked his chin.

Strange, Daniel. Very strange.

He immediately referred the incident to Jim Houston, the 'Oversman' in charge of the dayshift, who duly arrived some fifteen minutes later to carry out his own inspection of the blast-hole, and coal production in the heading was temporarily halted. About an hour later, Knockshinnoch Castle Colliery Manager, Willie Halliday, went underground to examine the problematic holing for himself, and instructed the men that a number of wooden pillars – or 'chocks' – should be hammered into position to augment the strength of the various props that were already in place to support the rather feeble calmstone roof of the heading.

Over the course of the following week, a total of eight hardwood chocks, each measuring a mere thirty-by-six inches, would be hammered into place in an effort to render the roof more secure. Both Johnny Bone, the Area Colliery Agent, and backshift Oversman, Andy Houston, were then duly informed that the blast had holed through from Number Five to 'the outcrop', and that coal production had been stopped for the time being. Neither Bone nor Houston actually visited the face of the heading personally although Ben Kennedy, the pit's Under-Manager, was dispatched to inspect the scene the following day.

It was then that the Agent instructed Apprentice Surveyor, Ian Murray, to survey the underground workings, in order to determine the exact position of the face of Number Five Heading and, critically, its depth from the surface.

Earlier that same year - in the month of April to be exact - Willie Halliday had been handed a detailed 'development plan' from the Sub-Area Planning Department. The plan was a bit speculative, but nevertheless suggested that Number Five should eventually reach just short of the Southern Upland Fault, at which point it would have at least 100 feet of cover from the fields above. The big problem was that the heading's projected position was based on one rather simplistic assumption, and that was this.

When the plan was produced, Number Five was rising at a gradient of approximately one-in-four. However, and as ought to have been predicted for a coal seam rising towards a major upthrow fault, the heading's trajectory soon began to increase very sharply indeed. In fact, later in July of that same year, the Coal Board's 'Quarterly Review' had then indicated that the face of the heading was now a mere 196 feet below the surface. And that was when the penny really ought to have dropped.

At this stage, the pit's senior managers had clocked that the coal seam, which had now begun to shoot upwards at about one-in-two, would actually hit the outcrop near the surface a fair bit short of the Southern Uplands Fault, at a location a few hundred yards to the south of the main pit shaft. Well aware of this rather sobering news, those in charge did not appear to have lost any sleep over its potential consequences.

Nor indeed were they in possession of all the necessary management information that might have enabled them to make a more enlightened decision. Specifically, the version of the development map they had been given, hand-traced by a junior office clerk from the original official plan now hanging innocently in a filing cabinet in the Coal Board's Dunaskin office, had a vitally important 'symbol' missing. That symbol should have borne the word 'peat', a veritable red-alert danger sign to any colliery planner. Not only that, but the peat symbol's rightful position would have been slap-bang on the surface above where Number Five was bursting to emerge from the darkness.

In the event, Murray's survey established that the actual depth of cover between the roof of Number Five Heading and the surface was nowhere near that which had been expected. In fact, it was a mere 38 feet, less than the height of the pit canteen's roof.

Later that same day, Senior Assistant Surveyor, Tom Brown, carried out his own survey on the surface directly above Number Five. During the survey, Brown instructed Murray to knock a small wooden peg into the lush green grass of the field, to mark the point immediately above the face of Number Five Heading. Murray was surprised how easily the peg went into the ground under the limited encouragement of his two-pound hammer. He also noted that the ground appeared to be 'a wee bit soggy underfoot'. However, it seems that he was not unduly concerned about the condition of the surface above the heading.

Halliday, Bone and Sub-Area Planning Engineer Donald Mackinnon then set off on a walkabout of the surface area, to see for themselves precisely where Number Five would hit the surface if it continued to be driven straight through. Apparently, not one of the three senior officials even noticed the presence of either moss or peat on the surface. Very strange indeed, considering that Messrs Bone and Mackinnon in particular had previous experience of working beneath such surface conditions in several other collieries.

For the next few days, the water from the stone-bed was simply allowed to continue flowing down into Number Five Heading, where a ditch was eventually dug to carry it into some old disused workings. Despite the miners' own concerns about the sodden working conditions, their protestations fell on deaf ears. They were relocated to two new areas on either side of the main heading, and told to get bloody-well on with it. Still, the water poured into the heading.

And before much longer, with it came the egg shells from the birds' nests in the reeds above.

THURSDAY, 7 SEPTEMBER 1950

6.00 a.m.

As Jimmy McCreadie set off to work in the breaking daylight, it was just another day. Another ordinary day.

Save for the rain, of course, which for two days now had been battering down on his humble Glengyron home, situated on the heights above the market town of Cumnock. As Jimmy's size tens swished their way through the two-foot-high pools that had already flooded the length of the old Skares-to-New Cumnock road, he let out a big hearty laugh at the sheer futility of the whole exercise.

'Jesus Christ!' he giggled to himself. 'Don't fa' doon Jimmy, you could droon in this stuff!'

Jimmy was a coalminer, first and foremost, and as tough and hardy as they came. However, it wouldn't be his coalmining skills that would be called upon today. Instead, it would be his superb training and the deeply-instilled self-discipline that now defined this most respected of men. Those were the very skills and qualities that had propelled him to membership of the local rescue brigade, that most elite and revered of organisations.

Jimmy had left school at the tender age of fourteen years to take up his first-ever employment position, this as an apprentice painter. Blow torches and paint brushes might have been the graith of choice for some, but Jimmy had simply detested that job, and with such a vengeance that he had lasted less than a week before chucking it. The following day, he sweet-talked the manager of his local Whitehill Colliery into hiring him. Within the hour, and as a very dubious reward, he then found himself at the pit bottom, rubbing shoulders with seasoned miners up to five times his own age. For Jimmy McCreadie, there would be no soft pit-head baptism.

It wasn't until a few years later that Jimmy landed a prestigious position in his local pit's rescue brigade, a real feather in every ambitious miner's cap. In the early 'fifties, every colliery operated by the Coal Board required to have its own rescue brigade, the size of its membership being proportionate to that of the workforce. However, for the aspiring Brigade man, there was one nasty little shock in store.

An absolute pre-requisite for appointment to the brigades was the successful negotiation of an exceptionally gruelling, tortuous training course at Kilmarnock Mines Rescue Station, under the unforgiving eye of Superintendent Willie Dick. Suffice to say that for the numerous hopefuls who sought to progress to the dizzy heights of brigademan, many more failed the course than passed, and for one very good reason. The job of the rescue brigademan was to save lives. As such, the Brigade was no place for star-struck shrinking violets, or anyone who might conceivably buckle under pressure.

Willie Dick's training regime was simply brutal. There in the station's Bonnyton Road HQ, the bushy-tailed aspiring rescue men had to spend four weeks scrambling around a specially-designed 'underground gallery', most of the time wearing a desperately heavy, cumbersome and claustrophobic breathing apparatus, innocently enough called *Proto*.

New Cumnock's Matt Burns, a veteran of the mines rescue service, recalled the training programme with a shudder:

'The *Proto* had a breathing bag at the front, down to about your belt, but my best pal was so wee that it kept hitting him on the testicles! You wore an oxygen cylinder strapped horizontally across your lower back, and a big helmet over your head with nose clips and a mouthpiece that you had to bite on. It weighed 56 pounds all-in, and just walking about with it on for any length of time left you completely knackered.'

Matt remembers a couple of the training ordeals in particular, both of them wearing and breathing through the energy-sapping *Proto* gear. The first was the *Harvard Park Test*, a version of which is still used today. It involved him having to step on and off a thirty-inch-high wooden box for a full five minutes non-stop, to the infuriating rhythm of a metronome stuck right in front of his face, after which two burly instructors grabbed him by the arms and sat him back down, absolutely exhausted and trembling from the sheer exertion. A doctor then took his heartbeat and pulse at regular intervals until his condition had returned to something near normality, in order to check that his 'recovery rate' was sufficiently robust for the job.

The second was the infamous hot corridor, or 'torture chamber' as it was less than lovingly dubbed. This was a long dark passage heated to a very high temperature and made extremely humid by huge infusions of steam. There, he had to make his way up and down the corridor in total darkness in the searing heat, whereupon hefty sandbags would be draped over his shoulders and various obstacles shoved in front of him all along the way, in an attempt to discover if his spirits might break under the physical and psychological stress:

> 'Quite a few of the men never made it,' Matt chuckled. 'Although me and my wee pal did. Mind you, his testicles were black-and-blue for a month!'

Jimmy McCreadie was one of the hardy souls who had managed to pass Willie Dick's ultimate test. So too was the late Eddie Smith, a highly experienced member of the rescue brigade in Connel Park's very own Bank Auld Pit. Leaving school also aged fourteen, Eddie had started his working life at Afton Brickworks before becoming a coal miner. Having lived to tell the tale of Kilmarnock Mines Rescue Station's legendary torture chamber, Eddie was then elevated to membership of the Bank Pit Rescue Brigade, in which he later progressed to the lofty heights of Brigade Captain, no less.

If the weight of expectation on a Brigade man was already very considerable, surely the responsibility that came with being Captain was simply awesome? Not a bit of it, Eddie insisted:

> 'It was just our job, and the job had to be done, simple as that. If there was an emergency, you had to drop everything and get there as fast as you could. There was no time for worrying about what could go wrong,

all that mattered was getting straight to the scene of the accident and helping those in trouble. We had all been very well trained for emergency situations, and discipline was everything. There could be men's lives at stake, and our job was to be there for them. They were our brothers.'

Jimmy's and Eddie's paths never did actually cross, their respective communities and work locations being all of seven miles apart. Even to this day, the nonagenarians never knowingly met each other, and Eddie's much lamented demise has now conspired to ensure that they never will. However, on that auspicious September weekend in 1950, they and their fellow rescue brigade colleagues from every direction of the compass would go on to perform a role of such selflessness and courage that the New Cumnock community will remember them for all eternity with the deepest of gratitude.

The rescue brigade men's remit was a very simple, but utterly crucial one, as Jimmy McCreadie recalled. Respond immediately to any emergency, home or away, whether working at the coal face, playing dominoes in the local pub or wrestling around in bed with the wife:

'You just had to be ready. When you became a Brigade man, the Coal Board would get the Post Office to install a special telephone line in your house. Whenever it rang, you had to get your bloody skates on. After that, it was all about your training. Training and discipline, simple as that.'

And so that morning, as Jimmy paddled his way through the knee-high puddles of rainwater towards Whitehill Colliery, Eddie did likewise en route to the Bank Auld Pit, the two strangers naturally assuming that today would be just another day. Another ordinary day of hacking the black stuff from its seams, and chucking it into the waiting hutches.

Neither Jimmy nor Eddie had any idea of what lay ahead on that fateful September day, none at all. They had not the slightest clue that today would witness the greatest-ever call being made on the training and discipline of Willie Dick's infamous torture chamber.

Nor indeed did those two young men realise that today would prove to be their ultimate test as human beings.

6.30 a.m.

At almost the same unearthly hour as Jimmy McCreadie left his terraced home in the Glengyron miners' rows, Jenny Walker departed from hers in Burnside near Connel Park, a good seven miles away from Glengyron as the crow flies.

Not that there were many crows flying anywhere that morning, of course, the enlightened creatures having had the good sense to shelter from the incessant deluge underneath the darkening autumnal foliage of the sprawling Ayrshire countryside.

'Run a pole, walk a pole!'

That was twenty-year-old Jenny's daily mantra, as she part-sprinted and part-marched her way between the big wooden telegraph poles that lined the pavements of Burnside. It was a technique that had succeeded in getting her to work on time every morning in life since she had left school some five years earlier. For Jenny, work was at the 'fab' new canteen in Knockshinnoch Castle Colliery, at the top of Castle Hill, right above Bill Wilson's farm.

One of three girls and six boys to father Tommy 'Pup' Walker, himself an Oversman in The Castle, and hard-pressed mother Mary, Jenny counted her blessings each morning that she had landed such a great little number as trainee cook in this spanking new kitchen, complete with its giant coal-fired stoves and all its armoury of pristine utensils. Perhaps even more importantly, and as a strikingly attractive young woman, Jenny was invariably if unwittingly the focus of frantic male attention every time her warm eyes sparkled in response to each coy miner's culinary enquiry.

'How's your moose soup the day, Jenny?' Dan Park and his pal Jock Clapperton would tease her.

'Fine, boys!' she would reply with a mildly embarrassed giggle, in acknowledgement of the fact that she understood the joke, even if her austere manageress, Miss Hyslop, did not. 'It should be weel-cooked by now!'

What they were referring to was the day when Jenny made a big pot of Scotch Broth soup and inadvertently left the lid off, thereby facilitating the unwelcome intrusion of one of the pit-head's resident mice, the poor creature immediately perishing in the searing heat of Jenny's incomparable mutton stock, on the surface of which it was found floating the very next morning. In the event, Dan and Jock were the only ones to be entrusted with Jenny's gruesome secret, and poor Miss Hyslop would eventually leave these mortal plains completely oblivious to the saga of the 'moose soup'.

Today Jenny, now an utterly charming 83-year-old lady, has absolutely no recollection of what kind of soup was on offer on the auspicious day that was Thursday 7 September 1950. What she does remember, though, was the main course she had prepared. And prepared unwittingly for the most enormous invasion of hungry mouths that the village of New Cumnock would ever witness:

'Beef stew, with carrots and onions, and mashed tatties on the side! And if we ran out, there would always be plenty of cheese and corned beef sandwiches for the men. They would never starve, we made sure of that!'

However, there was something else that Jenny remembered about that particular day:

'The rain that fell was unbelievable. It hadn't stopped for days on end, and the whole place was flooded, even the main roads.'

In addition to Jenny's dad, Tommy (Senior), all of her six brothers were employed as coalminers in The Castle, every single one of them. Tommy (Junior), Alex and Walls were due to go on the backshift that particular afternoon, while Archie, Jim and Willie would be working on the nightshift, or the 'tenshift' as it was often dubbed. One can only speculate about how Mary, the irrepressibly solid matriarch of the Walker family, actually managed to get to sleep each night, doubtless dreaming restlessly of her husband and sons toiling in the humid heat and omnipresent danger of the pit depths. Perhaps it was just the sheer effort of feeding a family of eleven and scraping the muck off the backs of seven of them before collapsing exhausted into her bed that kept her going, who knows?

However, for Mary Walker, sleep would soon become that most elusive of privileges.

9.30 a.m.

Only a couple of hours into the dayshift, another very strange thing happened down in Number Five Heading. The trickle of water, which had been flowing steadily from the hole at the foot of the land basin ever since the blast one week back, suddenly began gushing down the heading with a real vengeance.

So surprised and concerned about this latest turn of events was dayshift Fireman Tam McDonald, that he felt the need to report it immediately to his shift Oversman, Joe 'Tiger' Houston, who inspected the damage himself and noticed that the blast-hole had now widened considerably. However, Tiger wasn't unduly concerned by the increase in the hole's size, because the bed of stones behind it appeared to be in much the same position as before, and it still looked pretty rigid.

Tiger's immediate priority was to do something about the water, because it was now pouring into a couple of the areas where the miners were hacking at the coal face, and hindering their work. To combat the problem, he instructed one of the men to dig a gutter and confine the water to the heading itself. Having been informed of this latest set-back, Under-Manager Ben Kennedy duly arrived on the scene a few minutes later, only for his injured knee to prevent him from climbing up the remaining thirty-odd yards to the blast-hole at the face of the heading.

A quick discussion then ensued between Messrs Kennedy and Houston, after which it was agreed that one big question had to be answered without delay. Will the pit's pumps be able to cope with the water ingress and sustain the heading's vitally important coal production levels?

Of course, the real question that the miners themselves wanted answered was another one entirely. To hell with the pit's pumps and the Coal Board's productivity targets, is this heading now too dangerous for us to be working at all? It was a burning question that would never be answered by the men on high.

And so life returned to normal, or at least as normal as it could possibly have been in that most sinister of places, the doom-laden Number Five Heading. About one hour later, the cheese sandwiches were duly being washed down assorted throats with cold tea. By the time the pit horn had informed the men that it was time to get back to work and see out the second half of their dayshift chores, the water cascading down the heading was by then up to the knees of their moleskin trousers.

Every now and again, a slight fall of loose coal came rattling down the heading with the water, followed inevitably by a clatter of pebbles. Several times that morning, the falling debris even contrived to jam the belt conveyor, which on each occasion ground to a screeching halt, bringing production to yet another infuriating halt.

And so, in summary, the situation was now this. The earlier trickle of water had become a small waterfall. The blast-hole itself had tripled in size. The coal, stones and pebbles from the rain-drenched land basin that lay only a few yards above the miners' heads were tumbling continuously down the heading. The belt conveyor was jamming in response, rendering the Coal Board's productivity targets dead in the water. And still the pit's bosses did nothing.

Before much longer, it wouldn't only be their precious productivity targets that would be dead in the water.

12.00 Noon

Nobody in New Cumnock had ever seen rain like it.

For three days on end, it had been absolutely pelting down. The famous Afton Water had long since burst its banks as it flowed less than gently into the River Nith, which itself was at its highest level in living memory as it flooded the low-lying fields on either side of New Cumnock railway station. All across Ayrshire, umpteen rivers and burns were similarly overflowing, numerous roads were hopelessly blocked by muddy landslides and assorted seafaring vessels were being blown around the Firth of Clyde like the tiny plastic *Airfix* model ships that many an excited schoolboy always looked forward to finding in his Christmas stocking.

Hardly any of New Cumnock's seven-thousand-plus inhabitants even dared to set foot outdoors, as vicious gales drove sheet-after-sheet of autumnal rain into row-upon-row of council house windows, shattering countless prize greenhouses and ripping out unsuspecting tomato vines by the root. As the flood water continued its relentless cascade down the steep slopes of Pathhead, The Coupla and The Shillin' Hill to gather in a giant pond that completely blocked the village's main commercial street, everyone peering out from behind their curtains wondered if the deluge would ever end.

This was no ordinary autumn rainstorm. This was a monsoon by any other name.

'We'll soon be up tae the daisies!'

Those were the prophetic words of Bill Lee that still echo today in the ears of his daughter, Jessie. Bill was one of the village's many hardy coalminers who worked in nearby Knockshinnoch Castle Colliery, as also was Jessie's husband, one William Lopez, or Willie as he is still much better known around these parts.

Bill Lee had been referring to the desperate underground conditions in Number Five Heading, in which he and a dozen of his colleagues had been toiling away for some time now, and to which he would be returning on the backshift that very afternoon. It wasn't a prospect he was particularly relishing. He cringed momentarily when he remembered that his son-in-law would also be on the same shift that day, but quickly reminded himself that at least young Willie wouldn't have to work so close to 'the daisies'. In a few minutes' time, Bill would simply have to wrap himself up like the proverbial 'pish-hoose spicket' and brave the elements on the mile-long trek from his Dalhanna Drive home, swishing his moleskin trousers through the knee-high puddles in the howling rain until he reached The Castle pit-head.

There he would collect his metal token from timekeeper Sammy Brown, before being given the nod to walk into the mighty engine room and enter the giant metal cage. Sixteen men at a time, that was all the cage could handle, and as soon as the last man was in, the big steel gates would be hauled down with a mighty clatter that still managed to assault hardened miners' eardrums like a head-on car crash.

Like Bill, most of the miners in the cage were very experienced by that time, and the journey down into the bowels of the earth didn't really bother them anymore. The younger ones were a different story. They would simply close their eyes and grab onto the cold metal railings as if their very lives depended on white knuckles bursting through youthful skin. Bill knew only too well that the very moment the lever got released, his feet would be plunging at great velocity down a pitch-black shaft, while his stomach would still be somewhere up near the surface trying to catch up. When the cage eventually came to a juddering halt at the foot of the shaft, he would once again be incarcerated deep beneath the lush green land of his beloved New Cumnock.

However, it wasn't the half-mile depth of the pit bottom that was bothering Bill Lee and his neebors that day. It was the deeply unsettling thought that they would be working less than fifteen yards beneath the lumbering hooves of the cattle grazing on Bill Wilson's farm field above.

Fifteen bloody yards.

One of Bill's neebors, Jimmy Love, had just said something remarkably similar to his wife Ella that same morning, as their daughter Molly recalled:

'My dad was quite excited that day before he set out for the backshift at Knockshinnoch. You see, we had just bought our first electric washing machine, and it was due to be delivered later that afternoon. However, his excitement was tinged with sadness, because my mum had just suffered another one of her wee strokes – or 'TIAs', as they're called nowadays - and she was ill in bed.'

However, it was what Jimmy said to his wife that would live with Molly for the rest of her life.

'Don't worry, Ella, I'll be hame early yin o' these nichts. I'll jist walk oot by the De'il's Stane!'

The 'De'il's Stane' was the colloquial expression for the 'Devil's Stone', a huge boulder that had lain for millions of years on the surface just below the Laight farm, and straight above the latest outpost of Knockshinnoch's underground workings. And, of course, what Jimmy had been referring to was the fact that his own working area had now been driven so close to the surface that one of these days it might actually burst through, and he would just walk straight home for tea.

Sadly, Jimmy would never live to use his new washing machine. Tragically, he would never even see his beloved Ella again.

Meanwhile towards the end of the 'dayshift', Tom 'Toe' Melvin suddenly burst through the door of the engineers' workshop on the pit head, absolutely drenched to the skin. Toe's dramatic entrance was nothing unusual in itself, since every single day in life the burly engineer would do precisely that, bawling out his immortal words at the top of his gruff voice.

'Where's a' these f----n' cats?'

That would be the signal for the workshop's various rodent-hunting felines to bolt frantically out of the nearest open door or window at the very sound of the big man's booming voice. It was a well-worn routine, but it still made everyone in the workshop split their sides. Everyone that is, except the petrified cats themselves.

However, on this particular occasion, the likeable Toe uttered no such rasping rhetorical remark in his daily attempt to put the wind up his furry foes. Instead, he made a quite different announcement, this one to no one in particular but to everyone in general.

'The men on the backshift had better get their skates on if they're goin' back doon there the day! Something serious is going to happen in that place!'

Toe Melvin had just dumped his toolbag while scrambling to escape from a slight 'fall' of loose gravel at the foot of Number Five Heading in the south-eastern extremity of the pit's underground workings. And in those days an engineer and his toolbag were not easily parted. Within the next few hours, the same heading would contrive to become the most notorious of its kind in British mining history.

As Bill Lee's thoughts turned to his imminent hike towards Number Five, he knew only too well that the heading's extremely steep gradient and ridiculously close proximity to the surface had already rendered its condition potentially unstable. However, something else had occurred only a few days back, something which had made Bill even more twitchy. Namely, the shot of high explosives that had blown through the coal seam and dislodged the foot of the land basin above. Never before in his mining career had he ever known such a thing to happen, and he was worried. Very worried indeed.

Bill and his twelve other squad members were acutely aware of the dislodgement, because a steady stream of water had been pouring into the heading ever since, from the cattle field above. However, what none of them realised was that on the surface directly above Number Five lay something a great deal more sinister than a few unsuspecting cattle.

An enormous hidden lake of stinking, putrid sludge.

Bill Lee reflected briefly on the well-rehearsed pattern of the day that lay ahead. Having collected his metal token and stepped into the cage along with his neebors on the afternoon's backshift, they would be at the pit bottom in the blink of an eye. There they would all file out of the cage like ants from an anthill, and begin their trek along the well-lit main road in the direction of the West Mine area of the pit.

A few hundred yards along, the thirteen-man squad would make its customary right turn towards Number Five Heading. As soon as they left the main road to begin their ascent back up the 'dook', the electric lighting would slowly recede into the distance behind them, and their miners' cap lamps would then be their sole source of light. As they scrambled up the steep contours of an amazingly elaborate matrix of roads that always made Bill think of a huge rabbit warren, they would instinctively know that they were nearing the extremity of Number Five. The big giveaway would be the trickle of running water. It was the most sinister trickle of water that Bill had ever heard in his life. However, today of all days, he could never have known that this same familiar trickle would now sound more like a respectable waterfall.

As Bill left his great pal William 'Paley' Howat at the control panel of the belt conveyor which he operated to send the coal towards the waiting hutches, he opened his pit-bag and took a quick peek at his pit-piece, smacking his lips in anticipation. Three slices of local baker Glendinning's oven-baked bread on cheese and another three on homemade redcurrant jelly, and all soon to be washed down with a 'tinny' of strong Lipton's tea. Bill grabbed his pick-axe, and convinced himself that it would be piece-time in jig-time.

For Bill Lee and his neebors, their last supper was fast approaching.

1.30 p.m.

Nineteen-year-old May Robertson kissed her husband John goodbye as he headed out into the lashing rain in his moleskin trousers towards The Castle, to meet his younger brother Eddie for their backshift in the pit.

Married for two years by then, John and May were living in the attic of a friend's house in The Leggate. For the young Robertsons life was idyllic, even if that idyll was extremely hard-earned, as May recalled warmly:

'The attic was tiny, but it was home. We had an outside toilet which we had to share with our neighbours, and old newspapers for toilet roll! When John came home from work, the whites of his eyes would be glowing from the blackness of his face, and he would scrub the dirt off his moleskin trousers at the front gate. I would always have warm water ready for him in the metal bath, where he would wash himself and I would scrub his back. Some miners never washed their backs, you know, because they believed it was a sign of weakness! I suppose it was a kind of "manliness" thing. Life was very simple in those days, but it was a good life, even if it was all about survival.'

Jean McMurdo has very similar recollections:

'Life in the early 'fifties was all about the family unit. Basically, the men worked and the women stayed at home, particularly if there were children in the family. The whole day was structured around the man's work pattern, such as shift work in the pits. John worked mainly dayshift and backshift, but very few nightshifts, because as a "stripping-and-drawing" man down the pit, I think they tended not to strip as much coal on the nightshift. Our meals were prepared accordingly. For example, when John was on the dayshift, the main meal would be ready when he came home around three o'clock, but when he was backshift it would be on the kitchen table at half-twelve prompt, just before he set off to work. We lived in a rented room-and-kitchen in a big red sandstone building at the far end of The Castle. It was called "Gold's building", because it was owned by an old lady called Mrs Gold. The toilet was outside, and sometimes it got so cold that the pipes actually froze. Life was incredibly simple, but very satisfying, as was the New Cumnock staple diet. Tatties and mince, stewing steak, sausages-and-onion, and all with a lot more real meat content than the stuff you get today. Good hearty soups, and the only time you used rice was for rice puddings!'

So what did Jean remember about the afternoon of 7 September?

'Nothing at all, really. It was just another day. John picked up his pit-piece as usual, and off he went. He would have cheese in his piece nine times out of ten, and a flask of hot tea which he told me would always be stone cold by the time piece-time arrived! Oh yes, and I remember the rain. For the past few days, it had been absolutely torrential, and the roads were flooded. Every day, John would set off for Knockshinnoch on his bike, dressed in his pit boots, moleskin trousers, heavy working shirt and light singlet vest, but I can honestly say that I have no clear recollection of him leaving the house that particular afternoon. I must have assumed that despite the rain, it was just going to be another ordinary day, and that he would be coming home for his tea about ten o'clock as usual, as black as the Earl of Hell's waistcoat and with the whites of his eyes sticking out like car headlights. I would have water heating on the range as always, and he would scrub himself in the zinc bath in front of our coal fire, the water turning black almost immediately. But … he never … he never did come home that night.'

And so off into the Scottish monsoon and in the general direction of their assorted workplaces went Jimmy McCreadie, Eddie Smith, Jenny Walker, John Robertson and Jock McMurdo, along with over one hundred other unsuspecting souls, while their loved ones waited expectantly for their return home.

For some, that return would be a long time coming. For others, it would never come at all.

1.32 p.m.

Such was the volume of rain that had fallen on New Cumnock over the past few days, that some of the gaffers at Knockshinnoch Castle Colliery were beginning to entertain the idea that 'Tam Todd the Drainer' might just have been right after all.

Tam was a local drainage contractor, well-known for both his entrepreneurial skills in seeking out new work opportunities, and for his unfailing ability to deliver the goods whenever they did come along. Some months earlier, Tam had been digging a ditch at The Castle pit-head, and he had commented to the colliery's bigwigs that the fields down in the hollow beneath the Laight farm were becoming extremely boggy, and really needed draining. His well-intentioned, if quaintly opportunistic remarks had apparently fallen on deaf ears.

However, as the men in suits now observed the overflowing ditches spewing their guts out onto those same fields a little more than a penalty kick's height above the dozen or so men working in Number Five Heading, Tam's prophetic words were beginning to ring in their ears.

Bloody rain, they cursed. When would it ever stop?

And so, while the gaffers dunked their digestive biscuits into their cheap imitation-china teacups in the Dunaskin and Lugar offices, and scratched their ever-expanding backsides in tunnel-visioned denial, 129 men were already splashing their way through the deluge in the general direction of Knockshinnoch Castle.

The backshift was on its way.

As John Robertson began wading through the laughable depths of the waterlogged Dalmellington-to-New Cumnock road along the Leggate, clad in his trusty moleskins, big Jock McMurdo set off on his bike from 'Gold's building' in New Cumnock's similarly saturated main drag. A good fifteen minutes later, as John trudged his way up Castle Hill towards the pit-head, Jock came puffing up behind him, straining on the pedals.

'A fine day for the ducks!' John Robertson remarked.

Jock McMurdo just nodded breathlessly, as he dismounted his bike upon reaching the crest of the steep hill just outside the timekeeper's office. 'Soaked to the arse, and we're no' even clocked in yet!' he laughed.

There they met Willie Lopez and his father-in-law Bill Lee, together with Sam McCracken, a hardened miner who had plied his trade in the New Cumnock coalfield ever since leaving school as a fourteen-year-old. That afternoon, Sam had also jumped rather optimistically onto his bike, only to end up shoving the damned thing through the puddles until he reached the pit-head.

'You're there boys!' shouted Andrew McDicken, a New Cumnock worthy if ever there was one. 'The watter's fair runnin' doon the sheugh o' ma erse!'

Having started 'snibbelling the hutches' in the local mines as a bushy-tailed fourteen-year-old about half-way through the Second World War, Andrew was about as seasoned a coalminer as there was, and all of his neebors looked up to him. Living in Craigbank, he had earlier played alongside his three other brothers in the local juvenile football side of the same name, which he proudly claims once went an amazing three years undefeated. Now, though, Andrew's playing days were well and truly behind him, and the focus of his cultural attention was New Cumnock's 'big team', Glenafton Athletic, or 'The Glens' as they are still affectionately known around these parts to this very day. The previous Saturday, the Glens had continued their great run of early season form by walloping Whitletts Victoria 7-1, much to Andrew's delight.

'The Glens' gemme has been ca'd off already, would you believe it?' Andrew announced dejectedly, to whoever was listening. 'The watter's runnin' doon the slope o' Connel Park, and the bottom goalmouth's like a swimmin' pool!'

'Aye, so it is!' remarked Rab Cockburn. 'The weans were even sailin' their wee toy boats on it this mornin'!'

At only 22 years of age, Rab was one of the younger brigade, but clearly enterprising beyond his years. Having been transferred from the Bank Auld Pit to The Castle a year or so earlier, he had demonstrated the ingenious temerity to keep hold of his locker key, so that he could mount his bike after his shift in the latter and cycle back to the pit-head baths at the former, while his somewhat less resourceful neebors were still contorting themselves into their primitive little zinc baths.

'Right boys, collect your tokens and let's get on our way.'

It was the softly-spoken voice of Alex Clapperton, better known as 'Eck', one of the pit's Deputies and shot-firers. Eck's dulcet tones smacked of quiet authority, but never of the barking aggression that often characterised many of the Coal Board's big chiefs.

Having collected token number 230 as usual, Eck then issued his troops with the day's working instructions and ushered them into the cage. As the big metal gate came crashing down with that all-too-familiar clatter, the cage was released and its maximum cargo of sixteen hardy souls suddenly found their pit boots shooting down the shaft towards the pitch blackness of the pit bottom.

For most, it would be a very long time before they would ever catch the joyous sight of daylight again. For the others, it would be a privilege never to return.

2.05 p.m.

It was a good half-hour before the full backshift squad had finally reached the pit bottom, and for two very good reasons. Firstly, the cage had a maximum payload of sixteen. Secondly, no two members of the same family were ever permitted to travel on the one journey. At least, that's what the Coal Board's rulebook said.

It was for the second reason that the three 'Pup' Walker boys on the backshift had to travel separately, as indeed would their three other brothers and father Tommy 'Pup' himself on the nightshift a bit later on. That particular afternoon, the Walker siblings detailed for the backshift were Tom, who operated the joy loader, Walls who was the locomotive driver, and young Alex, a mere 'pit boy'.

The man in charge of all 129 men went by the name of Andrew Houston, the backshift Oversman. A tall, lanky middle-aged gent, anything that Houston lacked in muscular stature he more than made up for with his assured presence and quiet authority. He had already seen more than his fair share of drama in a life that had been well-lived, if punctuated with terrible heartache along the way.

A veteran of the Great War of 1914-18, he had served King and country with distinction and valour, as evidenced by his impressive medal collection. Houston had also witnessed terrible personal tragedy, his first wife perishing on the delivery table during the birth of their twins, one of whom was still-born, the other passing away a mere six months later:

'Andy Houston was a serious-looking little man,' recalled former Knockshinnoch stalwart Billy McMichael, 'but his sombre expression belied a really dry, infectious sense of humour. He was an exceptionally hard grafter, punctual to a fault and meticulous in his work, so much so that even the lazy ones liked him!'

High praise indeed. Houston's niece Anna Copland's recollections were similarly warm and affectionate:

'Uncle Andy was the complete gentleman, quite unlike the mental picture you might have of the rough-and-ready miner down the pit. A real family man with a heart of gold, but with a wicked sense of humour too. He was a great practical joker, and it was often difficult to tell whether he was actually being serious or just winding us up!'

However, on that auspicious September day, it wouldn't be Andy Houston's frivolous side that would define him. It would be his calm and assured leadership qualities, and his battle-hardened, raw courage.

Houston held his backshift team at the pit bottom for a few moments, while he hurriedly discussed the relevant operational matters with the day's 'double shifter', the official whose job it was to coordinate changeover arrangements between the dayshift coming off the job and the backshift about to pick up the baton. There then followed a quick pow-wow between Houston and his five backshift Deputies, in order that one very important legal requirement could be fulfilled, namely that each Deputy had to satisfy himself that his allotted district was safe for his men to enter.

To a familiar hand signal from the relevant Deputy, each squad then set off on foot along the 'West Mine Turn' towards its pre-determined work location. The West Mine Turn was the pit's main underground 'road' that eventually led to what was more or less a T-junction, about three-quarters-of-a-mile due west of the pit bottom. It was a high, wide and near-level 'stone-drift' road, and very well lit, courtesy of the mains electricity supplied from the pit-head cables that were fed by the power station at the Bank Auld Pit.

A few hundred yards along the West Mine Turn, Dan Strachan led his men into the darkness of the first road on the right, as they prepared to head back up the South Boig District's steep contours in the general direction of the dreaded Number Five Heading. Dan waved a quick goodbye to his opposite number Eck Clapperton, who reciprocated and continued marching his own team straight ahead. Neither Dan nor Eck could possibly have known that this rather businesslike wave of goodbye would ultimately prove to be one of tragic farewell.

The rest of the men all trudged past 'The Mech' (the mechanised section of the pit) on the left, which itself then led towards a steep slope called Waterhead Dook, without giving their whereabouts a second thought. 'Watterheid' was no longer a working area of the pit, merely a long, cavernous dook that led down to the huge barrier of coal that separated Knockshinnoch Castle from the even deeper recesses of the now completely derelict and hopelessly gas-contaminated Bank Number Six Mine. A few years back, a very small section of the 200-foot-thick wall of coal had been blasted away to leave a separation of only 24 feet between the modern-day Knockshinnoch and the abandoned Bank, in order to allow a narrow borehole to be drilled through to facilitate the drainage of troublesome water from the former colliery into the latter's powerful pumping system.

That September day, nobody could ever have known just how critically important that 24-foot wall of coal would later turn out to be. Never in their wildest dreams.

A hundred yards or so further along the West Mine Turn, two further dooks dived into the blackness. The one to the right was called Garrowscairn, which led down towards a particularly accessible section of the main coal seam, with all its glorious riches lying there waiting for the financial delectation of the Coal Board's unrelentingly demanding Directors. A seam hacked out by a squad of hardy miners, each of whom would be lucky if they managed to take seven-quid home to their wives at the end of yet another gruelling week's toils in the most hostile of working conditions.

The dook on the left led to a vitally important cog in the pit's operation, referred to as 'the endless rope'. A few yards further on, another dook veered at about 'one o'clock' to the right, this one called Lanemark.

'Big Jock McMurdo worked in my squad at the endless rope,' Eck Clapperton said. 'Wee Rab Cockburn too. Big Jock was a "stripping and drawing" man, that was his job. He worked with another wee neebor, but I can't remember his name. Their job was to strip the coal from the coal-face after it had been shot-fired, and load it into the tubs. They would then draw the tubs out to the endless rope at the roadend, or 'the lie' as we called it, where the 'dook runner' would collect them for transportation by the diesel locomotive along the West Mine road to the pit shaft. After Jock and his wee neebor had drawn the full tubs out to the lie, they would then draw the empty ones back in, and start digging again. It was a system that worked very well. Knockshinnoch was a very efficient pit, a proper production line before its time.'

When Eck and his men reached the T-junction at the end of the West Mine Turn, they all instinctively headed towards the familiarity of their allocated dooks. There they dumped their jackets and working shirts, and began scrambling down towards the various coal faces that only a few minutes ago had been vacated by their colleagues on the dayshift.

Now well into the deepest bowels of the vast colliery, the humid heat would be building up in synch with the diminishing ventilation, and a light singlet vest was all that was required. Some of the more 'gallus' men even stripped off their trousers as well, and set about toiling in their Co-op underpants, safe in the knowledge that the discarded garments would still be lying there for reclamation at the end of their shift.

And so the backshift squad of 129 miners had arrived at their assorted work locations, over half-a-mile below the rain-drenched fields of New Cumnock. All of them commencing their toils without delay, in order to maximise productivity for the Coal Board and, of course, the thickness of their pay-packets come the weekend. Some driving the joy loaders and the locos, some testing the air quality, some preparing to blast the coal seams asunder with 'Polar Ajax' dynamite for the coal-strippers to hack away with their pickaxes and bare hands in the near-total darkness of the pit depths.

And every single one of them looking forward to the steaming bowl of home-made soup that would be waiting on the kitchen table when they got home to their wives and bairns.

6.40 p.m.

As Dan Strachan went about his business in Number Five Heading half-way through the backshift, he found himself reflecting on his earlier discussion with Andy Houston.

Two of the wooden chocks supporting the roof of the heading had just been sent packing by the rushing water, washed away like soap suds down a kitchen sink. Strachan had reported the matter to Houston, and in turn the Oversman had gone back up to the surface to raise his concerns with Agent Johnny Bone, Under-Manager Ben Kennedy and Surveyor Robert Arbuckle.

'Whit are the gaffers sayin' about these two chocks that disappeared?' an invisible miner bawled to Strachan from the near-obscurity of the coal face.

'Buggered if I know,' he shouted back, 'I havenae heard a thing since.'

Suddenly, Strachan heard a very strange noise. It was loud and crunching, and came from further up the heading, swiftly followed by a low-pitched rumble. He froze in dread.

The men working at the coal faces adjacent to the heading immediately downed tools and caught their breath. In the 'stoop' to the west of Number Five, Jim Houston, Tam Houston and Bill McFarlane just stood and stared in the general direction of the heading, while to the east side, John Smith, Sam Rowan and Bill Lee did likewise. Further up the seam, Jim Love, John Murray and Jock White strained their eyes as they peered down into the blackness of the void. Not a word was spoken, not a single one. As experienced coalminers, every one of them instinctively knew that something was up, and absolutely nothing needed to be said.

A few moments later, and as quickly as it had begun, the rumbling suddenly stopped. The men immediately grabbed their pickaxes back up from the pit floor. After all, the size of their pay packets depended on hard graft and full 'tubs' of coal, not on idle chit-chat about what might or might not have happened just then. There were hungry mouths to feed.

Dan Strachan knew for sure that something was badly wrong, and sent a message to Andy Houston asking to speak to him as a matter of urgency. Houston asked Strachan to come out from the heading at once, in order to meet him at a point near the foot of the pit shaft, where he was duly informed that there had been a 'big fall' at the face of Number Five. Strachan went on to tell his gaffer that the fall had reached as far as 100 yards 'inbye' from the belt conveyor and that, very strangely, the water had now stopped flowing from the blast-hole. The Oversman then instructed his Fireman to return to the working area of Number Five and ensure that its condition was still safe and habitable for his squad of men to continue with their work.

Those would be the last words ever exchanged between the two men.

Meantime, Houston decided to climb back up to the surface via the steep incline of the adjacent North Rising Mine, rather than by cage up the pit shaft itself. From there, his plan was to wade his way through the flooded fields and locate the wooden peg that had been hammered into the ground by rookie surveyor Ian Murray, so that he could personally inspect the condition of the surface directly above the heading.

When Houston arrived at the location and began looking around the field in the lashing rain, Murray's wooden peg was absolutely nowhere to be seen. However, straight in front of him, he noticed something else entirely. Something that made him catch his breath.

It was a big 'sit' in the field. About ten yards long by five yards wide, a section of the field had sunk to a depth of over two feet. It reminded Houston of a giant wash-hand basin, and it looked strangely 'alive'. The earth was moving. Moving very slowly, almost imperceptibly, but it really was moving.

Houston immediately telephoned colliery Manager Willie Halliday, and broke the bad news to him. He didn't mince his words. There had been a bloody big fall in Number Five, and now there was a bloody big hole in the field directly above it.

Halliday instructed Houston to take three men out of the pit and get them to team up with two others from the pit-head. Their task was to erect a wooden fence around the hole in the field, because there was a hell of a lot at stake here. A right-of-way existed across that particular field, and God forbid, the farmer's cattle could stumble into the hole. Just think of the huge compensation claim that the Coal Board might have to face if that happened, and the hefty kick up the arses they would all receive from the suits. Perish the thought.

However, Andy Houston's own thoughts were elsewhere. A few yards beneath the hole in the field, to be precise, where thirteen of his men were busily grafting away in the sodden squalor of blissful ignorance. He marched purposefully back to the pit-head as fast as his skinny legs could carry him, and into the engine room.

The cage was waiting for him like an obedient puppy.

7.15 p.m.

Andy Houston followed Willie Halliday's instructions to the letter.

Before heading back underground, he had arranged for three intrigued coalminers to be brought back to the surface. There they met up with a couple of pit-head guys as planned, one of whom was Bobby Nairn, the colliery's larger-than-life blacksmith.

When the five bemused conscripts eventually arrived at the locus of the 'sit', they just stared at it in bewildered silence. To experienced coalminers, sits were nothing unusual on the land directly above operational workings. However, this wasn't simply a bog-standard sit. This thing was so big that you could have parked one of local transport businessman Sanny McKechnie's doubled-decker buses in it.

Bobby Nairn pursed his lips and blew. The resultant noise was not unlike that of the exhaust of the new Triumph Tiger 100 motorbike that all the young guys in New Cumnock seemed to be salivating about. Four others blew back in resigned accord.

'Right boys!' Willie Halliday shouted to the men, his voice in fierce competition with the torrential rain. 'Take the wood oot o' that cart over there, and get a fence up a' the way around that hole in the field. And make it quick, boys. Nae time tae lose, so get your arses movin'.'

'Aye-aye, Captain,' a familiar voice replied. It came from the diminutive, wiry-framed Andy Cunningham, and he looked less than impressed.

The Manager just glowered at his Conveyor Shifter, but said nothing. You didn't want to fall out with 'Handy Andy' when there was a job to be done, any job at all. Cunningham was one of the most versatile and technically gifted men in the entire colliery, and Halliday knew it. His neebors always insisted that Handy Andy could have constructed a Royal Navy aircraft carrier from a box of Swan Vestas matches.

The six-foot-high wooden stabs went into the sodden moss like a hot knife through Lipton's butter, nine feet apart as Bobby Nairn had decreed. The four-by-two-inch planks were then nailed on horizontally by Nairn himself, using his trusty old claw-hammer. In no time at all, the fence was nearing completion.

'We're runnin' oot o' wood, Bobby,' one of the drenched miners shouted from the far end of the field.

'For f--k's sake!' Bobby cursed in frustration, heaving the hammer down beside his toolbag. 'I'll go mysel' and get some mair. You lot get on wi' things till I get back.'

No sooner had the big smiddy's tractor disappeared into the saturated autumnal gloom than his neebors standing in the hollow of the field began to feel a very strange sensation beneath their feet. When they looked down, they could scarcely believe their own eyes. The grass was slipping away from under them.

The sit was sinking. Very slowly at first, but it was sinking, no doubt about it. Suddenly, the sides of the basin started to collapse in towards its centre. Big sods of muck from the banking on the far side began dropping into the blackness beneath, shearing the mossy surface and exposing yawning cracks in the hollow. The cracks rapidly expanded in all directions, momentarily rendering the basin with the surreal appearance of a giant dartboard. The fence stabs started tumbling like a row of dominoes, hauling the wooden planks down along with them. And then, the whole fence crashed out of sight and into the void below. Into oblivion.

The four remaining men just stood there, gawking. As more and more grass, moss and muck continued to collapse into the void, the sit expanded in all directions. The earth started twisting in a clockwise direction, rapidly increasing in centrifugal force until it took on the appearance of the local toddlers' favourite toy, the 'spinning top'. The field's contents then began to swirl and rip, before being sucked in towards the middle and plunging out of sight. Disappearing into the void like filthy water down a drain.

'Run, boys!' Halliday hollered. 'Run for your bloody lives!'

The men began scrambling away from the rapidly-expanding vortex as fast as their petrified legs could carry them, the grass giving way beneath their feet as they ran for dear life. All the while, the same vortex seemed to be trying its best to pull them down into the stinking gluey blackness of whatever hellish fate lay below.

By the time the men had emerged from Wilson's field and found themselves wading frantically through the overflowing ditch and onto the makeshift road below the pit-head, they thanked the good lord that their saturated boots were once more on terra firma. A few minutes later, they were back in the relative luxury of the engineers' workshop, all of them still gasping for breath and soaked to the skin.

What now, Willie Halliday conjectured? What the hell do I do now?

There was only one thing for it. Someone – anyone at all - simply had to go back down the pit at once, and get the men in Number Five Heading out of there. Thirteen innocent men up to their arses in water, toiling away in blissful ignorance of the swirling carnage that was erupting only a few yards above their heads. It simply had to be done, and without delay.

'I need one of you to go down in the cage right away, and get these men out of that heading,' Halliday said.

Andy Cunningham looked straight at his gaffer, the rainwater still dripping down his chin onto the wooden floor.

'I'll go, Willie.'

Everyone stared at Handy Andy, blown away by the sheer guts that the wee man had just displayed. There again, perhaps it wasn't guts at all. Perhaps it was just plain stupidity.

The recent fall below ground, and now the burgeoning subsidence above, could only mean one thing. A catastrophic cave-in was now highly likely, and the miners in Number Five were in serious bother.

And so too was Andy Cunningham.

7.25 p.m.

'You're there, Johnny,' Andy Houston remarked casually to the 50-year-old who was loading coal onto the belt conveyor, in a valiant effort to pretend that everything in the world was hunky-dory. He was kidding no one, and certainly not the battle-hardened old fox that was big Johnny Dalziel.

'Whit happened to you, Andy?' Dalziel enquired quizzically, as the beam from his cap-lamp illuminated the beads of water that were still trickling down his gaffer's face. 'Halliday shove you intae the Connel Burn, did he?'

Andy chuckled momentarily, before the reality of what was happening above their heads struck home again. 'I've just come down from the pit-head, Johnny. I don't think this rain is ever going to stop.'

The Oversman continued up the belt conveyor heading, leaving Dalziel to get on with things as if nothing had happened. There was simply no point in radiating the deep sense of foreboding that he felt in the pit of his stomach. He simply had to check out the underground conditions for himself, and take things from there. Andy Houston's heart was thumping faster than the pit pumps.

Discipline, Andy, he reminded himself. You've been through a hell of a lot worse than this before, and you always lived to tell the tale. Keep the heid man, you'll handle it. Had he known that the sit in the field above was by now a spiralling vortex of live muck, his inner voice might not have sounded so convincing.

When Houston had finally clambered all the way up the belt conveyor track's steep incline to the intersection with Number Five Heading itself, there stood the faithful Switch Attendant as usual. At 61 years of age, William Howatt was the oldest man in Dan Strachan's backshift squad.

'How you doin', Paley?' the Oversman enquired, attempting to make his rhetorical question sound as droll as possible in the circumstances. However, when it came to drollness, Paley Howatt had no equal.

'Fair tae middlin', Andy. You?'

'Aye, fine. If it wasn't for the bloody rain, that is. I left the pit-head half-an-hour ago, and I'm still soaked through to my Y-fronts! Everything seem all right up here, Paley?'

'You mean, apart fae a week's worth o' watter poorin' doon the heading, and a big fa' o' coal the length o' a fitba field? Aye, everything's fine Andy. Just champion.'

Houston continued trudging further on up the heading, his thigh muscles straining to the limit, courtesy of the energy-sapping one-in-two slope. I'm getting far too old for this malarkey, he muttered under his laboured breath. For a fleeting moment, the seasoned coalminer reflected on how much easier a life he could have lived if only he had converted his favourite hobby into a proper career. Stitching-and-sewing cloth garments, hardly the domain of the archetypal coalminer. Just for a fleeting moment though, as he quickly reminded himself that every one of his testosterone-charged neebors would have taunted him mercilessly about pursuing 'a wumman's joab'.

The Oversman turned and made his way cautiously into the return airway at the top of Number Five. He was now so close to Bill Wilson's cattle that he could have discussed last Saturday's football match with them. He rested both hands on his knees, and took a well-deserved breather.

What the hell was that?

Houston shot bolt upright, his wiry frame as rigid as if his old army Sergeant Major had just barked another spittle-laden command straight into his face.

And where's that cool air coming from, he asked himself, screwing up his eyes in puzzlement? It reminded him of the through-draught in his own house whenever someone left both the front and back doors open at the same time. The draught that would always be followed by a loud bang when one of the doors suddenly slammed shut.

This time, though, there was no bang. This time there was only silence. However, it was the most deafening silence that Andy Houston had heard for a very long time. In fact, ever since that fleeting moment of blissful solitude which immediately preceded the German shells exploding all around him some 30-odd years back, blasting the innocent bodies of countless young men all the way to kingdom come. And now, here he stood, not this time amid the blood-soaked trenches of the River Somme huddled together with dozens of shell-shocked troopers, but all alone in the eerie silence of a pitch-black coal mine.

The first thing that Houston felt was the sudden surge of pressure in his eardrums. The next was the enormous force of the blast itself, as the cold air belted him flush on the chest. Head over heels he went. Or arse over tit, as they used to say in the trenches.

And then, as quickly as it had happened, it was all over. Houston scrambled back unsteadily to his feet and picked his cap-lamp back up from where it had been catapulted onto the wet floor. His ears were still ringing from the sheer force of the blast.

'Jesus Christ!' he gasped, spitting the muck from his parched lips.

This was no blasphemous outburst from the deeply religious man that was Andy Houston. This was a desperate plea for his good lord to intervene in a day that had started out fairly normally, but which he now knew for sure was about to turn into something else entirely.

A cataclysmic disaster.

7.30 p.m.

Even someone of Andy Houston's vast experience had no idea what had just happened in the heading, none at all.

A blast of cold air? What was that all about? And where the hell had it come from? Suddenly the dawning realisation hit him. It was cold air, Andy, <u>cold</u> air! The clue is in the adjective, you idiot, he rebuked himself.

And in those humid, sticky underground conditions, that could only mean one thing. The cold air hadn't come from down here in the pit; it must have come from up there on the surface. Andy Houston's imagination started whizzing up through the gears like a test driver putting the brand new 1950 Morris Minor through its paces.

First gear; if the blast of air had come from the surface, then it must have been sucked in through some kind of aperture or opening, sucked in from above to equalise the air pressure below. Second gear; the only possible explanation was the big hole that Dan Strachan's shot had blown right through the land basin. Good God, Andy gulped, that was a whole week ago, and all we've done since then is to knock in half-a-dozen wee wooden chocks to hold the roof in place. Third gear; that's where the blast of air has come from, the land basin is starting to collapse! Top gear; please God, let that field be stable enough to hold. If it isn't … if it isn't … then the whole bloody lot might come in! And the rain, the torrential rain … oh my God!

Hands trembling at the very thought of where all this was leading, Houston took three deep breaths, thought of his war medals, and strode purposefully into the pit's furthest extremities. There he met John Montgomery. As the Oversman and his Belt Attendant were about to speculate on what had just happened, another figure suddenly came scurrying out of the darkness of the heading. It was old Jim Haddow, the backshift Switch Attendant. The beam of Houston's cap lamp was just sufficiently strong enough to let him catch the sight of Haddow's eyes bulging out of their sockets as if he had seen a ghost. Perhaps he had.

'Jesus Christ, Andy!' Haddow spluttered, tripping over his boots as he slithered his way towards him along the uneven surface of the pit floor. 'Did you feel that blast o' cauld air? It knocked me aff my feet. I landed on my arse, Andy, right on my arse!'

'You okay, Jim?' Houston enquired. 'You hurt yourself?'

'No, Andy, I'm fine … I think,' Haddow replied, his voice trembling. 'But the belt conveyor, Andy … the belt conveyor …'

'What about the belt conveyor?' the Oversman asked, not really wishing to hear the answer that was coming.

'It moved, Andy!' he replied through chattering teeth. 'The belt conveyor got shoved oot o' its bloody fixings, about ten yards at least … aye, and maybe even fifteen. I'm no' stayin' another minute in this place, Andy. I'm for oot o' here!'

'We all are, Jim,' said Houston, as calmly as his own voice would permit. 'We need to head back to the pit bottom as quickly as possible, and get back up in the cage. You two help me to get the message to Dan and his men in the heading. I'm going to phone the pit-head and tell them that we need to get everybody out of here. Okay, boys?'

Haddow and Montgomery nodded in grateful acquiescence, and began marching back down the heading behind their gaffer, still gasping from the shock of it all.

Suddenly, from behind them, came a terrific ear-splitting roar.

Instinctively, the three men hit the deck and assumed the foetal position, waiting for their own inevitable, awful demise. They had no idea what that particular fate might entail, but they just knew it would be akin to the fires of hell.

A blood-curdling creak began screeching down the full length of the heading, followed immediately by the dreadful sound of metal twisting as if caught in some huge industrial vice. The three men raised their heads and looked straight ahead, straining their eyes at the dreamlike vision in front of them. In the flickering beams of their cap lamps, it looked at first like one of the miniature railway trains that the children loved to play on at the summer funfairs on Ayr's Low Green, or even New Cumnock's own 'Castle Races'. However, Andy Houston, John Montgomery and Jim Haddow all knew one thing for sure.

This was no summer funfair.

'It's the belt conveyor!' Haddow shouted. 'Look at it! It's gettin' shoved a' the way doon the dook!'

'Holy Goad!' Montgomery gasped, grabbing at his hair in disbelief.

As the roar behind them turned into a deep, continuous low-pitched rumble, Andy Houston surveyed the scene in front. For an instant, he recalled the day away back in August 1916 when a German mortar bomb had blown his best mate's head-and-shoulders clean off his torso, as they crouched side-by-side on the gore-splattered banks of the Somme. That day, Andy had feared he was about to meet his maker.

Today, though, he was absolutely certain.

7.45 p.m.

Life is all about decisions. Or at least, so they say.

And at precisely quarter-to-eight on that infamous Thursday evening, Andy Houston had to make the most important decision of his life. Worse still, he had no more than a few seconds in which to make it. His dilemma was this. Up the way, or down the way, Andy?

The terrifying scenario that now confronted Andy Houston was defined by its exceedingly elaborate three-dimensional layout. Not only did a complex web of roughly level roadways shoot out before him in all directions of the compass, but so too did an even more bewildering 'rabbit warren' of headings and dooks upwards and downwards at umpteen different gradients.

In those few fleeting moments available to Houston, he had to recall from the deepest recesses of his consciousness all of those critical decisions that he had previously been called upon to make during the course of an incredibly dramatic life, and also the clinical rationale that had prompted him to make them. He hadn't called every one of those decisions right, that was for sure, but he had got remarkably few of them wrong, and for one very good reason. His experience of life had taught him the difference between blind panic and forensically astute judgement. In an instant, he once more instinctively deployed the latter.

Whatever ghastly hell-storm was coming towards the 129 men in the bowels of Knockshinnoch Castle Colliery was coming with a vengeance. The terrifying rumble was getting louder and louder, radiating an unearthly message of death and destruction. If its deep, low tone reminded him of the big bass drum in New Cumnock's renowned Silver Band, then its eardrum-shattering volume roared of one-thousand drummers.

Up the way, or down the way, Andy? Make your bloody mind up!

'Quick boys, this way!' he shouted above the deafening din. 'And don't ask any questions, just do it!'

And off Houston started up the slope of the dook on the 'rise' side of Number Five Heading, the one which he knew for sure led in the direction of the return airway from the main surface bore-hole. John Montgomery and Jim Haddow scarpered after him like obedient bloodhounds on a Marquis's foxhunt.

Houston ploughed on, with both Montgomery and Haddow scrambling willingly in his wake. Not a single word was spoken, the crunching of their miners' boots on the wet pit floor being the only discernible sound that could be heard in competition with the mayhem that was wreaking havoc down below. It was Haddow who broke the verbal silence.

'Where are we headin', Andy?'

'Up and over the top of the West Mine Turn,' replied the Oversman, breathing heavily. 'If we can make it to the return airway at the top of Garrowscairn Number Three, we can get down the dook to the far end of the Turn. I need to get a message to all the Firemen in the pit, and tell them to get their men to hell out of there.'

'But it'll take us a guid fifteen minutes to get to Garrowscairn, Andy,' Montgomery remarked, clearly unconvinced.

'Aye, fifteen if we're lucky,' added Haddow, now struggling to keep up with the pace.

'Well, what else do you two suggest, then?' the Oversman retorted impatiently, bringing their scramble for freedom to an abrupt halt. 'Come on, I'm listening!'

And if that rhetorical question hadn't already focussed their minds, then Houston's next statement certainly did.

'So far, we've been the lucky ones, boys, remember that. Just imagine what all your neebors are going through at the moment, back down there. And now we've got a job to do, a damned important job at that. We've got to get a message to all the men in the West Mine.'

Two cap-lamp beams nodded in resigned acceptance that Andy Houston had made the only sensible decision possible in the circumstances.

'Right then, so let's get moving,' the Oversman said brusquely. 'And no more blethering. We've got to get to these men without delay.'

7.50 p.m.

'Handy Andy' Cunningham leapt out of the cage like a gazelle with its arse on fire.

What the hell are you doing, man, he screamed at himself? Jesus Christ, Andy, when will you ever learn to keep your big mouth shut?

The enormity of his latest and decidedly *risque* act of valour had finally hit him, and hit him square between the eyes. Here he now was, half a mile under the ground and scurrying towards the hellhole that was Number Five Heading as fast as his legs could carry him, in the near-certain knowledge that an enormous cave-in was about to engulf the whole place. The big clue was the deafening din reverberating all around him.

The pit had always been a very noisy place, with the roars of the joy loaders, locomotives, coal cutting machinery and belt conveyors always just managing to get the better of the thumping pickaxes and swishing shovels. However, tonight was different. Tonight was defined by another background noise altogether. Low-pitched but high energy, distant but getting closer. The pit floor trembled under Cunningham's feet, and the wooden props shook like jelly-legged weightlifters as they strained to hold the roof in place.

In the distance, the mighty arc cutters still continued to rip through the coal seams. Likewise, the pickaxes and shovels clattered and clanked from every conceivable recess of Knockshinnoch Castle's vast expanses. The whole pit was teetering on the brink of disaster, yet it seemed that nobody gave a damn. And that was when the realisation suddenly dawned on Cunningham. I'm the only person in this whole damned place who knows what's about to happen.

Turn around now, Andy, his sensible voice counselled him. Turn around and get your arse back into that cage … right now! And then what, his alter ego retorted angrily? Just leave all your neebors down here on their own? Leave them with absolutely no warning about what's going to hit them any minute now? Leave them here while the floodgates of hell are about to burst open?

'Nae chance!' Cunningham roared out loud, as he scrambled on up the dook in the direction of Number Five. 'Nae bloody chance!'

About 300 yards further on, a solitary miner's cap-lamp suddenly emerged from the pitch blackness, its host strolling along towards Cunningham as if enjoying a Sunday School picnic on the banks of the Afton Water.

'Get out now!' Cunningham screamed at the shapeless figure beneath the lamp. 'Head for the cage!'

As the two miners' paths crossed, the forlorn figure spoke at last, but as if it didn't have a single care in the world. 'That's some racket back there.'

'Get out!' Cunningham screamed again. 'The whole bloody pit's comin' in! Move yoursel', man!'

Andy Cunningham had no earthly idea who the man was, nor indeed whether his verbal blast had even registered, but he had done his bit and could do no more. About 50 yards further along the road stood a much burlier figure, only this time one that he recognised immediately. It was Johnny Dalziel.

'Get out, Johnny!' he shouted, 'as quick as you can! There's been a big fall, and it'll no' be long till we're up tae our necks in it. Quick, Johnny! Head for the pit bottom. Now!'

Clearly confused, Johnny Dalziel stood transfixed at first, then began scurrying back in the completely opposite direction, clearly now in a bit of a stew.

'No' that way, Johnny!' Cunningham bawled. 'Head for the cage, for Christ's sake!'

'But my jaicket, Andy …' Dalziel mumbled, 'I need to get my jaicket …'

'Never mind your bloody jaicket, Johnny!' Cunningham yelled, as the old fellow disappeared from view back in the direction of the heading's belt conveyor. 'Johnny, just get out of here!'

Suddenly, a terrific roar erupted from the general direction of the heading, so enormous that it seemed as if planet earth itself had just been blasted asunder. Andy Cunningham caught his breath with such depth that he thought he might never exhale again. This was no routine underground landslip, he assured himself, not even a respectable cave-in.

This was Hiroshima and Nagasaki rolled into one. This was Armageddon.

Covering his ears with the palms of both hands, he stood and stared in the direction of the heading. He knew what was coming, and there was nothing he could do about it.

It was death itself.

7.52 p.m.

Somehow amid that near-infinitesimal split second of horror, Andy Cunningham allowed his memory to float back to a memorable science lesson he had learned during his adolescent years in New Cumnock Junior Secondary School.

'Light travels faster than sound.'

A very important lesson indeed, and one that for some reason had always stuck with him. And now as Cunningham braced himself for the silent vision from hell, he knew for certain that it would then be followed by the deafening roar from hell.

And down the heading it came, raging with evil vengeance, a huge river of sludge. Black, stinking, unstoppable, silently at first. Neither solid in the proper sense of the word, nor even liquid for that matter. Andy Cunningham just gawked at it in mesmerised shock for a single fleeting moment.

His granny's porridge, that's what it reminded him of! Thick and impenetrable, it used to stick to his breakfast plate like glue to a postage stamp, and his granny would tell him that it would stick to his ribs as well. Completely captivated in awe, the faintest nostalgic smile attempted to form on his parched lips.

It was the almighty roar that snapped Cunningham out of his trance.

'Oh God ... oh God!' he gasped, recoiling backwards and stumbling down onto his backside. He sat there staring in horror as the enormous river of sludge raged down the floor of the dook towards him, its incredible momentum immediately filling the whole expanse right up to roof level as it advanced at speed.

The voice in Cunningham's head was in fine working order. 'Get your arse oot o' here, or you're deid!' it screamed.

The problem was his legs. They were paralysed, hopelessly welded to the spot. Frozen with dread, he noticed two cap lamps, maybe three, diving into a side-heading to flee the raging torrent. A few seconds later, the same side-heading was completely sealed off by the unstoppable inrush, and the cap lamps had disappeared into what had instantly become an utterly impenetrable human tomb.

'Run Andy, run!' his inner voice screamed again.

This time his legs did begin to move, but they were trembling like jelly. Somehow he succeeded in scrambling back to his feet. He slowly began stumbling in the general direction of the pit bottom, like a drunk man being shown the door from Bridgend Bar after one too many on a Saturday night.

The sludge seemed to be hunting Cunningham down mercilessly, like a foxhound after its petrified prey. By then the stuff's evil contents were oozing out of every dook, heading and side-heading all along the roadway, resembling a monstrous facsimile of his mum's famous vanilla icing being squeezed from a giant 'piping bag'. Soon Cunningham's legs were pumping like those of an Olympic sprinter making a desperate lunge towards the finishing line.

By the time he had caught sight of the roof lights at the pit bottom, he was already waist-high in sludge and convinced that his heart was about to burst. Somehow he managed to grab hold of an overhead steel girder, and with one almighty effort, succeeded in pulling himself free. Then, by using his hands and arms like a well-trained chimpanzee to swing his torso from one girder to another, he eventually contrived to get ahead of the stuff again. When he eventually reached the main shaft, the palms of his hands resembled a pair of burst sofas, and his entire body was shaking in shock.

As Cunningham leapt into the empty cage, he looked back in the direction from which he had come. He had out-manoeuvred the sludge for now, but it was still advancing towards the shaft at unbelievable speed, casting aside everything in its path like spent apple blossom in a force-ten gale and filling up every single road from bottom to top as it did so.

This was his last chance. Up to the pit-head in the cage right now or die, Andy. A no-brainer, as the youth of today would say.

No sooner had Andy Cunningham burst into the relative security of the cage, than he immediately stepped back out of it again. If all those back-breaking but highly-rewarding years in the New Cumnock Coalfield had taught him anything, then it was this.

There's a lot more to life than saving your own arse. Saving your neebors' arses, for example.

Cunningham picked up the 'listening tube' on the telephone set and wound the handle, his hands still trembling.

'It's a disaster,' he spluttered down the line to Willie Halliday. 'A total bloody disaster, Willie. The whole pit's fillin' up, a' the way fae Number Five through the rest o' the South Boig. Flair to roof, Willie, flair to roof. Gie it another five minutes, and the sludge will have reached the winding shaft itsel'.'

'Just hang on, Andy,' Halliday shouted down the phone. 'I'll be down right away. Get a message to the Firemen in the districts, and tell them to bring their men outbye to the pit bottom immediately, failing which to the Old Knockshinnoch shaft.'

'But Willie …'

'Do it now!'

And down went the phone.

7.53 p.m.

If Walls Walker's job as backshift locomotive driver wasn't exactly the most riveting in the world, then it was certainly one of the most important in the depths of Knockshinnoch Castle.

Step one; pick up the empty three-quarter-ton tubs from the pit bottom, hook them onto the big diesel locomotive about 50-to-60 at a time, and drive them to the 'endless rope' for the coal-getters to collect and draw them to the coal face. Step two; take the newly-laden tubs back to the winding shaft for transportation to the surface. Step three; do the whole bloody thing all over again.

And again, and again.

It wasn't very often that anything exciting happened on Walls Walker's shift, save for the odd mechanical breakdown or the occasional daydreamer wandering carelessly across the rail track, depressingly rare incidents which Walker would always greet as welcome distractions from the mundane humdrum.

And, of course, if ever young Walls Walker needed a wee bit of distraction, then it was tonight of all nights. Anything at all, just to take his frantic mind off the thought of his wonderful Jessie lying stretched out like a beached whale on their second-hand settee. The visiting midwife's words to her were still ringing in his ears.

'Any day now, Jessie lass, any day now.'

Walker administered yet another silent self-rebuke. Jessie's about to go into labour any minute now, and here am I all cooped up in this shithole of a place, when I should be up there by her side. What a clown, Walls, what a bloody clown. If it wasn't for the money, I'd tell the Coal Board where to stick their job.

Walls Walker really needed a distraction that evening. Anything at all, anything just to stop him fretting about his beloved Jessie and their new baby-to-be. What he didn't know, though, was that once tonight's particular distraction had finally arrived, he would never wish to witness another. Never, ever.

Walker scratched the darkening stubble on his chin. What's that noise, he asked himself, a bit perplexed? It sounded a bit like a scene from that *Tarzan Of The Jungle* film which he had taken Jessie to see in Biddals' picture house, the one with the tropical waterfall cascading into the freshwater lagoon.

He leaned out the open 'window' of his cabin to get a better view of what was up ahead. All he could see were the exhaust fumes of Jim Serrie's loco in front, as the two pals and their precious cargoes rumbled along the West Mine's rail track, back towards the pit shaft. As Walker's backside bounced up and down on the wooden seat of his loco, he found himself perplexed by the strange noise. So familiar was he with the multitudinous sounds of the pit, he could have pinpointed the precise location of a flatulent miners' fart without even lifting his head.

What the hell's that bloody noise?

He stuck his head out of the cabin again to see if he could catch a glimpse of whatever was happening up in front, because it sure was getting louder by the second. Whatever it was, he thought, Jim would see it before he did, because the wee man's loco was now only a couple of hundred yards or so off the winding shaft.

The noise was getting closer. Much closer, and much louder.

Soon Walker couldn't even hear the roar of his own diesel engine. Something was seriously wrong, no doubt about it. When his loco rounded the final turn, his pupils automatically narrowed to allow them to adjust from the gloom of the West Mine to the dazzling overhead lighting of the pit bottom. However, it wasn't the sudden increase in 'lux' that took Walls Walker's breath away.

'Christ Almighty!' he gasped, as he slammed on the brakes of the diesel locomotive.

And there, before his very eyes, it came rushing down from the roof above the main roadway, an enormous putrid sea of blackness. And all of it bursting out from an old disused air-course, with a momentum so violent that the pit props and roof trusses were being blasted out of their fixings like splintering matchsticks.

Walls Walker froze, more in bewilderment than terror, gawking open-mouthed at the sight that confronted him. Ten seconds ago, he had been watching the tail-end of his mate Jim's loco puffing along the clear rail track in front. Now here he was, staring in disbelief at a river of God-knows-what erupting from the pit roof and surging along the road towards him.

The black stuff reached the loco's wheels before Walker had time to get his brain into gear. Instinctively, he thrust his foot out of the cabin door and shoved it into the sludge. It pounced at his pit boot like a starving python at a petrified rodent. Grabbing his moleskin trousers around the knee, he hauled his foot free. What the hell is this stuff?

Heart thumping, Walker looked along the road towards the pit bottom, only to discover to his horror that the same pit bottom was now completely blocked from view. All he could see was sludge. Hundreds and hundreds of tons of the stuff, possibly even thousands, and it had already filled the old roadway from the pit floor right up to the metal girders that lined the curved roof.

Suddenly, the brutal reality of the situation hit him right between the eyes. There was now no way back from the West Mine to the winding shaft at the pit bottom, absolutely none at all. The shaft was at one side of this enormous mass of muck, he was at the other, and so too were all of his unsuspecting neebors in the West Mine.

Cut off by a sea of sludge. Cut off from the outside world. Cut off from their waiting families. And, of course, Walker himself cut off from the new baby boy or girl who was about to make its spectacular entrance into this unforgiving, perilous world.

Almost sick with shock, Walker just stared at his pit boot. The sludge clung onto it like his mum's famous porridge to a wooden spurtle. There was only one thing for it. His heart still racing, he grabbed the handle of the cabin door and shoved. It wouldn't budge. He thrust his head out of the window once more. The sludge was now over the loco's wheels and rising.

Walker slid across to the opposite door and shoved again. He then leaned his back against the wooden seat and kicked the door open, just sufficiently wide enough to allow him to squeeze his torso out of the cabin. Momentary thoughts flashed through his mind. They were of a fully developed human foetus struggling to fight its way through the birth canal.

He made his decision in an instant. It was to run as fast as his legs could carry him back along the turf slope of the West Mine, and in the opposite direction to the winding shaft. As he ran, gasping for breath and sweat pouring down his cheeks, he suddenly heard a very strange noise behind him. It was a high-pitched metallic 'squeal', one that reminded him momentarily of the Glasgow-to-London steam train pulling into New Cumnock railway station. When Walker stopped to turn around, he could scarcely believe his own eyes.

Not only had his diesel locomotive and its cargo of 57 hutches been stopped in its tracks by the massive inrush of sludge, but it was now actually being shoved back along the rail track in the completely opposite direction. As metal wheels screeched on metal rails, the sludge continued to surge forward until, suddenly, the whole contraption got shoved right off the track altogether, at which point the hutches began to concertina into each other with a succession of thunderous 'bang-bang-bangs'.

Bewildered by what he was actually witnessing, Walker started bolting again towards the West Mine, only with a renewed vigour fuelled by real terror. A few minutes later, he was beginning to pull clear of the sludge, although he could still hear the deeply threatening rumble behind him as it continued to chase him for dear life. Was it beginning to slow down, Walker wondered? Because if it didn't, and managed to plough on until it reached the roadway's furthest extremity, then he and every other miner in the West Mine would soon be facing a very watery grave.

At last, he saw the welcome sight of a miner's cap-lamp in the distance. It transpired to belong to coalminer Jimmy McLatchie, who upon hearing Walker's breathless account of what had just happened and clocking the horrifying deluge coming his way, willingly agreed to join him on his frantic scramble to reach the higher ground at the far end of the roadway. A few minutes later, another lamp began to approach them. This one belonged to none other than Andy Houston himself, the Oversman having decided to walk out from the West Mine to see things for himself.

No sooner had Houston's eyes lit up at the sight of his two charges having made it along the roadway towards him, than that same beam of pleading expectation was immediately extinguished by Walls Walker's breathless message.

'I don't ken whit you're daein' oot here, Andy,' he spluttered. 'The road's blocked solid back there. Blocked fae flair to roof, an' the stuff's comin' this way fast.'

'So no way back to the shaft?' Houston asked solemnly.

'Nae chance,' gasped Walker.

Jimmy McLatchie nodded in accord. 'No' a snowba's chance in hell, Andy.'

And at that very moment, the wise 'auld heid' that was Andy Houston suddenly realised the awful truth. Every last man in Knockshinnoch Castle Colliery was trapped, and there was no way out.

Their workplace had just become their tomb.

8.35 p.m.

As Andy Cunningham stood trembling in shock and gasping for breath at the pit bottom, he surveyed the scene all around him. It wasn't the most encouraging situation he had ever encountered. The whole place stank like a public lavatory after a week-long council strike.

Behind him in the South Boig District of the pit, the roadways were already hopelessly blocked by the huge tidal wave of sludge as it continued to surge menacingly towards the winding shaft. Everywhere he looked, the stuff squeezed down every last heading and dook. Straight in front of him, it had also started spewing from the return airways above, and down onto the main track in the direction of the West Mine itself. The West Mine where 116 miners were still toiling away in splendid ignorance of the utter carnage taking place, as a whole farm field continued to crack and crumble down Number Five Heading into the void below.

Cunningham bit his lip and stifled a terrified tear. *This is where we all die.*

Suddenly, amid the incessant rumble of the sludge gushing out in all directions around him, he heard the familiar rattle of the cage descending. Out stepped Willie Halliday, a sight for sore eyes if ever there was one.

Their immediate task was clear. They simply had to find out if any possible escape routes remained open, because it looked as if every single road, heading and dook was now already full to the girders with sludge, or in the process of filling up very rapidly.

'Did you manage to get a message to the Firemen, Andy?' Halliday asked, more in pleading hope than realistic expectation.

'Nae chance, Willie,' Cunningham replied, shaking his head ruefully. 'No' even one o' them answered the phone. The bell's hard enough to hear doon these dooks at the best o' times, but with a' this noise ...'

'Bugger it!' Halliday muttered, looking all around as if expecting some kind of miraculous vision of salvation to manifest itself from the dark, damp stink of the pit bottom. 'Those poor bastards in the West Mine have probably no idea what's happening down here.'

Halliday and Cunningham then proceeded to explore the various potential egress routes, to try to find any possible means by which the men in the West Mine area of the pit might conceivably make it through to the winding shaft, and hence to the surface. Hardly a word was spoken about those who had been working in Number Five Heading itself when the sludge had come rushing in. After all, nothing really needed to be said, nothing at all.

Almost inevitably, every roadway and return airway that Halliday and Houston attempted to enter was already either choked full or filling up at an alarming rate. Three separate times during their futile explorations, both men managed to pull themselves free from the pernicious clutches of the advancing muck just before it succeeded in sucking them underneath.

Meanwhile, all around them, the constant booming rumble continued as the stuff gurgled relentlessly from every pit orifice, closer and closer to the shaft at the pit bottom. Every now and again, the occasional resounding 'crack!' interrupted the rhythmic tremor of the sludge's steady advance, as yet another enormous section of Wilson's field above imploded from the rain-drenched vortex into the depths below.

Next out of the cage was the Agent himself, Johnny Bone. The look of horror on his face said it all. Willie Halliday quickly briefed him on the situation, and Andy Cunningham tried to fill in the blanks. The blanks easily outnumbered the words of encouragement.

Trapped on all sides, and with the sludge now at the pit bottom and creeping menacingly into the winding shaft itself, there was nothing else that the three men could now do. Bone signalled for the cage to take them back up to the pit-head. By the time the winding mechanism had begun to take the strain, they were already up to their chests in the stuff, and with eyes closed in disbelieving terror, contemplating their imminent horrific fate. A moment later, they were being hauled upwards towards the surface.

When they arrived traumatised at the pit-head's engine room, they would not be the bearers of good news.

9.10 p.m.

'Where's Mister Clapperton?' shouted the young pit-boy, as he bolted towards the Mech section of the pit, trying desperately to catch his breath.

'Doon there son,' a voice replied from the darkness. 'Doon at the endless rope. Whit's wrong, son, you lost your play-piece?'

'What is it, lad?' enquired the refined voice of the section's Fireman, Eck Clapperton, his elevated position betrayed by the distinctive corrugated rim on his miners' helmet.

'There's been a big accident, Mister Clapperton!' the youngster gasped breathlessly. 'The Connel Burn is in! Yous have a' got to come oot, and make your way to the telephone station.'

'Says who?' Clapperton demanded, knowing full well the impact that this would have on coal production, and the dent it would make in his men's hard-earned pay packets come the weekend.

'It's an order … an order fae Mister Houston himsel', Mister Clapperton!' the lad spluttered nervously. 'An order tae a' the Firemen in the pit tae get their men oot, and head for the telephone station. You've no' tae argue, Mister Clapperton, you've just … you've just tae dae whit Mister Houston says!'

Clapperton pondered the message carefully. The Connel Burn is in? How the hell can the Connel Burn be in?

He knew that the little burn's trajectory took it past Knockshinnoch farm, adjacent to which was situated the opening to a relatively steep mine formerly deployed as the main coal transportation route from Old Knockshinnoch to the pit-head. However, these days it was only ever used as an occasional alternative access and egress road, although it also did a fine job as an auxiliary airway. In truth, the proximity of the mine's entrance to the normally gently-flowing Connel Burn – about ten yards, at most – had always troubled some of the more experienced miners. They realised that if the burn should suddenly go into really serious spate someday and burst its banks, the flood water could conceivably start pouring down the mine itself.

And so, as Eck Clapperton led his men towards the West Mine telephone station, he found himself pondering on how such a thing could possibly have happened. Sure, there had been a lot of rain over the past few days, in fact a hell of a lot of rain. And yes, the Connel Burn might well have burst its banks and started running into the old mine workings.

Surely, though, the problem couldn't be so bad as to prompt Andy Houston to call a complete halt to production, simply because of a wee bit of flood water? Good grief, that's what the pit's pumps were for. Houston wasn't normally one for overreacting whenever the going got tough.

However, as soon as Clapperton and his men emerged from the Mech section onto the main West Mine roadway, they could hear it.

'It' sounded uncannily like the ebb-and-flow of the Firth of Clyde lapping onto Ayr beach, many a coalminer's favourite family haunt on a glorious summer's Sunday afternoon. Aye, the Connel Burn could be in right enough, Clapperton and his men soon reluctantly agreed.

Meantime, it was the dook runner who conveyed Andy Houston's instruction to the miners toiling away in Garrowscairn No. 1:

> 'We were told to stop working immediately, and to come 'outbye' and head for the West Mine telephone station,' recalled Willie Lopez. 'We just assumed that there had been a fatality in the pit, since production was always brought to an immediate halt anytime somebody died.'

Andrew McDicken's recollections were almost identical to that of his shift neebor and great pal, Lopez. However, McDicken seemed to remember that the messages delivered to the men in Garrowscairn were a bit less clear, at least initially:

> 'The dook runner's first message was for us to head for the pit bottom. It was only when we had started walking back up the dook that the instruction got changed, and we were told to make for the West Mine telephone station instead. At that stage, we had no idea that there had been a cave-in, but we knew that something was badly wrong. The problem was that we had already eaten all our pit-pieces and drunk most of our water. You see, you just had to keep drinking water down there, because you were hacking out the coal and shovelling it into the hutches in really hot conditions. And then there was the coal dust. Most of the time, you couldnae even see for stoor!'

Meanwhile, Andy Houston was already retracing his steps back towards the West Mine telephone station, accompanied by Walls Walker and Jimmy McLatchie. Houston's shoulders were already beginning to sag heavily from the sheer weight of responsibility they were now carrying. The good people of New Cumnock had a name for such a condition.

'Humfy-backit', they called it.

Not only did the battle-scarred Oversman know for sure that he and his men were now hopelessly trapped half a mile underneath the New Cumnock fields, but he was pretty damned certain about something else as well. All thirteen men who had been working in the immediate vicinity of Number Five Heading had perished already.

And one of them was Jimmy. His own brother.

Hardly surprisingly, Andy Houston's mood was by then a very sombre one indeed. However, there was simply no time to lose. He just had to get his act together, because well over 100 lives depended on strong leadership and clarity of thinking. He had been tested many times before in the most harrowing of circumstances, Houston reminded himself, and he had never fallen short of the mark, not even once. Somehow, he had to raise his game and do it all over again, because today would be his greatest test.

In the distance, he could just make out the gathering speckles of light, as 115 miners began to congregate at the West Mine telephone station to learn the awful truth.

'Think, Andy!' he whispered under his breath, as he approached his charges. 'Come on man, think! What are you going to say to your men?'

Words of inspiration were not coming easily.

9.50 p.m.

Andy Houston's authority over his men was never gained from barking and bawling at them. It was borne out of quiet authority and hard-earned respect.

Once the remaining miners on Thursday's ill-fated backshift had been summoned from their respective workplaces and made their way in remarkably orderly fashion to the telephone station, they instinctively shuffled themselves as calmly as possible into the shape of a captive audience. Some parked their weary backsides down on the pit floor, while others just continued standing as if they were waiting for a bus. The former were clearly more conducive to learning their fate than the latter, whose bus would be a long time coming.

The area in which the men had been instructed to gather wasn't all that cramped as such, but neither could it have been described as cavernous in size. Nor indeed was it exactly the lap of luxury, but it would simply have to do for the time being. A matter of a few hours at worst, most of them imagined. However, Walls Walker, Jimmy McLatchie and Andy Houston knew different. After all, they had seen it for themselves. An ocean of sludge coming this way, and coming fast.

The 'assembly area' was about 45 feet long by eighteen feet wide, with a relatively smooth pit floor (known as a 'pavement') underfoot, along which ran the locomotive's rail-track. The curved metal-girder-lined roof was about fifteen feet high at its apex. This particular locus of the pit had always been known as the West Mine telephone station. Alas, the grandeur of its title completely belied the primitive crudeness of its non-existent facilities, as Willie Lopez reflected:

'The West Mine telephone station? There was nae telephone "station" at a'. It was just a phone hingin' on a wa'!'

And on that wall hung a rectangular-shaped metal box, inside which was located a telephone set consisting of a winding handle, listening tube and mouthpiece. From the bottom of the box ran a thin black telephone line that was stapled onto the wooden fixings of the coal wall and all the way along the three-quarter-of-a-mile journey back to the winding shaft, then up the shaft to the pit-head. At least it had done, until one of the farm fields half-a-mile above their heads had decided to enter the equation and rip out every last subterranean man-made structure by its roots.

Andy Houston knew that there was simply no chance that this puny little telephone wire could have withstood the enormous force of the inrush, not a hope in hell. Good God, even the steel-reinforced, six-inch-thick power lines that fed every major section of the pit had been snapped like rotten twigs, and left dangling like the wife's split-ends after a cheap hairdo gone wrong.

Houston eyeballed his charges as best he could in the faint glimmer of the light generated by a sea of cap-lamps.

'Right boys, gather round, and listen very carefully.'

He proceeded to instruct them to turn their lamps down to 'emergency setting', explaining his reasoning in the simplest of terms. They were going to be here for a while. Quite possibly, a bloody long while.

A deathly silence descended, save for some nervous breathing in the foreground and that all-too-familiar malevolent low-pitched rumble in the background. Every last man stared at Houston, hoping for the good news, but instinctively expecting the bad. It was the bad they were about to receive.

The Oversman began his explanation, his tone as calm and reassuring as he could muster in the circumstances. He told them that there had been a huge cave-in at Number Five in the South Boig District, and that the amount of stuff that had collapsed into the pit was colossal.

When a voice from the back asked, 'what kind o' stuff, Andy?' Walls Walker retorted, 'sludge – black, stinkin' sludge.' Walker then proceeded to tell the men about the enormity of the sludge's volume and force, and how the inrush had somehow succeeded in shoving his loco and all of its tubs backwards along the rail track. As soon as the men began to start hollering question-after-question at Walker, Houston decided that enough was enough.

'Right, boys!'

Silence descended once more. The men really needed a leader, and like it or lump it, Andy Houston was it. He cleared his throat, and proceeded to make the most important speech of his life.

He began by telling his men that he was about to give them the complete picture, warts and all, and that no matter how this whole incident might pan out, he would always be completely honest with them and tell them the full story, good or bad. Had it not been for the continuing rumble in the background, they might otherwise have heard a pin drop.

He proceeded to emphasise that he himself had only very limited information at his disposal by this stage. What he did know was that there had been an enormous fall at Number Five, and it had almost certainly had catastrophic consequences for the thirteen men working in that section of the pit. It was clear that 'Bill Wilson's field' immediately above the heading had now caved in, and that its contents seemed to be crashing into the pit's workings in the form of a semi-solid, semi-liquid sludge. The sludge had then burst through the South Boig road-end, and also through the roof of the pit at the old disused air-course a few hundred yards along the West Mine Turn. It had blasted itself into the pit by unstoppable force of gravity and at terrific speed, filling up every roadway, heading, dook and air-course in its path, all the way from pavement to girders.

As the miners listened open-mouthed in disbelieving shock, those who had earlier been standing were now slumping down on the pavement one by one, as the horror of their predicament began to hit home. They now knew to a man that they would be going nowhere soon.

Houston then told his men that there were two matters of immediate concern. Firstly, their normal egress route to the winding shaft at the pit bottom had been completely blocked by sludge. Secondly, the stuff was still making its way inbye towards them, although the signs were that its momentum was beginning to slow down a bit. He explained that it was because of the sludge's continued progress into the pit depths that he had ordered everyone to gather here at the telephone station, the highest point on the West Mine roadway.

A nervous voice piped up from the near-darkness. What about the other winding shaft, the one at the foot of Old Knockshinnoch pit? It was a voice that enquired more in hope than expectation. The shaft had always been recognised as an emergency escape route in the event of a catastrophe such as this, so surely the men could head in that direction? No chance, Jimmy McLatchie interjected. The only route to Old Knockshinnoch was from The Castle pit bottom, and the whole road was now 'stapped tae the gunnels wae bloody sludge'.

The men's anxieties began to rise by the second, as did the volume of their protestations. So we're trapped in here, like rabbits in a snare? Worse than that, we're trapped under the ground. Buried alive, for Christ's sake! What if we don't get out? Who's going to look after Betty and the weans? What do you mean, 'what if we don't get out?' The gaffers up there don't even know where we are, for Christ's sake!

And so it went on, as the Oversman and his bewildered charges attempted to gather their thoughts. Suddenly, a youthful voice piped up from the shadows.

'Is the telephone workin', Mister Houston?'

Houston let out a despondent sigh, shaking his head ruefully. No chance, son, not a hope in hell. What a bloody stupid question.

The brutal reality of the situation had already belted everyone else in the guts, and now it was Andy Houston's turn to let down his own guard and feel the awful pangs of dread for himself. Here they all were, trapped in this hellhole, half-a-mile beneath their beloved New Cumnock and their precious families. Buried alive, with almost no hope of anyone ever finding them, let alone actually getting them out.

Suddenly, Houston was hit by a dawning realisation. He was 'it'. He was the man in charge, the man who was supposed to be demonstrating leadership. Give yourself a bloody shake, Andy, he rebuked himself silently. Thirteen men have almost certainly perished in Number Five, swept away by the enormous inrush of sludge, and drowned like unwanted kittens in a sack. And here you are, feeling sorry for yourself. Give yourself a bloody shake, man!

And then the very next moment, the back of his head was again slumped heavily against the damp coal wall. Oh, Jesus Christ, Jimmy is dead. My beloved

Jimmy. As the Oversman buried his head in his hands, over one hundred distraught miners did likewise.

'Haw Mister Houston!' the same youthful voice persisted from somewhere in the mirk. 'Are you sure the phone's no' workin'?'

Andy Houston cringed at the futility of the boy's utterly inane question. No way could a flimsy little telephone wire have withstood the sheer force of such an enormous cave-in. He lost his customary cool.

'I'll tell you what, son. If you think the phone could still be working after everything that's just happened here, then why don't you try it yourself?'

The youngster got up, and walked over to the telephone box as calmly as you like. He opened the door, lifted the listening tube out of its cradle and wound the telephone handle. A few seconds elapsed, then a few more.

The young miner suddenly broke the silent tension. 'Hello!'

Andy Houston's head shot up, and every other set of eyes immediately followed his gaze.

'Aye, we're fine, Dougie! But you'd better tell Halliday that we're stuck doon here, an' we cannae get oot.'

Andy Houston shot to his feet, and ripped the tube out of the bemused lad's fist.

10.30 p.m.

As the activity on the Knockshinnoch Castle Colliery pit-head accelerated from frantic to feverish, the people of New Cumnock prepared to retire for the night in splendid ignorance.

There were beds to turn down, children to kiss goodnight and late-night suppers to put on the kitchen table for the men coming off the backshift, before sleep could descend like a cool autumnal mist. However, for the good folks of the village, sleep, that most basic of human privileges, would soon become impossibly elusive.

When Johnny Bone, Willie Halliday and Andy Cunningham were eventually dragged out of the cage, gasping for breath and saturated from shoulders to feet in muck, they somehow managed between them to splutter out the few words that were needed to warn of the unfolding catastrophe down below.

As they did so, a bell began to ring on the pit-head, immediately followed by another, then another still. Those were the bells controlled by the men underground, who traditionally rang them to convey a series of messages to the surface. Now the same bells were ringing of their own accord, their wire terminals short-circuited by the watery sludge below. Ringing in desperation, screaming their desperate screams for help.

All hell broke loose on the surface. By ten-thirty, The Castle pit-head resembled Glasgow's Sauchiehall Street in the January sales, and the switchboard in Miss Veitch's Post Office telephone exchange in her village-centre upstairs flat had become hopelessly jammed with outgoing calls from the colliery's red-hot phones.

Within minutes, most of the calls were being diverted to neighbouring Cumnock's much larger Hearth Road telephone exchange, as frantic attempts were made to notify all the relevant authorities. The local sub-area and area managers in the Dunaskin and Lugar offices; the Coal Board's top brass in Ayr, Dumfries, Edinburgh and even the national HQ in London's Hobart Street; all of the Ayrshire police constabularies; the fire authorities in New Cumnock, Cumnock, Kilmarnock and Coatbridge; The National Union of Mine Workers (NUM); His Majesty's (HM) Inspector of Mines. You name them, and they all had to be given the sobering news without delay. Everybody and anybody who had a legitimate locus or a legal right to know simply had to be contacted at once. Particularly those who might conceivably have the foggiest idea of how to get those poor miners out of that pit.

And in the latter regard, the Mines Rescue Service had to be put in the picture as a matter of the utmost urgency. In a wonderfully coordinated operation, the 'special' Post Office telephones began ringing in synch in the homes of umpteen rescue brigade men all across the county of Ayrshire.

As Eddie Smith got the call on his shift at the Bank Auld Pit instructing him to await the emergency transportation that would whisk him to The Castle to take charge of his hastily-assembled rescue brigade, Rab Hyatt prepared to do likewise with his Highhouse team and Willie Jolly with his Whitehill squad. Simultaneously, a whole host of other Brigade men were being hustled either from their own shifts or out of their sound slumbers, from such places as Muirkirk and Mauchline in the local vicinity, to the more far-off corners of the county like Stevenston and Dailly.

By then, Willie Dick and his elite team of mine rescue men were already winging their way from Kilmarnock towards Knockshinnoch. However, it wouldn't be Dick who would assume the role of top dog in any rescue plan that might somehow be put into operation. That awesome responsibility would sit firmly on the shoulders of one Willie Dyer, the head honcho of Coatbridge Mines Rescue Station, Scotland's only 'A Station'.

Dyer's Coatbridge team members were the recognised national mines rescue 'experts', and all coalmining emergencies were routinely coordinated by the men from Lanarkshire. The team was staffed by a permanent core of full-time officers and trained rescue personnel, and it would be Dyer's job to plan and oversee the well-established, four-pronged strategy that was deployed in every colliery incident in the land - surface control; management control; underground control; and rescue control.

This was emergency planning at its best, and if the trapped miners were ever to have any chance of seeing their families again, it would bloody-well have to be.

10.40 p.m.

The village of New Cumnock slept peacefully.

Save, of course, for the 'late bedders' who were still up and about waiting for husbands, brothers and sons to return any minute now from the backshift. Another quick glance at the clock on the wall verified that it was time to heat up the beef-and-onion stew, or slice the cheese onto the bread ready for toasting under the grill.

Ten-thirty had already become ten-forty. A heartbeat later, and it was ten-fifty. As numerous pairs of eyes stared anxiously at the walls, the New Cumnock clocks began to strike eleven, even if not all quite in perfect unison.

Where is he? ... if he doesn't get home soon, the sausages will be sticking to the frying pan ... it must be the rain ... the roads are still flooded, so stop worrying ... aye, that'll be it ... but he's never been this late before, Willie ... for Christ's sake Agnes, would you stop fidgeting and sit down? ... you're jumping about like a hen on a hot girdle.

And so it went on, as a sea of progressively worried faces began to peer from behind assorted curtains through the rain-lashed windows. Something's not quite right here. Something's up tonight.

As May Robertson sat upstairs in her attic bedsit, the penny suddenly dropped that husband John was never as late as this:

'I didn't think anything of it at first. John had been on the backshift
with his younger brother Eddie, and any number of things could have

87

delayed him. Just at that, the door opened, and in walked my cousin. I could tell by his face that something had happened, and he told me there had been a serious accident at the pit. The next thing I remember was being taken to John's parents' house. They told me I could stay there until John came home. I must admit I was frightened to think about how it might all turn out, but my attitude was just to wait and see how things developed.'

Jenny Walker had already gone to bed around ten o'clock, in order to rise well-refreshed in good time for the following morning's dawn start at The Castle canteen:

'I realised that young Alex hadn't returned home by the time I was nodding off, but I never bothered about it all that much. I just thought that he might have been offered another couple of hours' overtime, or something like that. For some strange reason, though, I don't remember Tommy and Walls being late.'

However, Jessie Lopez received the news with a shudder:

'My sister and I had been visiting an auntie, when all of a sudden the pit horn started going off. We all stopped talking and just looked at each other for a moment. Then my auntie said, "There must be something wrong at the pit!" I just covered my face with my hands and said, "Oh please don't say that."'

Meanwhile, Jean McMurdo was sitting in her chair waiting for husband John to come home, secure in the knowledge that both hot water and hot food would greet him the moment he walked through the front door:

'I was knitting a wee woollen suit for the baby, and I noticed John was late. It didn't worry me, though, because the roads were badly flooded and John always cycled to his work on his bike, so I just assumed he was having a bit of bother pedalling home through the puddles. Then my mother appeared at the door, which was a very unusual thing for her to do at that time of night. I asked her what was wrong, but she just kept flannelling and blethering about everything under the sun.

Suddenly John McKechnie - the garage owner next door - burst in shouting, "it's no' a fall, it's a flood!'"

And that was the first Jean knew of the accident, although her own mother had heard the grim news a good bit earlier, but just didn't have the heart to break it to her. She had probably heard the pit horn as well, but daughter Jean had not:

'The Castle was about a mile away, and my favourite wee wireless set was sitting on the shelf playing music while the baby slept in his wooden cot, so I could never have heard the horn. When my dad then appeared with Jenny McDonald from over the road, the mood deepened. Jenny's brother Ronald was on the same shift as John, so we knew that the two of them were trapped. I just couldn't go to bed, and sat up all night with Jenny. I never once doubted that John would be coming home soon, and I was certain that he would just walk in the front door any minute. However, as time went on, Jenny began to sow some seeds of doubt in my mind.'

And so, as the awful news began to break and the villagers of New Cumnock prepared themselves for the worst night of their lives, an army of Coal Board top brass and mines rescue experts rushed from all points of the compass towards the pit-head at Knockshinnoch Castle Colliery.

The lives of the trapped miners now lay entirely in their hands.

11.10 p.m.

Fireman Eck Clapperton was in absolutely no doubt:

'If that telephone line hadn't held up, we knew it would have been curtains. It was a miracle that such a flimsy wee wire could have withstood the enormous force of the inrush.'

Willie Lopez's take on the situation was identical:

'We realised the situation was bad, but once we learned that the telephone was working, we knew we had a chance. That was a very important moment for us all, because it gave us hope and kept us calm.

There was never any panic at that time, in fact I don't even remember feeling any real concern.'

Oversman Andrew Houston had been in a very sombre mood, exhausted by his flight from the inrushing sludge and saddened by the near certainty of his brother Jimmy's demise in Number Five Heading. However, the moment that telephone contact with the pit-head had been established, the miners' spirits improved dramatically. So too did those of Houston. He was now very much in charge, and it was his telephone. His, and his alone.

The Oversman immediately set about demonstrating his position of command with quiet but firm authority. He instructed Andrew McKnight, the backshift electrician, to start taking an account of events as they unfolded. Better known to the miners by his nickname of 'Doch', the electrician's task was to deploy his trusty pencil and standard blue-covered NCB notebook to write down anything of significance that might happen. McKnight was also charged with the responsibility of logging each miner's name and age in the same notebook.

And that was when the crushing fact was established that all the men who had been working in Number Five were unaccounted for, every last one of them. Missing were Dan Strachan, Fireman in charge of No. 5 Section; the Section's Shot-Firer, John McLatchie; Switch Attendant, William Howatt; Loader Attendant, Johnny Dalziel; and the nine miners who had been grafting at the coal faces in the vicinity of Number Five, namely Jim Houston, Tam Houston, Bill McFarlane, John Smith, Sam Rowan, Bill Lee, Jim Love, John Murray and Jock White.

As the already black mood darkened further, a small group of men eventually plucked up the courage to try walking outbye along the West Mine Turn, back in the direction of the pit bottom, in order to see the sludge for themselves. Despite Andy Houston's reservations about the futility of this exercise, he nevertheless gave them his permission, and off they went. It would be a journey of despairing fascination for Willie Lopez:

'The stuff was still moving, advancing into us, although it was starting to slow down. It was as if it had run its race. I never went too near it, mind you. The further on we walked, the deeper it got, fluid-like in appearance but full of peat and moss. There was no way we could have got anywhere near the pit bottom, because it must have been right up to the roof there. A big "dung midden", that's the best I could describe it. A great big dung midden.'

Seasoned miner Matt Sanderson's own description of the sludge was equally vivid and sinister:

'It was moving inbye at a slow creep. It had lost its momentum and just rippled over anything lying on the floor of the mine. It reminded me of the tide coming in at Ayr beach.'

Sam McCracken described the stuff as 'about 70% slurry, 30% peat' and noticed with trepidation how it piled higher-and-higher towards the roof of the vast main roadway the further back it went, completely blocking the road to the pit bottom.

Andrew McDicken was intrigued by the sludge's consistency, noting that 'it looked really slimy, a bit like soft clay I suppose.'

However, it was something else entirely that made Rab Cockburn shiver in dread, because the tidal wave of sludge had by then reached very close to the dook that led to the endless rope section of the pit. The same dook in which he, Eck Clapperton, Jock McMurdo and the others had been toiling on the backshift, and from which they had made their hurried exit only a few minutes back. Clearly, they had just had a very, very fortunate escape.

In truth, the men's communal stroll outbye to see the sludge for themselves had achieved two constructive objectives. It had passed a bit of time, and it had given them something to do rather than sit on their backsides fretting about how this dire situation might eventually play out.

However, that same short stroll had also delivered a much less positive message to them. It had well and truly established that there was nothing else they could now do to get themselves out of this desperate predicament.

Absolutely nothing.

11.30 p.m.

While the cages at the foot of the main shaft were clearly the principal means of egress from Knockshinnoch Castle Colliery's vast labyrinth of underground workings, it was well-known that the only other way out of the West Mine was through the overhead return airway that led from the same area of the pit.

The auxiliary escape route from the West Mine was, in effect, the exact same one along which Andy Houston, John Montgomery and Jim Haddow had scrambled just a few hours earlier, only in reverse. The route would have taken the men steeply uphill in an easterly direction, and towards the locus of the inrush itself, Number Five Heading. From there, it would have sent them back downwards to the top of the North Rising Mine, and further down towards what was known as the Black Band Mine, from which an old road would be waiting to lead them upwards to the foot of the Old Knockshinnoch shaft. At least, that was the theory.

Alas, the brutal reality of the situation proved to be somewhat different, after the Oversman had given the go-ahead for an exploratory party of volunteers to try out the emergency escape route for themselves. Led by Garrowscairn Section Fireman Archie Crate and turf coal Fireman Sam Capstick, the party soon discovered that a mere thirteen feet along what should have been an open road, the whole place had already become hopelessly blocked by sludge. The various individuals were then detailed to check out all other connecting roadways and airways.

Matt Sanderson and his long-time friend Robert Loy quickly established that two other downhill connections were completely cut off by the sludge, so they continued up the sole remaining roadway in their designated area, only to find that the far end was also blocked solid. Their findings mirrored those of the other volunteers in the party, and the decision was soon taken to abandon their explorations and return immediately to base.

Sanderson's own futile journey was dominated by one particularly weird and unsettling sensation:

'There was a strange, loud, hollow, eerie sound. It reminded me of the picture house film, where the well-muscled man strikes the large brass cymbal [Rank Organisation]. The noise had a constant rhythm, and was loud and clear. I was never able to fathom out the reason for this sound.'

Knockshinnoch Castle's workings, so intimately familiar in every one of the five human senses to its exclusively indigenous workforce, had changed completely. It would never be the same again.

And so the volunteers trudged back 'humfy-backit' to the West Mine telephone station to brief Andrew Houston on the dire status of the would-be auxiliary escape route. True to his word, Houston then duly conveyed the full story to his charges, warts and all as promised. The men had already known, from Walls Walker's earlier dramatic account, that the main West Mine roadway towards the shaft at the pit bottom was blocked from floor to roof. Now they had just learned something even more gut-wrenching, namely that the emergency egress route to the Old Knockshinnoch shaft was also completely cut off.

The situation was now desperate. On one side of the men, countless tons of sludge continued to seep menacingly towards them. On the other lay a mighty wall of coal and rock that separated them from the long-time derelict and firedamp-contaminated Bank Number Six Mine. In Matt Sanderson's own words, the miners were now 'inside the barrier'.

They were trapped in a pitch-black subterranean tomb from which they might never escape. Now their only possible hope of survival lay at the mercy of a flimsy little telephone wire.

And, of course, in the hands of the best-trained and most courageous mines rescue service in the world.

11.45 p.m.

Sam Capstick was never one for throwing in the towel. The mood of the 116 trapped miners was as low as the depths of the pit itself, and Sam knew that something had to be done to lift it.

'Andy, I think it might be worth havin' another go at findin' if there are any other roads still open to the old shaft,' he whispered in Houston's ear. 'After all, the alternative is just tae keep sitting around daein' nothin', an' feelin' sorry for oursel's. And lot o' bloody good that'll dae us. Whit dae you think?'

The Oversman pondered his shot-firer's proposal in silence for a few moments, before nodding. Capstick immediately shot to his feet, and addressed the men.

'We've gi'en up far too easy, boys! Let's have anither go at findin' a way oot. I need four or five men to go wi' me. Who's up for it?'

Heads bowed in silence, the sheer futility of Capstick's appeal for volunteers already seemed to have defeated its fine intentions. However, no way was he prepared to take 'no' for an answer.

'Come on boys, for f - - - 's sake!' he shouted in frustration, immediately getting the reaction he was looking for. 'Whit's the point o' sittin' here on our big fat arses, when we could be doin' something aboot it? There are thirteen men missin'. Thirteen o' your ain best pals!'

A sea of hands went up right away. Capstick calmly chose his four volunteers, and off they went, the glow from their cap-lamps slowly fading into the distance. Houston wound the handle on the telephone, and informed Halliday accordingly.

Not even an hour had elapsed before Capstick and his men trudged wearily back to the telephone station. The rest of the miners could already see from their colleagues' demeanour that this had been another exercise in sheer hopelessness. When Capstick shook his head, no words were necessary.

The telephone rang. For a full two minutes, Andy Houston found himself listening rather than talking. The only thing he said before hanging up was, 'right, Willie'. He then turned to face Andy McKnight.

'Get your notebook, Doch,' he told him, 'and write this down.'

The men fell silent again, eavesdropping nervously on the ensuing conversation. Houston spoke directly to McKnight, only very softly and painstakingly slowly this time, while the latter licked the lead in his pencil and scribbled furiously. A few minutes later, the phone went down.

The Oversman then turned to speak directly to his men, taking no prisoners. All possible means of escape to the pit shafts were now completely blocked by sludge. Bill Wilson's field was 'in', and the stuff was still seeping further inbye. The sludge had now risen up the main shaft itself, and the gaffers had tried to clear it, but the task was proving impossible. The main West Mine roadway was choked to the girders, as were all other roads to the shafts and even the return airways too, and the sludge was creeping ever closer towards the trapped men. While they were in no immediate danger, clearly the main air supplies from the surface had been cut off, and the air wouldn't last forever. However, the rescue brigades were now arriving in force on the pit-head, and the top brass were working on an escape plan. Any questions?

The men just sat there, open-mouthed. Any f - - - ing questions? Aye, here's one for starters, Andy. What about the air quality? In other words, the dreaded 'firedamp' gas, that most infamous enemy of coalminers? Houston knew a hell of a lot more about the production of deadly methane than he needed to tell his men, so his response was brief and reassuring. No firedamp for the time being, boys, the atmospheric pressure in the West Mine is too high.

Houston was fully aware that methane was non-toxic and therefore a non-asphyxiant as such, other than in very high concentrations, where if its presence

94

were to reduce the percentage of breathable oxygen from the normal 21% in fresh air down to 16% or less, asphyxiation would soon occur as surely as night follows day. This was extremely unlikely to happen down a coalmine, though, other than in quite exceptional circumstances. However, these were indeed truly exceptional circumstances, and absolutely anything was now possible. The real problem with methane, though, lay not in its toxicity, but in its flammability. In the 5% to 15% concentration range, methane was extremely inflammable, and even the tiniest spark could kick off a disastrous chain reaction where the methane/oxygen mixture would flash-burn, then spontaneously ignite the coal dust-fuelled atmosphere, which could result in an enormous explosion.

However, even though Houston's men were blissfully unaware of the chemistry behind the dangers of firedamp, they still knew to trust the wire-gauze-and-glass-protected flames in their 'Glennie lamps', which turning from a low blue hue to an increasingly tall yellowish flicker, would immediately inform them whenever its concentration was beginning to approach the dreaded 5%.

The Oversman had also clocked that the huge inrush of sludge that had cut off the men's escape routes had actually contrived to render the production of firedamp considerably less likely – at least, for the time being. Methane gas itself is released naturally from the decay of organic material in the production of coal, and is held in place in the coal seams by the surrounding 'hydrostatic pressure' of trapped water droplets in the coal itself, and by the 'lithostatic pressure' of the overlying rock formations. Therefore, since no airways were now open to the surface, the combined pressure in the Knockshinnoch Castle pit depths was presently very high indeed, although any sudden release of that pressure would have the immediate effect of releasing the methane from the coal seams, with almost inevitably devastating consequences. Like digging an escape tunnel, for example.

Houston knew that he would need to choose his next words very carefully indeed.

FRIDAY, 8 SEPTEMBER

Midnight

As Walls Walker sat on the wet pit floor fretting about poor Jessie and agonising over whether or not she had already given birth to their new baby, something else was troubling him very deeply.

What the hell had happened to his fellow locomotive driver and good pal, Jim Serrie? One minute, Walker had seen him driving his loco towards the pit shaft, and the next an avalanche of sludge had buried him from view.

Meanwhile up on the pit-head, Serrie was asking the self-same question about his close neebor, Walls Walker. One minute, he had been hauling his cargo of full tubs towards the pit bottom, with Walker doing likewise only a couple of hundred yards behind, and the next … the next, the whole bloody world had caved in on top of them.

'I was the nearest man to the fall,' Serrie was able to tell his gaffers. 'I heard a rushing noise, and saw loose muddy sludge bursting through the walls. I turned and ran, shouting to the others as I went. Over my shoulder, I could see the muck coming faster and faster towards me.'

Amazingly, Serrie and a total of seven others in the immediate vicinity of the pit bottom had contrived to beat the sludge and scramble into the cage, where they were then hauled up to the surface. The others who managed to escape were John Stevenson, Jim Holland, Andy Whiteford, Sam Hill, Henry Fordyce, Tam McAughtrie and Walter Simpson.

Driving Superintendent Stevenson informed the beaks about 'pug driver' Serrie approaching him just seconds before the inrush.

'Jim said he wanted me to see stuff which was coming out of a dook leading to an old working. We went along to a turning about 100 yards from the pit bottom and were met by mud oozing out of the dook. As we looked at it, it came away with a burst and we had to run for our lives. We ran to the pit bottom, and gave the alarm and came right up.'

As Willie Halliday and Andy Cunningham had already discovered to their incalculable personal relief, the area around the foot of the main shaft hadn't yet been engulfed by the sludge as it burst through in all directions. They had all made it to the surface, thank God, but now the sludge had not only reached the pit bottom; it had actually risen some sixteen feet up the shaft itself.

Serrie shuddered when he thought of what might had been for him, and now almost certainly was for Walker and the others. Buried alive in a dark stinking hellhole, with no food or water, and little or no hope of survival. Buried alive, and pondering the unimaginable horrors of a slow, lingering death.

It was the sea of blue lights flashing through the rain-lashed canteen windows that snapped Serrie out of his living nightmare. That and the near-continuous screaming of the petrol engines, as a seemingly never-ending cavalcade of emergency vehicles thundered along the Leggate, before turning left into Knockshinnoch Road and up Castle Hill. By then, Colliery Square had begun to look much more like a city centre amusement park than a rural pit-head.

Here comes the cavalry, Serrie muttered to himself.

About a quarter of a mile away, an army of men was wading its way down the hill from the pit-head in a south-easterly direction towards Bill Wilson's field, or more precisely, what was left of Bill Wilson's field. Some of them were miners employed at The Castle, some worked in other local collieries, and others were simply volunteers from the locale. They were only given one piece of advice.

'Be careful, boys! The hole in that field is gettin' bigger a' the time, so watch your step for Christ's sake!'

As the men splashed their way knee-high through once-lush grazing fields that had now been converted into bottomless bogs by nearly three days of incessant rain, the downpour continued without mercy. The only light available shone weakly from the cap-lamps of the miners, as they all made their way closer and closer to the scene of the inrush, with neither moon nor stars to help illuminate their path.

'Watch yoursel's, boys!' shouted Toe Melvin. 'We're nearly at the "sit" in the field, so one short step at a time. And where's that f - - - in' lighting, Geordie?'

Suddenly, a deep yellow glow tried its best to illuminate the surrounding terrain, as electrician George Paton's exhausting task of running a power line all the way from the pit-head to the emergency spotlights they had erected at the locus of the inrush had finally borne fruit.

The men immediately stopped in their tracks and looked straight ahead at Wilson's field. There was no Wilson's field.

'Jesus Christ!' a lone voice gasped from the crowd. 'That's a quick road tae Australia down there.'

What had once been a couple of acres of fresh green grass was now a mass of blackness. Where the blackness began and where it ended, nobody could possibly tell in the half-hearted beams radiating through the deluge from the emergency lighting and the miners' cap-lamps. They would have to wait until daybreak to get a more accurate picture of the extent of the inrush.

However, there was something that simply couldn't wait until daybreak. Something just had to be done to stop this huge hole in the field from getting any bigger, and to prevent even more of the surface from collapsing onto the heads of their neebors down below.

Something to plug up this hellish hole.

12.40 a.m.

If local mines Agent Johnny Bone and Knockshinnoch Castle Colliery Manager Willie Halliday had ever harboured any pretentions about taking control of the hastily-arranged emergency meeting, then these were well and truly knocked out of them the very moment the big chiefs began to appear. The line-up of senior officials arriving on the scene was like a veritable 'Who's Who?' of the mighty National Coal Board.

David McCardel, the Area General Manager had already assumed command, flanked on either side by Baillie Alexander McDonald, his Area Production Manager, and Eric Richford, HM District Inspector of Mines. As Bone and Halliday both stood to attention awaiting instructions, Superintendent Willie Dick of Kilmarnock Rescue Station and his second-in-command, Terry Morran, paced the floor impatiently beside Willie Dyer, the Coatbridge Rescue Station supremo, bursting to get bloody-well on with things. Even Lord Balfour himself, Chairman of the Divisional Board, would soon be on the scene, the assembled top brass were duly informed.

McCardel invited everyone to take their places at the makeshift conference table. He then opened the discussions by asking Bone and Halliday to outline the current status of the situation, as best they could. By the time they had done so, every head in the room was shaking in disbelieving horror, the various anguished expressions only partially camouflaged by the huge pall of tobacco reek that hung in the air like a lead balloon.

The best news that Halliday could give them was that, quite unbelievably, the telephone connection between the Knockshinnoch pit-head and the 116 men trapped down below at the West Mine telephone station had somehow contrived to hold up. Therefore, ongoing two-way verbal contact could still be maintained between those in charge on the surface and those buried underground. Only for as long as the connection held up, of course.

Halliday was also able to report his latest telephone discussion with backshift Oversman, Andy Houston. Opening his blue-backed NCB notebook, the Pit Manager proceeded to give them the gist of it.

Houston and the other miners were now assembled at the far end 'junction' of the West Mine Turn. Fireman Andy 'Doch' McKnight had been charged with the responsibility of keeping a record of events as they unfolded. McKnight had already taken a meticulous note of the names and ages of those assembled. Including Houston and McKnight themselves, there were 116 miners gathered there, in total. Halliday had informed Houston of the names of the eight individuals who had managed to outflank the sludge inrush before it had engulfed the main shaft. From Halliday's information and Houston's original rota, both had thus been able to establish that there were thirteen men in his backshift squad still unaccounted for, all of whom had been working in the South Boig district's Number Five Heading.

At this juncture, McCardel asked Halliday if Houston had been able to give him an accurate status report on the trapped men's present position, in relation to any possible escape routes to the surface. He nodded solemnly, and the others instinctively knew what was coming.

Halliday proceeded to brief his colleagues on the disastrous consequences of the colossal inrush from Bill Wilson's field down into Number Five Heading itself. He advised them that, in his opinion, the thirteen men working near the heading had almost certainly either perished already or had now found themselves irretrievably trapped by the sludge. Furthermore, his own first-hand account, and those of Bone, Andy Cunningham, Jim Serrie and the others who had made it back to the surface had convinced him that the sludge had now completely sealed off access from the east side to the main shaft. However, when Halliday then told the big chiefs that the shaft was now totally cut off from the West Mine as well, that revelation was met with gasps of horror.

If the inrush had come from the east of the shaft, Halliday was quizzed, then how the hell can the shaft possibly be blocked off from the west as well? On account of the sheer quantity and force of the sludge, the Pit Manager retorted. Not only had it blasted its way down the heading and filled up every roadway in its path until it reached the pit bottom, but it had also burst through the walls at the South Boig road-end and through the overhead return airways down onto the main West Mine roadway on the west side of the shaft. Worse still, Halliday added, Houston had already despatched two separate exploration teams to identify any possible means of emergency escape to the 'second egress' at the Old Knockshinnoch shaft, only to find that every single nook and cranny was full to the gunnels with sludge.

Halliday sighed heavily as he summarised the situation. The thirteen men working in Number Five Heading had almost certainly been overpowered by the inrush, and all contact with them had been lost. The 116 men now gathered together at the West Mine telephone station were trapped on all sides, and with no means of escape.

Every head in the room sank in despair.

However, when the Pit Manager then said, 'except one', the heads suddenly bounced back up again from the notepads. Let's hear it, the boffins chorused, their radar-like gazes focused on Halliday's heavily-drawn facial contortions, and their pleading ears hanging onto his every word and syllable.

This time, it was Johnny Bone's turn to do the talking, and Willie Halliday's to start unfolding a giant map and spread it across the table. The map was of the whole New Cumnock Coalfield, and it was so large that some of the officials had to pick their notepads and pencils back up from the table to allow its full display.

Bone described the plan as 'a huge long-shot, but the men's only hope'. Essentially, it was this. Andy Houston had already assured Bone and Halliday that there was no chance of the men reaching either the main shaft at the pit bottom of The Castle, or the auxiliary shaft at Old Knockshinnoch. Neither could access be gained to the old North Rising Mine. In short, all egress routes were now hopelessly blocked by sludge. Not only that, but such was the sheer quantity of the sludge and the distance it had travelled inbye, that it would take 'several months' for rescue workers to clear a path to the trapped men. Therefore, there was only one possible way out.

Through the huge barrier of coal that separated the Knockshinnoch workings from those in the adjacent Bank Number Six Mine.

Bone explained that the coal barrier was at least 200 feet deep, but that several years back this depth had been reduced to only 24 feet at a point where an old drainage borehole had been driven through. Technically, it was feasible for this section of the coal wall to be 'holed', by the Knockshinnoch miners digging from one side and the rescue brigades from the other. However, there were three problems, all of which were very considerable, possibly even insurmountable.

The first was that Bank Six had not been worked for many years, and so it was anybody's guess what the condition of the old roadways would be like. The second was that the same old roads on the Bank side fell far short of the coal wall adjacent to Knockshinnoch, except at one specific location. Finally, and possibly most worryingly of all, one of the main reasons for the earlier abandonment of Bank Six was that its workings had been plagued by the dreaded firedamp gas, and it was almost certain that the same old workings would now be full of the stuff.

'What's the alternative, Mister Bone?' enquired McCardel.

'There is no alternative,' the Agent replied. 'That's it.'

'Mister Halliday?' McCardel continued, turning to fix his steely gaze on the Pit Manager.

'No alternative, Mister McCardel,' the Manager agreed. 'This is our only hope. It's this way or nothing.'

McCardel eyeballed everyone in the room. The heads began nodding in resigned acceptance of the solitary option on the table. It wouldn't be so much a long shot, more a laughable attempt to perform a bloody miracle.

'Bank Number Six it is, then,' said McCardel, slamming his leather-bound notebook shut. 'So let's get on with it.'

1.10 a.m.

Jimmy McCreadie's 'special' telephone bell had already interrupted his late evening's audio entertainment well over an hour ago.

It was the BBC *Light Programme*, one of the very few British radio stations available on 'the wireless'. Jimmy had been in a very relaxed mood that evening, after a particularly productive day at work, hacking out the 'guid coal' from Whitehill Pit's main seam. Chilled-out, as the kids of today would probably say, but chilled-out in a way they could never understand.

Suddenly, the front door of his home in Cumnock's Glenlamont had burst open, as in marched Willie Jolly, his next door neighbour and erstwhile Captain of the Whitehill Rescue Brigade. Willie would always have knocked first, but this time he hadn't bothered, so Jimmy just instinctively knew it was 'a big one'.

'Accident at Knockshinnoch, Jimmy,' his Captain had announced ruefully. 'And a bloody serious one, so shift your arse.'

Soon afterwards, both Willie and Jimmy had jumped into the back of a Frew's coal lorry despatched from its depot in the quaint little village of Sorn, before uplifting the rest of the Whitehill Rescue Brigade from their variously scattered abodes. In the blink of an eye, they were approaching the pit-head at the Bank Auld Pit in Connel Park.

'Whit the hell are we doin' here, Tam?' Willie Jolly bawled impatiently, leaning over towards the lorry driver's side window. 'The accident's at The Castle, no' here!'

'F - - - ed if I ken, Wullie,' the driver shouted back. 'I'm just daein' whit I was telt.'

Jolly and his men leapt back out of the Frew's lorry, to be met by an elderly gent wearing the neat pin-striped suit, off-white shirt and dark tie that was the standard uniform of 1950s' officialdom. Jolly had no earthly idea who the old guy was, nor indeed did he really give a damn for that matter.

'Mister Jolly, take your men to the baths at once to get their medical examination,' the stranger-in-the-suit commanded. 'You all need to pass the doctor … before you can go in.'

'Go in where?' snapped Jolly. 'Whit the hell's goin' on here?' I thought the accident was at Knockshinnoch?'

The next thing Jolly, McCreadie and their fellow Brigade men knew, they were all standing in their Y-front underpants in the damp chill of a wet autumnal New Cumnock night. A team of doctors and nurses then set about sticking stethoscopes on their chests, blood pressure bands around their arms and wooden spatulas over their throats.

'Right boys,' announced the wiry, bespectacled doctor in charge of the medicals. 'You've all passed, so now put your gear on and make your way to the opening at Bank Six. Quickly, now.'

Willie Jolly continued pulling on his standard-edition flameproof rescue overalls, then raised his right arm in polite but firm protest.

'Sorry, doctor, but my team take their instructions from me, and naebody else. That's the way it works, and until somebody explains to me why we're a' here an' whit the hell's happenin', they're going naewhere.'

'The pit's caved in, Willie!' a familiar voice boomed out from the opposite corner of the room. 'One hundred and twenty nine men trapped, some feared dead, but the majority hopefully still alive.'

The unmistakable voice belonged to none other than Willie Dick, the highly-respected 'heid bummer' from Kilmarnock Mines Rescue Station, not only the custodian of the station's infamous torture chamber, but its torturer-in-chief.

Dick immediately updated Jolly on the situation, and then briefed him on the task in hand. It was for his own Whitehill Brigade to descend the depths of the long-abandoned, firedamp-contaminated Bank Number Six Mine, and explore whether there was any conceivable way of reaching the coal barrier that separated Bank from Knockshinnoch. And by the way, 'some others' will be joining you, Dick added tellingly.

After a detailed study of the New Cumnock Coalfield's underground plans and a quick discussion between Superintendent Dick and Captain Jolly, the latter collected his men and briefed them on their mission. Jimmy McCreadie remembered the briefing as if it was yesterday:

'Willie Jolly told us to go and check out our *Proto* gear, then wait for his instructions. He said that we didn't need to bother about carrying the stuff down the dook, because a designated 'helper' would do it for us. I couldn't believe my luck when I found out that my own helper was to be Robert "Rancher" Grant, a great hero with the local football team, Glenafton Athletic. And me a Cumnock Juniors' supporter too!'

The *Siebe Gorman Proto* apparatus had been around since 1914, and even as late as 1950 it was still the world's foremost 'industrial breathing set'. A breathing bag was worn on the chest, and an oxygen cylinder was strapped horizontally across the lumbar region of the back, providing a minimum of two hours of oxygen, with an additional twenty percent 'in reserve'. The *Proto's* carbon dioxide absorbent, known by its trade name of *Protosorb*, was contained loose inside the bottom of the breathing bag restrained by a perforated cloth, and a 'cooling cannister' was attached to the front of the bag to reduce the heat produced from the chemical reaction when the carbon dioxide was absorbed. The *Proto* had two wide breathing tubes that ran from the breathing bag to a strapped mouthpiece with accompanying nose clips, safety goggles and miners' helmet. And then there were its seven separate valves, the use of which could only have been mastered after many weeks of intensive training. The whole *Proto* apparatus weighed in at 56 pounds, roughly equivalent to half a sackful of coal, an utterly exhausting load for most mere mortals, but certainly not for hardy, seasoned Brigade men like McCreadie:

'The *Proto* was no problem, none at all. You see, that's where your training came in. And for bye, the only thing we were interested in was getting these men out of there. They were our brothers.'

The cavalry had arrived, and without the merest shadow of a doubt, it was the best-equipped and most courageous cavalry on the planet.

1.15 a.m.

When Area Manager David McCardel reclaimed his seat at the head of the makeshift conference table, everyone else in the room dived into theirs so quickly that a neutral observer could have been forgiven for thinking that it was a game of musical chairs.

The teacups had been refilled, the sandwiches had arrived from The Castle's famed canteen, and the bladders had been well and truly emptied, so it was now time to get back to business. It would be the most important business that anyone in the room would ever conduct in his entire life, even if he lived long enough to receive his personal telegram from King George. The only people missing from the earlier session were Kilmarnock Rescue Station Superintendent Willie Dick and his Deputy Terry Moran, both of whom were already making their final preparations to lead an advance reconnaissance party down into Bank Number Six Mine. As the frantic chatter in the room faded instantly to a respectful hush, the only sound to disturb the silence was that of the incessant rain continuing to lash against the office windows.

'Right,' said McCardel. 'Let's get down to business. We have some very important decisions to make, and we have very little time in which to make them. There are well over one hundred men's lives at stake here.'

Every head in the room nodded solemnly, and the discussions recommenced. Never before in their lives had these men required to take such monumental decisions in such a short space of time, and with so little reliable management information available to inform them. Given the completely unique circumstances of each and every individual coalmining incident, the Coal Board did not enjoy the luxury of a pre-ordained magical master plan. Nor indeed was there any other external source of brilliant, received wisdom available to dictate how such an enormously difficult situation ought to be tackled. This was decision-making at its most intellectually and psychologically demanding.

However, the big chiefs sitting uncomfortably beneath the rows of dazzling fluorescent ceiling lights knew that they did have a few very important assets on their side, which if they made the right decisions here in this very room, might possibly contrive to save those same lives. They had the considerable knowledge and sharp intuition of the men around the table. They had the high-level skills and raw courage of the rescue brigades waiting on the pit-head for their instructions. And, of course, they had the amazing fortitude and irrepressible spirit of a coalmining community in its time of greatest need. However, there were another couple of things that wouldn't go amiss either.

The good grace of the Almighty, and a great slice of luck.

Within fifteen minutes, the Coal Board officials had decided on the organisational arrangements required to put the rescue plan in action. They had no possible way of knowing whether the decisions they had made around the table would ultimately prove to be the right ones or not, but the very fact that they had been arrived at unanimously gave each of them the confidence they would need when they faced their own teams in a few minutes' time. This was 'it', and there was now no turning back.

The rescue mission was effectively split into three distinct, but very closely coordinated operations, all geared towards a highly ambitious attempt at getting the trapped men out through the old Bank Number Six Mine.

First of all, there was an immediate need to establish and maintain effective verbal communication between the various Coal Board officials directing the operation and the trapped miners underground. A Headquarters Base would be established in the Knockshinnoch Castle pit-head offices, with a telephone point being set up at the surface crater in Wilson's field. This arrangement would allow for telephone discussions to take place between the Knockshinnoch pit-head and those at the locus of the inrush itself, in addition to those already ongoing with Andy Houston and his men gathered at the West Mine telephone station down below.

Secondly, an operational base would be set up at the Bank Auld Pit's offices, situated only a hundred yards or so from the opening to Bank Six Mine. Another telephone point would then be hooked up in an underground base to be established at the foot of the main Bank dook. This arrangement would then facilitate discussions between the Bank's base and the rescue brigades once they had made their way down into the old mine's workings, in addition to those between the Knockshinnoch Headquarters Base and both the troops at the crater and the trapped miners themselves.

Unfortunately, that left one critical 'missing link'. Due to the distance involved over the rugged moorland, there could be no telephone link between Knockshinnoch and Bank pit-heads, meaning that any information conveyed from one to the other would have to be delivered by a 'runner' on foot or by motor vehicle, a huge challenge for everyone involved. In the meantime, Mister Charles Fleming, the well-known manager of the village's Commercial Bank, had volunteered to coordinate all telephonic communications between the pit-head and the outside world, a truly mammoth and critically important task in this most intricate chain of command.

Thirdly, and arguably most urgently of all, a team of senior Coal Board officials was detailed to take 'all practical measures' to stop, or at least minimise, the inrush of surface mud and sludge that was still cascading from the ever-expanding crater above, down into the pit workings below.

Meanwhile, as the rescue services continued to arrive in their droves with their blue lights flashing and emergency bells ringing, the world's media circus had already decided to join the party, notebooks in hand. Soon afterwards, the low-flying aircraft began circling above The Castle pit-head, in order to transmit their *Pathe News* film reels to the television sets and cinemas across the length and breadth of Great Britain, and beyond.

With the Knockshinnoch Castle pit horn now blaring continuously as well, the bedroom lights gradually began to make their startled appearances, all the way from the miners' rows in Burnfoot to New Cumnock's brand-new housing schemes. As desperately worried faces peeked wearily between half-drawn curtains, an eerie glow fought its way through the rain-drenched night-time sky, to illuminate the towering horrals of Knockshinnoch Castle in a ghastly grey-bluish shroud. Those who witnessed that dreadfully surreal apparition were left in absolutely no doubt that a terrible human catastrophe was unfolding before their very eyes.

And for the few who had somehow managed to sleep soundly through the 'wee sma' hours' of the morning, they would learn the awful truth very soon.

1.30 a.m.

By about half-past-one on the Friday morning, the devastating news was beginning to drip-feed its way into the New Cumnock homes. Very, very slowly, though.

These days, of course, whenever a major incident occurs, the whole planet knows about it within half-an-hour. Sky News immediately puts the big story on a continuous loop accompanied by written sub-titles, so that anyone with a television set can not only discover what has just happened, but watch live camera footage and listen to witness interviews as well. The same story is simultaneously fed into the world-wide-web, in order that every single person who owns a computer, laptop or smart-phone can pick it up in a heartbeat. Even the less technologically-minded can easily catch up on events, courtesy of relatively inexpensive phone calls or texts from every corner of the globe.

However, on that cold September morning, the world's population had no such brilliantly effective means of communication available, not even those residing in Great Britain, one of the wealthiest and most technically advanced nations on earth. There were no computers, and no internet. Black-and-white television had not yet been fully developed for commercial production, and so hardly a family in New Cumnock possessed a TV set. Likewise the telephone, whose ownership in those days was almost exclusively limited to large organisations and local businesses, but certainly not family homes. Even the national newspapers like *The Daily Record*, *The Glasgow Herald* and *The Daily Express* ran headline news stories which, by definition, were semi-historical even by the time they had arrived on the doorstep of McKechnie's newsagents' shop in New Cumnock's main street.

And so communication relied almost entirely on two things, namely the radio – or 'wireless' set - and word of mouth. However, at that unearthly time of the morning, the lucky ones were still fast asleep. Sadly, it wouldn't be long until sound slumbers would be disturbed and peaceful lives shattered.

May Robertson, Jessie Lopez, Jean McMurdo and the various others who had already heard the sickening news were beside themselves with despair. The reality was that it would be daybreak at the very earliest before the whole village found out about the sheer magnitude and scale of the awful events unfolding at Knockshinnoch Castle.

By the time the local children had reached the school gates and their parents arrived at the factory doors, New Cumnock would be in a state of bewilderment and terror. For everyone directly connected to the local coalmining industry, a pernicious wave of shock and grief was just waiting to pounce like a heartless tomcat on a helpless rodent. However, almost every single abode in the entire village would soon be recoiling in horror at the nightmarish mental vision of a husband, son, cousin, uncle, colleague, neighbour or friend having been buried alive under the ground.

And for Pup and Mary Walker, make that three beloved sons.

2.05 a.m.

The original army of around 50 off-duty miners who had earlier made their way to Wilson's field had now almost doubled in size, while volunteers young and old continued to arrive from every corner of New Cumnock and beyond.

As they made their way towards the crater, some having marched up Afton Road and others down from The Castle pit-head itself, the rain still lashed down, driven into their faces by an unforgiving gale. Not a solitary soul even thought of the warm bed they had just left behind. All they cared about was getting those poor bastards out of that pit, whether they were friends, neighbours, loved ones or strangers.

By this time, three Coal Board officials had arrived on the scene to take charge of the proceedings. However well-intentioned they had been in following McCardel's crystal-clear instructions, it turned out to be a futile exercise in crowd control. As the men in saturated suits stood there at the crater under the anaemic glow of the hastily-assembled spotlights, bellowing out orders at the top of their voices in the windswept torrential downpour, not a single soul could hear a word they were saying.

The truth was that it really didn't matter a damn what messages the frustrated officials were trying to convey, because everyone gathered around that crater just instinctively knew what had to be done. It was simple. The bit that was missing from Wilson's field had collapsed on top of their neebors down below, and the bits of the field that were still clinging on for dear life would soon start doing the same, unless something was done immediately. Formal instructions were superfluous, since the task was so blindingly obvious.

Fill up that bloody hole before the rest of the field falls in and suffocates the miners trapped down below.

In the rain-drenched early morning half-light of the crude makeshift spotlights and weakly glowing miners' cap-lamps, the big problem was that nobody could really tell for sure where the 'cratering' had begun and where it had ended. All they knew with a reasonable degree of confidence was that the initial inrush had occurred at the locus of the original 'sit' in the field, the location of which Bobby Nairn and the others who had earlier tried to erect the doomed fence were able to point out fairly accurately. That was why the spotlights had been erected there, and it was where almost all of the miners and volunteers had now gathered. Furthermore, from what everyone could see for themselves, it looked like an absolutely colossal hole, about 30 yards long by 20 or even 25 wide, and God-knows how many deep. Very soon, and without any need for the dubious wisdom of officialdom, the word got around. Plug it up with anything and everything you can lay your hands on.

So, off the local farmers went to collect their tractors, horses and carts, together with the haulage contractors to fetch their lorries, trucks and vans. Meanwhile, the masses of foot soldiers began gathering up every piece of solid material they could find lurking in the sodden darkness of the immediate countryside foliage.

Back came the cavalcade of vehicles, this time laden with all sorts of weird materials and assorted junk, all of them stopping as close to the crater as they dared, from where the volunteers began unloading the stuff and carrying it to the very edge. Then down it all went, every last item and contraption heaved straight into the blackness of the abyss.

Bale after bale of straw and hay. Pit timber by the cartload. Whole mature trees and thick bushes ripped from their roots by the farmers' tractors. Huge boulders and smaller rocks that had lain for centuries on the rural terrain. New pit props just prepared in the pit-head's own woodshed. Planks of wood and sheets of plywood from local homes galore. Whole sections of corrugated iron from neighbouring farms and smallholdings. Even pit hutches that should have been descending in an orderly fashion down the main shaft were now being flung unceremoniously into a gaping hole in a peat bog.

As the rain-drenched volunteers continued to haul the stuff towards the crater with hands so numb that they could barely even feel them, the various public authorities were preparing to set up a range of emergency operations aimed at halting the inflow of moss, peat, muck and watery sludge into the ever-expanding chasm.

Every available engine from the local fire brigade services had made its way to Wilson's field, where portable petrol pumps were already waiting to keep them fuelled up for as long as necessary. Umpteen ditches were hand-dug around the perimeter of the field, to try to stem the inrush of surface water flowing into the crater. The adjacent burn, which had already burst its banks, was dammed up, and a number of surface drains were also closed off by the fire brigades, who then set about pumping the diverted water at an incredible rate of 750 gallons-per-minute into the nearby Afton Water. The local public works contractor, Wimpey Limited, was deployed to do everything it could to shore up the sides of the crater.

Meantime, The Castle's electricians were already in the process of setting up auxiliary power supplies and running electricity cables from the pit-head down to the field, to provide much-needed additional lighting along the way, particularly at the crater itself. Simultaneously, the colliery's engineers had set about assembling a huge conveyor belt, which would run from the two massive 'pit bings' that dominated the skyline to the south-west of the pit-head, all the way to the crater itself, a good half-mile away. Its purpose was to facilitate haulage of vast quantities of 'dirt' from the bings, in order that the stuff could then be chucked in to help plug up the abyss.

This was community spirit and peer organisation at their most supreme. Perhaps the whole operation was best summed up by the words of one particular observer, who in keeping with the humble fortitude of this proud community, insisted upon remaining anonymous.

'Men moved in darkness and in the pouring rain. I saw nobody directing them, but they all knew what they were doing and why – and they went on doing it. Hardly anyone spoke a word. It was a silent army, working in silent discipline.'

This wonderful silent army would continue working in silent discipline until dawn had broken over the New Cumnock hills. Only then would they realise the full horror of Wilson's field.

2.20 a.m.

'Haw Andy!' a cynical voice piped up, as the men lay sprawled out on the cold, damp floor of the West Mine telephone station.

'Whit's goin' on up there? Bugger a', as far as I can see. They'll a' be sittin' aboot on their big fat arses, smokin' their pipes and scribblin' wee notes to yin anither, while we're stuck doon here like cats in a bag.'

Andy Houston's reply was a masterpiece of polite, but necessary dismissal.

'I very much doubt it. Half of Ayrshire is now on the pit-head, working their fingers to the bone, to try and get us out of here. We're the ones sitting on our backsides at the moment, but unless I'm very much mistaken, we won't be sitting on them much longer, because we'll soon need to dig a hole through a bloody big wall of coal. We just need to wait until we get the instruction to go in, so please just keep calm. Be patient.'

Back came the immediate retort, the same lone voice this time trying to save face by signalling more genuine concern than casual cynicism.

'That's fine, Andy, but whit happens if I don't get oot o' here. The wife'll be left tae feed the weans hersel', and we've got three o' them.'

This time a different voice spoke, one which made everybody sit up and pay attention, because it belonged to none other than big Wull Gray. Having played centre-half for the past five years for New Cumnock's famous junior football team, Glenafton Athletic, big Wull was local hero number one.

'Your wife's got three weans tae feed, has she? That's bugger a'. We've got either seeven … or maybe even eicht!'

The whole place fell about laughing. Big Wull might not have remembered exactly how many children he had fathered, but he knew it was more than three. And he certainly knew how to take the fear and tension out of a very trying situation.

In the hours and days to come, humour, that most elusive of gifts in a desperate crisis, would become an essential quality in keeping up the peckers of the trapped men, some of whom were as young as eighteen years of age.

Andy Houston smiled quietly to himself. He was now long enough in the tooth, and sufficiently well experienced in matters of life and death, to know that many different human emotions and responses would be played out in this searing drama. He also knew that the real heroes would emerge from the shadows, and he realised that their strength of character and self-discipline would be crucially important in keeping everyone focused on the task in hand. One, which for now, was simply to await developments as calmly as humanly possible.

The leaders would lead, and the followers would follow. That was the way it worked in the army, down the pit, and in every other facet of life that Houston had ever encountered. Indeed, it was this particular order of the universe that had been the deeply infuriating mantra of his old army sergeant-major.

'Either lead, follow, or get out of the f - - - ing way!'

Andy Houston knew exactly how desperately serious his men's present predicament was. He was pretty sure that thirteen of them had died already, and that one of them was Jimmy, his much cherished brother. Houston was exhausted, physically and mentally, and of course he wasn't getting any younger. However, he also knew that his men would need a real leader if they were ever to stand a hope in hell of getting out of this place alive. And like it or lump it, Andy old boy, you are it.

Big Wull Gray had now emerged from the shadows as another tower of strength at Houston's elbow. Very soon, others would follow.

2.40 a.m.

With the temporary headquarters base at Knockshinnoch pit-head now very much up-and-running and overseeing every aspect of the embryonic rescue operation, the real activity was by now being waged on two fronts.

Down at Wilson's field, the drenched volunteers continued their determined quest to plug up the crater, as the emergency services ploughed on with running their electricity cables and conveyor belts to the locus of the inrush, deploying their fire hoses to divert the still-rising flood water, and generally doing everything humanly possible to secure the sides of the crater itself. In their heart of hearts, though, most of the volunteers just instinctively knew that it was an exercise in sheer futility, since all around them they could hear the cracks and rumbles of yet more sections of the field disappearing into the jet-black void. However, the alternative was simply to give up altogether on the men trapped down below, and that was something that those hardy souls could never do.

Meanwhile, the activity on the pit-head at the Bank Auld Pit was becoming more frenetic by the minute, as the vast army of emergency vehicles, news reporters and rescue brigades was hastily diverted from The Castle to the Bank Auld Pit. Still, the volunteers continued to arrive at both pit-heads in their droves. People of all ages, shapes and sizes. Soon their number topped three-hundred.

In the words of the Daily Record's report that same morning:

There were many women and even children among the huge crowd at the pit-head. They stood in grim-faced groups discussing the accident, and asking for news of progress. Many who could only stand and wait because of the very large numbers of volunteers for rescue work and fetching material to fill the hole, were miners who could hardly conceal their anxiety to give a hand.

The volunteers at the Bank Pit were assembled together, and briefed on the job they would be given to do, but only when the time was right. It was an absolutely crucial one, they were assured. Under the supervision of the Brigade men, they would be expected to fetch and carry the rescue apparatus down from the pit-head to the foot of the Bank dook and onwards inbye to the furthest area of the old workings that were still free from firedamp gas. At that point, almost a mile-and-a-half into the bowels of the mine, a manned station was already being set up, this to be called the 'Fresh Air Base'. After reaching the Base, the volunteers would hand over their allocated piece of equipment to a designated rescue brigade member, thereby having helped him to conserve the energy he would surely need to make his onward perilous journey through the old gas-filled roadways. Thereafter, each volunteer would uplift an item of spent apparatus, and carry it all the way back up the dook to the pit-head, where he would be rewarded with a well-earned slap on the back, a plate of home-made soup and a lit cigarette.

One of the volunteers that morning was that Bank Six veteran, James 'Dick' Armour himself:

'I wasn't a brigade member at the time, but they were desperate for men who knew the layout of Bank Number Six Mine, and of course I knew it like the back of my hand. My job was to carry oxygen cylinders down the old mine to the Fresh Air Base and back. It was a very simple job, but it was bloody hard work, I can tell you! However, it was vitally important for the brigade men to save their energy, because they would need every ounce of strength they could muster.'

Inwardly, Dick harboured his own thoughts on whether the rescue brigades would ever manage to get the trapped men out of there alive:

'I thought that it might be possible to dig a way through the coal barrier and get the men into the Bank side, but there was no chance of getting them to the Fresh Air Base through all that gas, not a bloody hope in hell. The problem was that Bank Six was always full of firedamp, and of course that was the reason they shut the mine down. In fact, back in 1942, the mine's Manager and his Deputy were killed in a huge gas explosion down there. So it really looked an impossible task, but we simply had to give it a go, because there was nothing else for it.'

Another volunteer was Bob Dickson, himself a Knockshinnoch miner:

'I had been on the dayshift on the Thursday, and got back to my house in Mounthope Avenue about half-two in the afternoon. It was just like any other day, and I thought nothing of it. Whenever I was on the dayshift, I always went to bed early. Suddenly in the middle of the night, I heard somebody banging on the door. Outside was a group of men, and they were chapping all the doors, telling everybody that there had been a big accident at the pit, and that they needed every pair of hands they could get hold of. We really thought my father must have been involved, because he was supposed to have been on the "tenshift" that night. It was a good bit later before we found out that he was okay. In fact, he had never even managed to get down the pit at all because of the accident, but he just stayed on at the pit-head to help. Of course, the problem was that we didn't know that at the time. Anyway, I got dressed and walked up with some other men to The Castle, to see if I could help. It was pitch-black and the rain was still pelting down. The whole place was in turmoil, and the operation to fill up the crater was already well under way. Then somebody gave me a lift in a wee van up to the Bank Pit, and before I realised what was happening, I was in the pit baths getting changed into my working clothes. I knew that they were looking for men with a lot more experience than me, but they needed as many pairs of hands as they could get.'

In the meantime, the rescue gear had started arriving from all over Ayrshire and beyond, where it was taken into the operational base at the Bank pit-head. The preparations had been made, the telephones were now fully manned, the crater was being attended to, the rescue brigades were primed and the biggest volunteer army in British mining history was ready-and-waiting to do its business. All they needed now was for Willie Dick and his advance rescue party to resurface from Bank Number Six Mine.

And, God willing, with some good news.

2.55 a.m.

Willie Dick's exploration party had been down in the depths of Bank Six for almost four hours. It had been an extremely hazardous journey for the men involved, while for those on the surface waiting to hear the news, good or bad, it had been the longest four hours of their lives.

As Captain of the Bank Auld Pit Rescue Brigade and in light of his extensive local knowledge of the old mine, Eddie Smith had been handed the critically important role of guiding the expedition in its attempt to reach the coal barrier that separated Bank from Knockshinnoch. Even at this very early stage, this was the moment of truth for the whole rescue plan, and everybody knew it. One critical question had to be answered. Can we reach the coal barrier from the Bank side, or not?

So off the exploration party had set, led by Willie Dick and Terry Moran from the Kilmarnock Mines Rescue Station. With him were George Rowland, HM Inspector of Mines; Davie McParland, Manager of Bank Number Six Mine; Eddie Smith and his Bank Rescue Brigade of four men; and Willie Jolly and his Whitehill Brigade of three others. Some two hours later, they had been joined by Coal Board Area Production Manager Alex Macdonald and Eric Richford, District Inspector of Mines, for whom the tension of waiting on the surface had become too much, triggering them to go down and see things for themselves.

The original team had set off in the black of the night with high commitment, but low expectations. This was Bank Six after all, an infamous old mine that only twelve years earlier had witnessed the tragic demise of five young men in their prime. And one that had been so plagued by flood water and deadly firedamp gas that the decision had been taken seven years back to abandon it once and for all. Worse still, though, it had now lain derelict for those same seven years. If this was to be the trapped miners' last hope, then God help them.

Whitehill Colliery Rescue Brigade's Jimmy McCreadie recalled the perilous journey with crystal clarity:

'We didn't get clearance to go down the dook until our *Proto* gear had been thoroughly checked. It was a bloody heavy big thing to hump around down a pit, but there was no alternative. Firedamp isn't lethal as such, but the higher the concentration, the less oxygen there is in the atmosphere, so the *Proto* was absolutely essential. A breathing bag in front, an oxygen cylinder lying horizontally along your back, a metal helmet with your safety lamp on top, and the breathing tubes attached to your mouthpiece, with your nostrils clamped shut by nose clips. The *Proto* gave us two hours of oxygen, which we knew we would definitely need, so we didn't turn the supply on until we hit the gas. All I can really remember about the layout of Bank Six was that the main dook was very steep, about one-in-three, then level for a good bit, and then back up another steep dook until we eventually reached the barrier. The place was soaking wet and there were quite a few obstacles here and there – roof falls, rough pavements, big puddles of water and that sort of thing - but it wasn't nearly as bad as we had expected.'

And, of course, there was another huge challenge for the rescue men wearing *Proto*. That challenge was how to communicate effectively in such a dark and sinister place:

'You couldn't speak at all. Your nose clips were clamped shut, you were biting on your mouthpiece, and so you couldn't say anything, not a bloody word. We had three ways of communicating – a wee hooter on your side, hand signals, and scribbling messages on the walls with bits of chalk!'

Of the three, by far the most structured and reliable communication medium for mines rescue personnel was the simple 'hooter', and it operated via a formal code that was followed rigorously by every Brigade man in the land. Essentially, it worked as follows.

The Brigade Captain led the way, the team members followed, and the Vice Captain brought up the rear. The Captain would convey any one of a total of five commands to his troops by dint of a specific number of 'toots' on his hooter, immediately after which the Vice Captain would repeat the coded signal to ensure that all Brigade members had clearly heard and fully understood the command. The sophistication of the technique lay in its simplicity:

One toot:	'HELP!'
Two toots:	'STOP!'
Three toots:	'ADVANCE!'
Four toots:	'RETREAT!'
Five toots:	'ATTENTION!'

One of the Captain's many other important duties was to check each brigade man's oxygen pressure gauge every twenty minutes, reducing this to ten minute intervals when working in hot conditions. If, for any reason, one member of the team had to evacuate all the way back to a Fresh Air Base, he would never be allowed to go it alone and the entire team would retreat with him.

In short, this was a communication strategy based on a few very simple rules, but rules which had to be adhered to rigidly, meaning that it was a strategy which really worked.

Eddie Smith's take on the journey down into the bowels of the old mine was based on an intimate knowledge of its now derelict workings:

'For some reason, we were refused permission to use the "man-rider", so we had to walk the whole way down. It was about half-a-mile down the dook to the mine bottom, then about another full mile after that to the coal barrier that separated us from Knockshinnoch. Mind you, it wasn't an easy mile-and-a-half, because the old mine hadn't been worked in years. There were all sorts of things lying around here and there, and with your *Proto* gear on, it was really hard going. Mind you, the general condition of the road to the barrier was amazingly good, and the roofs and walls were still quite sturdy. The only real problem was the gas, but it was a very, very big problem. The firedamp levels were exceptionally high, and the only way we could think of getting rid of the gas was by bringing in big industrial extractor fans. That would then have caused another huge problem, because if methane is present in the atmosphere in the five-to-fifteen percent range, it is extremely explosive, and one single spark from a fan's electric engine could have blown up the whole mine.'

The exploration party had set about its job with resolute determination, and soon the various rescue brigades would follow in their footsteps. Loose falls of coal would have to be shovelled off burst pavements, crumbling wall-faces hastily repaired and dislodged pit props battered back into place. In the event that a rescue might actually be attempted – and that was by no means certain - the trapped miners' potential exit route had to be cleared and secured to present them with the fewest possible obstacles. So far, so good.

It was only when the team made it to around 500 yards from the coal barrier that the first real setback arose. Eddie Smith clocked the problem from the very moment that his 'Glennie' lamp's flame began to rise from a low blue glow in its base to a snaking yellow flame up the insides of the glass. It was a clear sign that they had hit a wall of deadly gas, and the whole mission was now in serious jeopardy.

As the presence of firedamp was conveyed down the line in wordless code, the men stood and waited for further instructions. While they did so, the only sounds to split the deathly hush were the drip-drip-dripping of innumerable little streams of water running down the pit walls into the massive puddles that punctuated the pit floor, and the men's own deep breathing.

Eventually the message came back up the line in the form of three 'toots', commanding them to 'advance'. After another exhausting half-hour trek through the muck-splattered ruts and puddles, the team eventually came to an impenetrable wall and could go no further. It had been one hell of a journey, but they had made it. They had reached the coal barrier. On the other side was Knockshinnoch, where Andy Houston and his men now lay trapped on all sides.

The 'four-toot' command was then given for the advance exploration party to 'retreat' back to base. They still had approximately 45 minutes of oxygen left, and 30 should take them back to the 'safe' area of Bank Six, where a giant white cross had been chalked on the pit wall to indicate the fresh-air limit. There they would be given the nod to remove their *Proto* headgear and start breathing normally again. When they did, they would also be able to speak to each other once more. However, only one question would be on their lips. Okay, we now know we can clear the road, but how the hell are we going to get those poor survivors through one-thousand yards of deadly firedamp gas?

One member of the Bank Pit Rescue Brigade summed it all up when he eventually emerged exhausted from Bank Six. Asked for a comment by the waiting newspaper reporters, he didn't mince his words.

'Gas is raging down there. It can only be moved slowly, and any attempt to hasten the process might have fatal results.'

The moment that Messrs Dick, Moran, Rowland, McParland, McDonald, Richford, Smith, Jolly and their crews had set foot back on the surface, the aforementioned senior officials were immediately whisked away by the Coal Board's top brass into a couple of waiting vehicles which took them back to the Knockshinnoch HQ for de-briefing.

The tension in the room could have been cut by a knife.

'The Bank roads are fine,' Willie Dick announced before his backside had even hit the chair. 'The old workings are in remarkably good order, considering that they haven't been used for so long. We managed to get right up to the coal barrier, the one that that separates Bank Six from The Castle, without much difficulty. There have been a few dislodgements along the old roadways - missing props, slight roof falls, broken girders and pipes, that kind of thing – but nothing that the boys won't be able to deal with.'

If the sighs of relief were huge, they were also ridiculously premature. The Kilmarnock Mines Rescue Station Superintendent continued, his steely gaze blazing from the stark contrast of white eyes against coal-black face.

'We have two very serious problems, gentlemen. Problem one; from where we're suggesting we set up the Fresh Air Base all the way inbye to the coal barrier, the whole place is full of gas, the methane concentration ranging from a few percent at the Base itself to as much as 50-percent at the far end. Problem two; the gas-filled roadways stretch almost 1,000 yards. We managed it reasonably well in our *Proto* gear, but we wouldn't have got ten yards without it.'

After a very brief discussion around the table, Willie Dick summed up the current situation as concisely as he could in the circumstances.

'This is the position, as I see it, gentlemen. The men are trapped by sludge on all sides, except one. Their only hope is Bank Six. They could certainly cut their way through the coal wall at the old borehole, but they'd need to do it from the Knockshinnoch side only, and be bloody careful while they're at it. Explosives and even power drills are completely out, with all that gas lying there on the other side. We'd have to be extremely careful digging from the Bank side, because one single spark and the whole bloody mine goes up. Then what do we do once they hole through, and the gas starts flowing through the hole from Bank into Knockshinnoch? We have to think of a way to control that situation, because the pressure will automatically equalise once the breach is made, and the gas will definitely be on the move sooner or later. Finally, and even if we do manage to get the men through to Bank Six, they'll have to walk through more than half-a-mile of gas, then another mile-and-a-half after that to the Bank dook.'

So what are you saying then, Superintendent?

'What I'm saying is this. Firstly, the trapped men really need to dig the hole by themselves and from their side only if possible, and with hand-rickety drills, picks and shovels only. Secondly, once the coal barrier is holed through, we need to control the gas flow somehow, in order to protect the men's air quality for as long as possible. Thirdly, and most urgently of all, we need to get that bloody gas in Bank Six pumped out right back as far as humanly possible, before we can even think about bringing the trapped men from The Castle side into the Bank side.'

As eyes rolled skywards and cheeks puffed out in disbelief at the terrible predicament facing everyone in the room, Willie Dick made one final pronouncement.

'And by the time we're ready to move, those poor bastards will have been down there for days on end, without anything to eat or drink. As soon as that hole has been driven through, we need to get some food and water into Knockshinnoch.'

3.25 a.m.

Fair play to the gaffers on the pit-head, backshift Oversman Andy Houston thought quietly to himself, as his men lay slumped on the cold, damp floor of the West Mine telephone station in the dim glow of half-a-dozen cap-lamps set for emergency lighting. They have been true to their word, that's for sure.

Houston was thinking about Willie Halliday's solemn promise that he, or at least one of his senior colleagues at The Castle's emergency pit-head HQ, would phone him every fifteen minutes without fail, and right on the dot. Every fifteen minutes it had been then, indeed even to the extent that the men would suddenly stop talking as the magical moment arrived, praying that the bell would start ringing. However, Houston asked himself for the umpteenth time, what exactly had those same telephone calls actually achieved for his men?

Absolutely nothing, sweet bugger all. Other, of course, than delivering some kind of ethereal reassurance that at least the pit-head and the pit depths were still in verbal contact with each other. The natives were becoming restless. Very restless.

Andrew McDicken summed up the mood perfectly:

'We were very relieved that the telephone connection was still holding up, but to be honest, there wasn't much happening as far as we could see. The Coal Board officials were phoning Andy Houston every quarter-of-an-hour, but the message was always the same. Nothing doing yet, boys. It was bloody frustrating.'

Indeed, Andrew's feelings about the escape plan itself were similarly equivocal:

'I really wasn't very hopeful at first, not at all. You see, I knew that area of the pit like the back of my own hand. I knew fine well that we could get down Waterhead Dook to the coal barrier, no problem at all. It was only a twenty-minute walk from the telephone station. I was also fairly certain that we could dig our way through the barrier, and in jig-time too if it came to it. However, the problem was always going to be on the other side. That side hadn't been worked in donkeys' years, and we knew the old roads would be in a hell of a state. Worse still, we realised that Bank Six would be contaminated with gas, in fact stapped to the gunnels with the bloody stuff. It was also a near two-mile walk from the coal barrier to the Bank dook. No, it wasn't a very encouraging picture, if I'm being honest. The thing was, though, that it was our only hope. And if we didn't try it, we'd still have been lying there till they eventually dug our bodies out. I suppose it was an easy decision, when you think about it.'

Easy decision? Not only were the trapped miners literally stuck between a rock and a hard place, but they were faced with an absolutely awful dilemma. Either go with the plan and risk near-certain death by agonising asphyxiation on the other side, or stay where we are and perish from thirst, starvation and probably mass psychological breakdown as well.

Sam McCracken's thoughts were very similar. He and his neebors had also become very familiar with the layout of the Waterhead area in years gone by, as a result of some of them having rather naughtily stripped the 'forbidden' coal at the boundary with Bank Six Mine. However, they also knew from chatting to their mates who had worked in Bank Six that the mine was now seriously contaminated with firedamp. Therefore, like his neebor Andrew McDicken, Sam wasn't particularly relishing making his escape through the old mine. However, he knew that it was Hobson's Choice. Do it or die, simple as that.

Willie Lopez felt a bit more positive that things would eventually work out fine, although he acknowledges that his mood was perhaps influenced by his relative lack of knowledge about the physical conditions of the area in question:

'I worked in Garrowscairn Number One, so I was a stranger to that area of the pit. Garrowscairn was up to the right at the end of the West

Mine Turn, while Waterhead Dook was away down to the left near the mechanised section, and I had never been down there in my life. When we heard about the plan to dig ourselves out through the coal barrier into the old Bank Number Six Mine, I got quite excited about it. The truth is that I just wanted home, and I had no idea how bad the conditions would be on the other side. Andy Houston told us that the rescue brigades and volunteers were arriving from all over the country, and that really made me feel quite optimistic about the whole thing. The mood among the men was generally quite good at that stage, and confidence high that the brigade men would soon get us out of there. Mind you, some of the other boys were a lot less hopeful. It was quite a tricky situation we were in, you know.'

A masterpiece of understatement, Willie. He was sure of one thing, though:

'It all came down to the telephone lines holding up. No question about it. If that wee telephone wire hadn't held up, there would have been a completely different atmosphere down there. In fact, I wouldn't even like to think about it.'

Yes, the natives were becoming restless, but their spirits and strength of character were holding up, just like the old telephone wire itself had somehow contrived to do. However, they badly needed some good news from the pithead.

And good news would be a long time coming.

4.40 a.m.

Fight or flight. The most basic law of survival across the entire animal kingdom spectrum.

From the hostile tomcat standing his ground and hissing defiantly at the advancing pit bull terrier, to the herd of terrified wildebeest scattering in blind panic at the distant roar of an invisible lion, all species react in different ways when faced with a crisis. And, of course, within every species, an individual deals with each challenging situation in its own way.

In a manner of speaking, the Knockshinnoch scenario contrived to present itself as a microcosm for that particular law of the universe. By around quarter-to-five on the Friday morning, 129 coalminers had last seen daylight some fourteen hours ago, some of whom were now probably dead already, and the rest in full knowledge of the horrifying truth. They were now buried alive. If ever there was a situation that would test the mettle and nerve of a group of human beings, this was surely it.

Fight or flight, then, what was it to be?

The mood was still very calm among the 116 men trapped at the West Mine telephone station. Remarkably so, considering their terrible predicament, and the near-certain demise of thirteen of their trusted neebors and close relatives.

Most of the men just lay around on the damp floor, some of them deep in conversation about the merits and demerits of the proposed escape plan itself, and others empathising with each other about the plight of Nelly-and-the-weans, or just blethering about the forthcoming Glenafton Athletic-versus-Auchinleck Talbot football match. Indeed, anything they could come up with, just to take their minds off the horror of the situation. Meanwhile, the rest wandered up and down the roadways, some chattering to each other in small groups, and a few on their own, fretting and fidgeting.

However, what struck Andy Houston was the manner in which the men were now speaking to each other. It was almost in a whisper, and not in a way that attempted to conceal the various conversations from prying ears, but one that smacked of humble respect, of an almost 'religious' decorum. Houston sat all by himself, observing the dynamics and listening attentively. A church congregation, that's what it was like. And a lot more like a funeral service than a baby's christening.

His mind began drifting back to his days as Oversman in the Bank Auld Pit, and to Number Six Mine in particular. Good God, it was in a bad enough state all those years ago, so what the hell is it going to be like now? Dark and soaking wet, pit props dislodged, steel girders lying rusted on the floor, wooden trusses rotting in giant pools of flood water, roof falls and huge piles of rubble galore. And the gas, that bloody gas.

No wonder the previous owners had shut down the old mine before the industry eventually succumbed to nationalisation. It wouldn't have lasted a day under the Coal Board's new productivity-at-all-costs regime, not a single day. Falling to bits, flooded to hell, and a veritable gas chamber.

And now it's our sole exit strategy, our only way out of this damned place. Houston's head hung heavily once more, hidden from his men's gazes by the long, eerie shadows of the pit depths. How would they react to this desperate situation, especially as time wore on? Fight or flight, Andy, he reminded himself.

The question was, though, who would fight and who would flee?

4.45 a.m.

Right on cue, the telephone rang. It was Halliday again.

Andy Houston lifted the receiver, his heart rate rising as usual. Please God, don't let this one be yet another 'nothing to report', he begged under his breath. There were a few moments of silence before the Oversman eventually got a word in.

'Okay, Willie, hold on a wee minute', he said, covering the mouthpiece with the palm of his hand, before signalling to Andy McKnight, his shift electrician and erstwhile scribe. 'Get your notebook and write this down. And word for word, Doch.'

As Houston spoke, the body of men fell into a respectful hush. McKnight began scribbling furiously, only once stopping momentarily to sharpen his pencil with the trusty old pocket-knife his father had given him for his tenth birthday. At last something was happening, Houston sighed with a modicum of relief, his thoughts silently echoed by those of every other man in the West Mine. Essentially, the message from the pit-head was this.

Umpteen rescue services had now arrived, both at Wilson's field and at the Bank pit-head, and the whole place was buzzing with activity. An army of one-hundred-plus volunteers was now beavering away to plug up the crater in an attempt to put a stop to any more sludge finding its way into the pit. Willie Dick and Terry Moran from Kilmarnock Rescue Station had just returned from Bank Six, accompanied by Eddie Smith's Bank Rescue Brigade and Willie Jolly's Whitehill team, plus the inspectors of course. The good news was that they had managed to scramble all the way up to the coal barrier between Bank and Knockshinnoch, and had found the old roadways to be in remarkably good condition.

However, the bad news was that they had found gas, something they would have to address urgently. Very soon, another brigade would be going down the Bank dook, together with dozens of volunteers whose job it would be to fetch-and-carry the brigade men's equipment up and down the dook. Industrial extractor fans were now being brought down Bank Six to get rid of the gas, and they too would be carried down the dook by volunteers. In the meantime, a 'Fresh Air Base' was being set up about a half-mile from the coal barrier.

After the message had been relayed in full to Houston and written down verbatim by McKnight, the Oversman began reading back the shift electrician's handwritten notes to the men, in order that each and every person could hear the full story for himself. The mood lightened immediately, to the point where a couple of characters who were well-known for their raucous shenanigans even started putting their jackets back on, ready to walk out. Houston then informed them of Halliday's parting words.

'Andy, this is going to take a long time, possibly even running into days. We need to get rid of all that gas before we can even think about attempting a rescue.'

And that was when the jackets came straight back off again.

5.00 a.m.

As Andy Houston sat slumped on the pit pavement, there was one thing he found himself having available in abundance. Thinking time.

His imagination slowly climbed through the gears once more, until it finally reached overdrive. Everything had been calm again, ever since the news about a possible rescue plan had broken from the pit-head. How long will the mood last, though, he wondered?

Even if things do go as smoothly as humanly possible for the rescue brigades, the whole operation will take days. Days without food, days without water, and days for the men to start fretting and panicking about their ever-diminishing chances of survival.

And then, of course, there's the gas. That bloody firedamp, the miners' greatest enemy. Just how the hell would the brigade men manage to clear over half-a-mile of gas from a maze of decrepit old pit roads that had lain spewing the stuff out for nearly seven years? Good God, it would be a bloody miracle if they even managed to drag those huge industrial extractor fans a-mile-and-a-half down a long-abandoned mine, and with no haulage facilities to assist them, let alone help them to clear out millions of cubic feet of noxious gas.

And if they couldn't get rid of the gas, then what? Sure, the brigade men had their *Proto* gear, but the trapped men had absolutely nothing. Even if the bosses managed to collect a few *Proto* sets, it would take weeks to train the men on how to use them properly. An impossible task, totally impossible.

As Houston's imagination continued to crank up, his next thoughts turned to the telephone connection, the men's sole remaining means of contact with the outside world. Ever since the moment that young apprentice Dougie Blackwood's voice had miraculously answered from the pit-head, that puny little telephone wire had been the trapped men's one-and-only lifeline. However, the signal had always been rather feeble, and Houston had clocked that it was now getting noticeably weaker, although he had said nothing to his men.

Halliday's decision had been to call Houston every fifteen minutes, but to keep the calls as short as possible to save energy. In the meantime, electrician Andy McKnight had hatched an ambitious back-up plan to maintain the telephone's capacity by using the remaining available charge from the batteries of a few miners' safety lamps. All fine and dandy, thought Houston, but if the connection should eventually fail altogether, then their last lifeline would have evaporated forever, and there would be no way left to coordinate the rescue brigades' fine intentions with the trapped miners' futile efforts at finding an escape route.

And, of course, there was always the little matter of food and drink, or to be more precise, the complete lack of each. Save, of course, for the big drum of water that the pit's engineers routinely deployed to clean their working tools, its surface covered by an inch-thick film of engine oil. No, Houston thought wryly, for essential food and drink, read imminent starvation and thirst.

He shuddered as he contemplated the inevitable end-game. He had read about such things before. Cannibalism, it was called. Who would be the first starving predator to attack, and who would be his horrified prey?

Suddenly, there was a distant crack, followed by a menacing rumble. In immediate response, the emergency beams from a sea of cap lamps shot upwards towards the pit roof.

'Whit the hell was that?' a voice sounded nervously from the body of men.

They all looked at Houston. He knew immediately what it was, but said nothing. They knew too, and took his silence as an affirmative. The crack-and-rumble was all-too familiar to the Oversman. It was another section of Wilson's field breaking away and tumbling into the pit, no doubt about it. This one seemed a lot more remote than the one that had almost killed him the previous evening, but the noise was sickeningly unmistakable.

A lone miner's frame rose from the unearthly shadows and stretched its legs. 'I'm goin' for a walk back along the West Mine Turn, tae see whit the sludge is daein'. Whae's comin'?'

Another miner arose, then another, and within a few minutes a group of about a dozen or so found themselves strolling wearily along the main roadway. They soon found that the sludge had advanced slightly in the last couple of hours, but only by a few yards. Still the stuff rippled along the floor in the direction of the West Mine telephone station. Even more worryingly, it continued oozing down from the return airways straight above their heads. Nobody said a thing, but everybody knew what that crack-and-rumble had been. The rest of Wilson's field was doing its best to collapse down into Number Five Heading, and the sludge was still coming. Coming to get them.

Some of the men set about constructing a 'barricade', at a location about 100 yards inbye from the point where the sludge had already reached. Pit props were flung together in a heap, coal and rubble were shovelled off the pit floor on top of them, and items of clothing got chucked in as well. Even parts of Walls Walker's demolished locomotive tubs were ripped off and heaved onto the pile, in an attempt to create the barricade.

'Away an' don't be sae f - - - in' stupit!' came a cynical cat-call from the midst of the doubters, as they observed the futility of the whole exercise. 'If any mair o' that field comes in, the sludge'll blaw a' that rubbish away like snaw aff a dyke!'

Andy Houston observed the proceedings in silence. Not one of the men building the barricade believed for a single moment that this pathetic little pile of junk could possibly withstand the terrific force of another inrush of sludge. However, they had simply felt the need to do something to take their minds off the pernicious evil closing in all around them. Anything at all.

The Oversman knew for sure that if the sludge did suddenly surge forward again, it wouldn't only come at them along the West Mine Turn itself. It would also erupt upon them from the saturated headings and air courses above their heads, cutting them off on all sides. Even if they somehow managed to escape by scarpering into the mechanised section, or down the dooks of Lanemark and Garrowscairn, the sludge would then hunt them down mercilessly until the whole pit was 'stapped tae the gunnels'.

Maybe we won't need to worry about the gas suffocating us after all, Houston reflected morbidly. And maybe not even about perishing of hunger or thirst.

Maybe the sludge will get us first.

6.00 a.m.

As Dan Park trudged dejectedly up the garden path of his Dalhanna Drive home in New Cumnock's rapidly-expanding new housing scheme, he wasn't best pleased. The early morning rain fairly pelted down onto his head.

Dan's father, Archie, pulled the front door shut and barked at him. 'That face o' yours would curdle milk, Dan, it really would. Put a smile on it before the bus comes, or you'll be walkin' tae the pit.'

'My place is at the screes along wae a' my pals, faither,' mumped Dan. 'I'm no' goin' tae the engineers' shop. You can a' keep your apprenticeships.'

'Aye, you'll be bloody goin'!' snarled Archie. 'I had tae pu' a lot o' strings tae get you a stert as an apprentice, an' you'll be there first thing this mornin', believe me. Even if I have tae come ower tae the screes masel', an' pu' you oot by the lugs!'

Five-foot-eight Dan turned to argue the point, but took one good look at his infuriating old man's six-foot-three frame and immediately thought the better of it. Dan knew in his heart of hearts that all his father really wanted was to give him the best possible start in his Coal Board career, and hand-picking rocks from coal wasn't it. Far better to learn a proper trade, Archie had counselled his son, and Dan instinctively knew that he was right. Furthermore, learning two trades rather than one was simply an opportunity not to be missed.

However, Dan had also realised something else entirely, something a great deal more scary for a mere slip of a lad. The moment he walked in the door of the engineers' shop on The Castle pit-head that morning, his youthful shenanigans would be a thing of the past and a regime of strict vocational discipline would for evermore become the order of a long, hard day's graft. In short, there would be absolutely no hiding place under the watchful glare of Sanny Allardyce and Geordie Paton.

'Mornin' Archie, mornin' Dan.' It was the sleepy voice of Tam Campbell, as the wee man shuffled his way up the hill to catch the bus that would take him to his factory job in the nearby village of Catrine. 'That's a bad yin at Knockshinnoch.'

Archie and Dan just looked at each other a bit quizzically, before turning back towards Tam again. 'Whit are you talkin' aboot?' Archie enquired hesitantly.

Wee Tam's reply hit him right between the eyes like a bullet from Smith and Wesson's very latest hand gun, the '36 revolver'.

'Oh, did you no' hear? The pit's fell in.'

Not another word was spoken between the three men until the bus had screamed its way up Dalhanna Drive to pick them up. Nor indeed was a single syllable uttered among the bewildered passengers inside, only the bus conductress's 'fares please' splitting the deathly silence. The whole busload was in shock. Everybody knew why, but nobody really knew when or even how it had happened. Dan Park will never forget the tension on that ten-minute bus journey, nor the scene that awaited him the moment he arrived at his destination:

'When we got to The Castle pit-head, the whole place was in chaos, pure bloody chaos. There were people running around everywhere, every last one of them carrying something or other. They were either scrambling down the hill in the direction of Danny's Brig with their hands full of stuff, or coming back up empty-handed looking for more to carry. I couldn't understand it at all, until one of the boys told me that it was Wilson's field that had "fell in". I'll never forget the mood at the pit that morning. It was total shock. Everybody was running here, there and everywhere, yet hardly a word was spoken. It was a heavy, heavy atmosphere that morning.'

'Run a pole, walk a pole!'

Trainee cook Jenny Walker once more found herself deploying the tried-and-tested mantra that had always got her to work on time. It was Friday morning, and Jenny always liked Friday mornings, because they were immediately followed by the glorious Saturday and Sunday morning 'long-lie-ins'. Only till half-seven, mind you, because Jenny and her two sisters would then have their weekend household chores to get on with, under the quiet but authoritative supervision of their wonderful mother, Mary. However, that morning, young Jenny just instinctively knew that something was badly amiss:

'I knew from the minute I stepped onto the pavement that something was wrong. It was still raining very hard, and I wondered if it was ever going to stop. The first thing I noticed was the amount of traffic on the road, far heavier than usual. Cars, vans and lorries, but a lot of police vehicles, fire engines, ambulances and that sort of thing. That was the first time I even thought about something being wrong at the pit. It was only when I walked into the canteen that my worst fears were confirmed, because it was then that the cleaners told me there had been a big cave-in at the pit. I knew then that Walls, Alex and Archie were stuck down there. It was a huge shock, but strangely enough it was my work that kept me going, simple as that. Miss Rennie was there keeping us busy as usual, and Doctor Dobson from the Coal Board, and Sister Rennie the Coal Board's nurse too. Normally the canteen was a very busy place, a really happy place with a lot of banter and laughter, but that day it was a totally different atmosphere. Very tense, and very sad. But you just had to get on with it.'

New Cumnock historian George Sanderson, himself a Knockshinnoch miner who had earlier been on the dayshift, would remember for the rest of his life the moment that daylight finally broke through the gloomy, watery skies above Wilson's field:

'The sight that slowly unfolded before my eyes shook me to the core. It was unbelievable. We had been working all through the night, over a hundred of us, throwing everything we could get our hands on into the hole in Wilson's field. The only lights we had to direct us in our work were Geordie Paton's emergency spotlights and our own cap lamps, and we thought we had been getting on fine. Then when daylight started to break, the whole scene began to reveal itself for very first time. It was incredible. The area we had been filling in was about thirty yards square, and we had flung a lot of stuff in there, an awful lot of stuff. When daylight broke through, the scene honestly took my breath away. Hardly anyone spoke. Straight in front of us lay this huge crater about the size of a football pitch, maybe even bigger, and about 50 feet deep. It was black, jet black ... and enormous. I remember looking at where we had chucked in all the rubbish to plug up what we thought had been most of the hole, and it was this fraction, this tiny wee fraction of the whole thing. It looked ... it just looked ... pathetic.'

The local paper, the *Cumnock Chronicle*, summed up the sense of shock around the crater, in its own inimitable way:

As the first faint streak of light broke above the stricken village, it became apparent that the efforts of the night had been pitifully inadequate. The 200 hutches of straw had made little or no impression on the source of the trouble, and to complicate matters still further, the ground at the edge of the crater showed signs of breaking away.

While George and his neebors began trudging despondently back up the hill towards the pit-head, those just arriving for Friday's dayshift had already learned that the winding shafts were now blocked solid by sludge. Today at The Castle there would be no dayshift, no backshift and no nightshift. In fact no shifts at all, and for a very long time to come.

As the miners milled around the pit-head in wordless confusion, they were joined by the volunteers who had spent all night and morning chucking half of New Cumnock down the hole in Wilson's field, while the cold autumnal rain battered down onto their heads. The omnipresent hustle-bustle of the *Collier's Symphony* had now been replaced by an aura of ghastly silence that screamed of utter helplessness.

A swish of bicycle tyres and a distant 'thud' caused a few heads to turn in the direction of the canteen. It was McKechnie's paperboy making his daily delivery of morning newspapers. And there lying on top of the sodden pile was a copy of the *Scottish Daily Express*. It bore a rather unforgettable headline:

129 MINERS ENTOMBED IN PIT DISASTER

The few still-slumbering villagers of New Cumnock would soon learn the awful truth for themselves, as word-of-mouth spread at the crack of dawn, and assorted daily newspapers exploded through unsuspecting letterboxes bearing similarly horrifying headlines. For the first time in many months, the media's blanket coverage of the Korean War had suddenly been relegated to 'page two'.

Suddenly, the sound of an engine could just be heard from the sky above, becoming louder and louder by the second, as another low-flying aircraft came into view underneath the early morning cloud-line. A few moments later it roared over The Castle's pit-head in a southerly direction, before banking to the right and circling all around the crater in Wilson's field.

The world's media moguls were already sharpening their pencils. Soon the quaint little Ayrshire village of New Cumnock would be playing centre-stage to the greatest drama on earth.

7.30 a.m.

The wireless sets in New Cumnock were tuned into the nation's favourite radio station, the BBC *Light Service*. It was breakfast time, and the devastating announcement from the posh toff's gratingly-irritating public schoolboy voice had just kicked his captive audience in the guts, killing off any few remaining appetites:

> If, as is feared, there is little hope for the one hundred and twenty nine men, this will prove to be the worst mining disaster since Gresford.

It was a brief, matter-of-fact broadcast that plunged a dagger into the hearts of each and every New Cumnockian sitting at their kitchen table that morning.

Almost exactly sixteen years earlier, a total of 266 men and boys had lost their lives in Gresford Colliery, near Wrexham in Wales. The Gresford Disaster had been a catastrophe of hitherto unimaginable proportions, still all-too-fresh in the memories of the old stagers in New Cumnock's mining community, who clearly remembered not only its terrible human cost, but its root cause too. A gas explosion.

An explosion of the dreaded firedamp gas to be precise, and one so enormous that only eleven bodies were ever recovered, all of them charred beyond recognition. Firedamp, the very same stuff that now filled the old workings of Bank Number Six Mine itself, a perilous journey through which just happened to be the trapped Knockshinnoch miners' only possible hope of ever seeing their families again. The collective mood in the village that morning could hardly have been more morose.

It was the Coal Board's Area Production Manager who made the big call himself. We have to get rid of the gas, Alex McDonald had implored the rescue teams on their second descent of the old Bank Six Mine. Somehow, and as quickly as humanly possible, we just have to get rid of that bloody gas.

If the old mine workings had transpired to be in much better condition than first feared, then the firedamp levels had sure been a hell of a lot worse than anyone ever expected. Strangely enough, an old-fashioned booster fan still remained operational at a location around 100 yards inbye from the foot of the Bank's main dook, this having been left in place to maintain adequate ventilation for the old disused mine's water pumps. However, the advance party had also found that the further in they advanced, the higher the methane levels were beginning to rise, soon reaching close on twelve percent of the atmosphere, a truly explosive concentration.

The task ahead was therefore an extremely daunting one. In essence, it was this. Locate and deliver at least another two industrial extractor fans to the gas-filled inner recesses of Bank Six. In other words, somehow devise a plan to haul a couple of huge, cumbersome metallic contraptions down through a maze of old derelict and firedamp-polluted mine workings that hadn't seen human form for seven years. And into the bargain, do so without the aid of any mechanical haulage facilities whatsoever.

How could such a thing ever be achieved, the exasperated members of the extended rescue squad implored the Area Production Manager? How the hell could they get industrial machines of that size down from the surface, then through all the old workings, and finally up into the roadway and all the way to the coal barrier? It would be damned-near impossible.

'Damned-near, but not impossible!' McDonald had snapped. 'I'll carry the bloody things myself, if necessary! Now let's get moving.'

Alex McDonald got his way as usual. By eight-o'clock on the Friday morning, some twelve and a half hours after the inrush, the first auxiliary fan was finally shoved into position. The switch was thrown, and the engine roared into action at the first time of asking. McDonald closed his eyes. Thank the lord.

All around, a dozen men lay on the ground gasping for breath, on account of the sheer monumental effort that had just been undertaken. Having hauled the huge contraption all the way down from the Bank pit-head to where it now stood with all the haunting mystique of an ancient Druids' stone monument, the men were exhausted, utterly and completely exhausted, some of them close to losing consciousness.

The incredible effort of transporting the machinery had been absolutely backbreaking. The extractor fan itself measured six feet high by three feet square, and weighed in at just over a quarter of a ton. The distance from the Bank Mine's surface opening to the Fresh Air Base was just over a mile. It had taken the men nearly three hours to manhandle the gigantic beast down the main dook, then up and down through the rabbit warren of old derelict roadways, while others hauled the rest of the auxiliary equipment that would be needed to power the engine and kick-start its furious action into the massive invisible wall of firedamp. Essentially, this entailed electrical switchgear to operate the fan, extendable canvas tubing to propel the pressurised air up the roadway and, incredibly, over a mile of thick electrical cable to carry the high voltage from the Bank Power Station on the surface down into the deepest recesses of the old mine workings below.

At various points in the marathon journey, the fan had been carried two-at-the-back and two-at-the-front, while every now and again the great beast had actually been strapped across the shoulders of a willing burly coalminer while three of his neebors attempted to take its massive weight from the rear. The men had worked in groups of four, and in strict disciplined rotation, each team unable to prevent thumping heads on broken girders, scraping weary limbs on the fan's metal casing, and tearing flesh from strained fingers, before eventually dropping exhausted onto the pit floor while another team took over. The whole ridiculous ordeal would have demoralised most adult human beings to the point of abject surrender, but to those hardened coalminers and courageous volunteers, defeat was simply unthinkable. Their neebors' lives were at stake, and that was all there was to it.

And so there it now stood, this immense man-made contraption, sucking viciously at the deadly gas for all it was worth. The canvas tubing was gradually extended one section at a time, and within a few minutes it had stretched almost 70 yards into the gas-filled roadway that led towards Knockshinnoch.

'If we can get right up to the coal barrier,' McDonald had assured his troops 'then with a wee bit of luck, The Castle men will be able to walk straight home for dinner.'

Everyone had nodded as enthusiastically as their aching limbs and bursting lungs would allow, but all of them knew that it wasn't going to be quite that simple. McDonald was trying to keep the peckers up, his own very much included. There would be many twists and turns before all of this was done and dusted, that was for sure. And in addition to several million cubic feet of lethal firedamp, another great enemy now lay in wait, and the men all knew it. The rescue brigades simply had to get the trapped miners out of that hellhole before the firedamp levels started building up on the Knockshinnoch side too, as they most certainly would whenever the breach was made in the coal barrier.

That great enemy was time itself.

9.00 a.m.

'The pit's fell in!'

It was the scream of a horrified schoolgirl, as her classmate and near-neighbour walked through the big gate into the playground of New Cumnock

Junior Secondary School, or the 'Toon School' as it was more commonly dubbed. 'There's men trapped doon the pit, an' yin o' them's your uncle!'

That September Friday morning, the recipient of the gut-wrenching news bulletin was a thirteen-year-old schoolgirl called Jessie, who insists that her surname must remain anonymous:

> 'I ran home and told my mum, who hadn't heard a thing about it. She immediately grabbed her coat and told me she was going up to the pit to find out how her brother was, leaving me in charge of my own wee brother, who was only four years old at the time. I can't remember how long she was away, but it was a good wee while.'

Astonishingly, Jessie's mother had still known nothing about the disaster some fourteen hours after the incident occurred, and she wasn't alone in her blissful ignorance. However, by then the news was certainly beginning to get around. For the rest of the morning, tiny tears would pour down distraught children's faces, as terrified mums wept in hand-wringing despair.

Meanwhile down below in the bowels of the earth, it had been fifteen minutes since the pit-head had last made contact with the West Mine telephone station. Fifteen minutes and thirty seconds, to be precise. Sixteen. Sixteen minutes and thirty seconds. Seventeen …

Suddenly the bell rang. Andy Houston nearly jumped out of his skin. If his weary old legs weren't all they used to be, then his reflexes were still in fine working order.

'Hello,' said Houston, much more nervously than ever before. He noticed that his voice was shaking, so too the hand that held the telephone receiver. Pull yourself together man, for Christ's sake.

'Hello, Andy,' Willie Halliday's voice replied. It seemed a lot further away than the last time. The Pit Manager spoke again, but Houston didn't catch his message.

'Sorry, Willie,' the Oversman replied, 'but the line's a wee bit crackly. Can you repeat that?'

'All I said was nothing new to report, Andy. How are you and the men bearing up?' It was as if Halliday was phoning from Australia. Perhaps he was, and who could blame him.

'Aye we're fine, Willie. Everything's calm for now, although one or two of the younger lads are starting to feel it a wee bit. Asking questions all the time, you

135

know what I mean? Questions I just can't answer. It would be nice if you could tell us something. Anything at all, Willie.'

'Just tell them that work is proceeding as planned, Andy. Tell them that we're still working on an escape through Bank Six. Tell them it's like Paddington Station up here, everybody working their arses off to get them out of there.'

'Okay, Willie, will do. Any word on when things are likely to start happening at this end?'

'No, not yet. Just be patient, Andy, you'll be the first to know. Now hang up and save the battery.'

The phone went dead again, perhaps for the very last time. There again, perhaps not. After all, who the hell could possibly tell how this whole saga would play out? Halliday would return to his desk, his cup of tea-and-two-sugars in one hand, and his Capstan cigarette in the other. How Andy Houston and his men longed for the same glorious privilege.

Just be patient, Andy. Easy for Halliday to say, sitting up there with his bloody tea and bloody cigarettes. And breathing fresh air, cool fresh air.

'Whit did they say this time, Mister Houston?' It sounded like the voice of a schoolboy, a voice as yet unbroken by puberty. 'They gonnae get us oot o' here, Mister Houston?'

'Aye, son,' the Oversman replied, mustering a show of such brash confidence that even he wondered where the hell it had come from. 'They'll get us out through Bank Six. It might just take a wee bit of time, son.'

If there was one thing that Andrew Houston detested, it was people lying through their teeth. He covered his face in shame.

10.50 a.m.

As Archie Park walked into the engineers' shop on the Knockshinnoch Castle pit-head, the two men he was looking for were nowhere to be seen.

Geordie Paton and Sanny Allardyce, chief electrician and chief engineer respectively, were down at the crater in Wilson's field. Of course they were. All that Archie had wanted was a wee quiet word with each of them, to find out if his son, Dan, had turned up willingly for work that morning, or slouched in like a truculent little bastard.

However, both Paton and Allardyce clearly had much bigger things on their minds. Like trying to fill up an enormous crater, for example. For now, the customary high-ordered discipline of the engineers' shop had been overtaken by feverishly spontaneous activity, as hordes of people scrambled around in all directions.

'Where the hell have you been, boy?' Archie barked, as young Dan jumped out of the back of a Coal Board lorry. 'I thocht you were supposed tae be stertin' your apprenticeship this mornin'?'

'I ken, faither!' Dan shouted back in exasperation, his arms waving around in annoyance at his old man jumping to the wrong conclusion. 'I turned up at the engineers' shop first thing like you telt me, but then got sent up tae the Bank Pit tae see if I could dae anythin' tae help.'

'Right, Dan, that's fine,' said Archie, quickly realising the prematurity of his all-too-hasty outburst. 'So whit have you been up tae a' mornin', then?'

'Makin' tea, faither,' Dan replied, a bit embarrassed.

'Makin' bloody tea!' his father retorted. 'Here's me tryin' tae get you a guid stert as a pit engineer, an' a' you've done this mornin' is learn how tae make bloody tea! Your mother could have taught you that at hame! An' how tae darn bloody socks as weel!'

'It was for the men in the rescue brigades, faither, no' for me!' young Dan snapped back, deeply hurt. 'I've spent the hale mornin' fillin' big urns wi' boilin' water, an' cairryin' them ower tae the pit baths, so that the Salvation Army can gie cups o' tea tae the rescue men an' volunteers comin' back up fae the pit bottom. The Salvationists think I've done a great joab. Even if you don't, faither! An' I havenae had a break a' mornin', no' a single meenute. I've no' even had time tae have a pee, for Goad's sake.'

Archie Park recognised the folly of his impulsiveness, but stopped well short of apologising, for that was not the miners' way. Archie was deeply proud of his wonderful wee Dan, but strict masculine discipline was the order of the archetypal father-son relationship, not sissy emotional guff like saying sorry.

'Right, Dan, you've done weel enough for noo,' he conceded. 'So away an' eat yer piece, an' drink a moothfu' o' that lovely tea you've been makin'. Oh aye, an' see when you're finished? You'd better have a pish as weel!'

As Archie Park walked back towards the Bank Auld Pit to continue his own efforts in the rescue operation, he didn't even crack a smile, not even when he turned to roar one final remark from a distance.

'An' Dan! See when you're bye wi' eatin', drinkin' an' pishin', go an' take a walk doon tae Wilson's field. It's best if you see things for yoursel'.'

11.10 a.m.

'Shut the fan down!' a frantic voice bellowed from just inside the roadway. 'Shut the fan down right now!'

A bemused electrician just stood and stared. What the hell is he on about? We've cleared the roadway to 300 feet already, and things are going as well as we could ever have expected. Why stop now?

'Sorry, Mr McDonald, can you repeat that?'

'Shut the fan down! Right now, I tell you! Right damned now!'

The electrician pushed the stop button, and the speed of the extractor fan's engine was soon dropping like a Bedford lorry approaching a red traffic light. In an instant it was completely silent, as indeed were all the volunteers at the Fresh Air Base. McDonald's next words had better be good, the men all thought simultaneously, as if in communal telepathic communication.

They were very good indeed. The Area Production Manager had just clocked something that the others hadn't, something rather important. The concentration of methane gas in the roadway towards the barrier had been inordinately high, indeed in excess of 50% of the atmosphere at certain points. This in itself was no real problem to the rescue brigade men in that area, because although such levels of methane would have reduced the oxygen content to such an extent that it would have made 'normal' breathing completely impossible, the rescuers were wearing their self-contained breathing apparatus, the trusty *Proto*. Furthermore, methane's much-feared propensity to explode spontaneously when ignited – as had happened with such devastating consequences in the Gresford Disaster – could only ever occur at levels between 5% and 15% of the atmosphere.

However, a truly horrible thought had just struck Alex McDonald, and it was this. With the contaminated air now being sucked from the roadway by the giant extractor fan, some of the residual gas would somehow contrive to find its own way elsewhere in the mine. And where would it go? Straight down the return airway towards the Fresh Air Base itself, that's where. And, of course, generating a potentially explosive methane/air mixture while it did so. Worse still, it could then waft right into the path of the extractor fan itself, complete with its open engine.

McDonald just shook his head. What a bloody idiot, he cursed inwardly. Certainly, the extractor fans, like all other electrical equipment used in the pit, were always kept superbly well maintained, and any malfunction that might have caused the electric current to 'arc' was highly unlikely. However, his words to the men in explanation of his precipitate action left no one in any doubt about what had caused him to push the panic button.

'With the gas now coming straight back into our faces, one little spark and we'll all be blown to hell.'

Two of the volunteers that day were George Harvey, from the neighbouring village of Auchinleck's Highhouse Colliery, and Bob Dickson, himself a Knockshinnoch miner on a different shift from the trapped men. Harvey was about to find out just how dangerous a situation he had stumbled into:

'I had been working on the backshift at Highhouse the night before, and I had then cycled up from Auchinleck to New Cumnock with my wee pal "Murphy" on the Friday morning, just to see if we could help. My father was already up there with the rest of the Highhouse Rescue Brigade. When he saw Murphy and me, he told us to go and get some "pit claes" on, because they needed volunteers to carry stuff down the Bank Mine dook. Murphy and I ended up carrying drills. Big drills for extending boreholes to help the brigades break through the coal barrier. They were really heavy big things, about four feet long with drill-bits attached to them, but I was as fit as a fiddle in those days, and I could carry two-apiece no bother. It was about 800 yards down the dook, then I'd say about half of that again up to the Fresh Air Base, which was as far as you were allowed to go. So down the dook we would go, with the big drills under our oxters, and every time you got back up to the surface the Salvation Army folks would hand you a plate of soup and a cigarette. Before long, Murphy and me were carrying big planks of wood down the dook. By that time there were men lying all over the pit floor, dropping with exhaustion. It was bloody hard work, especially for my father and the brigade men working with yon big sets of breathing apparatus on. Suddenly, a cry went up. "Get out! There's gas in here! Run for it!" And off we all went, scrambling through the old roads and back up the dook! It was quite a frightening situation.'

Dickson's own experience was almost identical:

'The entrance to the Bank dook was really steep. Steep enough that you could rumble down if you weren't careful. It flattened out a bit at the bottom, then started rising again as you made your way up to what they called the Fresh Air Base. Every time we went down the mine, we were led by a deputy, who told us what to do. At one stage, we were up the rise near the Fresh Air Base, and the deputy held up his Glennie then started bawling and shouting. "Run! There's gas in here! Run for your lives!" It was only then it dawned on me that we were in a fairly dangerous situation, because up until then the thought had never even entered my head. I ran back up that bloody dook as fast as my legs could carry me!'

In the event, and after taking stock of the ensuing panic, Alex McDonald signalled over to District Inspector Eric Richford, and the pair of them disappeared into a side-heading for a few minutes, deep in private consultation. Meanwhile, a few of the volunteers still stood milling around the foot of the main Bank dook waiting for further instructions and praying that the methane levels in the old roadway wouldn't start escalating again, undoing all their good work. When the two gaffers eventually re-emerged from their hurried confab, it was McDonald who addressed the troops.

'I want you all to know that by clearing the main body of gas from the roadway, we cannot prevent some of it from blowing back in towards the fan, and that any sudden malfunction or spark could ignite it. Mr Richford and I have discussed the matter, and while we recognise the dangers concerned, we see no alternative but to proceed as before.'

McDonald had spotted the danger – a methane/air mixture and electrical sparks were not good bedfellows – and Richford had concurred. However, the two of them could offer no alternative to what nowadays we would call 'Plan A'. The plain fact of the matter was that there was no 'Plan B', none at all. They would therefore have to take a chance, a bloody big chance at that, and if anyone was unhappy they could leave immediately.

No one did, and the electrician pushed the fan's start button once more.

11.30 a.m.

Being reared in a coalmining community did many things for a lad's transition from childhood to adulthood, most of them exceptionally good. Save perhaps for a developing propensity to puff cigarettes by the packet-load, neck Younger's Pale Ale by the gallon and curse like a trooper. The more abstinent and God-fearing excepted, of course.

Hardly surprisingly, a working class upbringing also led to the development of countless great characters, the vast majority of whom headed 'doon the pit' the moment they hit their fourteenth birthday. Almost inevitably, the pits ended up being full of such larger-than-life characters.

One such was coalface worker and father-of-two, Dave Jess. Dave wasn't just larger-than-life. He was even larger than larger-than-life, as many an elderly coalminer or anyone else who ever had the privilege of making his acquaintance will gladly testify. And the truth is that it was probably just as well for the miners trapped in Knockshinnoch Castle Colliery that Dave was in their midst. Indeed, it was almost as if he had been planted down there by the Almighty himself just to keep up their spirits, with his outrageous sense of humour, raucous tales and unfailingly optimistic outlook on life itself.

Andrew McDicken and Willie Lopez were only two of the many miners who were glad to have him by their sides. At one stage, Andrew could scarcely believe his ears:

> 'There were all were, stuck down the pit, and Dave Jess tells us to go and get ourselves some grub to eat! His latest idea was that Wullie and me should walk over to the area of the pit that we called the "engine room" and see if we could find any scraps to eat. That was where the men who worked there ate their pit-pieces, and quite often they would fling their crusts onto the belt conveyor. So Dave thought it might be worth our while having a wee look to see if we could find anything lying about on the pit floor.'

So off the two of them went. A few minutes later, Willie caught the sight of his great pal, Andrew, emerging from behind the belt conveyor, holding his singlet vest out in front of him:

'His vest was full of crusts, bits of orange peel, and things like that. Mines was too, but Andra' had far more than me. I'll never forget what he shouted to me when he came out from behind that belt conveyor. "Haw Wullie, your tea's ready!" The pair of us laughed for ages at that one!'

The two likely lads then immediately high-tailed it back to the telephone station, where they proceeded to share their dubious spoils with a few others who managed to pluck up the nerve to scrape the 'blue moold' off the hardened crusts, and get stuck right in.

'How's yer dinner, Wullie?' McDicken enquired with the customary glint in his eye.

'Fine, Andra', fine,' was Lopez's repost. 'No' as guid as oor Jessie's shepherd's pie, mind you, but it'll dae for noo!'

As the starving miners chortled and teased each other over the highly questionable contents of what they were now nibbling, one of the younger pit boys grabbed his water bottle and made a beeline for the big wooden barrel that was sitting about 30 yards or so inbye towards the opening to Lanemark dook. It was the engineers' barrel, and the water could well have lain there stagnating since time began. On top of it remained its ghastly one-inch-thick film of oil, grease and dirt.

'And where do you think you're going, son?' It was the unmistakably articulate voice of Andy Houston.

'I need a drink, Mister Houston,' the lad replied. 'Ma mooth's fair parched.'

'You're not the only one, son,' Houston told the lad sharply, as the others homed in on the developing dialogue. 'Put the bottle back down, and listen.'

Turning to his troops, the Oversman then issued a telling instruction to all of them.

'Boys, the water in that barrel is heavily polluted with oil and God-knows-what-else, and it will make you very ill if you drink even a mouthful. You can wet your lips with it, if you feel you really have to, but only wet them, boys. And absolutely no drinking. Everybody understand?'

As the last remaining crusts scraped agonisingly down parched throats, silence and gloom once more descended like a huge black cloak. First one whisper, then two.

'Naw, I'm no' singin' masel', nae chance.' It was the unassuming voice of John Robertson, a highly respected man who was well-known for his staunch religious beliefs.

'Come oan, John, you stert it, an' I'll join in,' his fellow church-going friend and neebor, Sam McCracken cajoled him. 'Gaun yoursel'!'

Suddenly, the words of a very familiar hymn began to flow from John Robertson's cracked lips. Quietly at first, in fact almost apologetically, but gradually gaining in confidence and volume. A few moments later, and true to his word, Sam McCracken joined in too:

> *On a hill far away stood an old rugged cross*
> *The emblem of suff'ring and shame;*
> *And I love that old cross where the dearest and best*
> *For a world of lost sinners was slain.*

For the God-fearing miners at the West Mine telephone station, the familiarity of the tune and lyrics resided in its popularity at the Sunday morning church service. For the others, it presented as a powerful message of hope and faith, a hymn often sung to comfort grief-stricken relatives at a loved one's funeral.

As the redoubtable Robertson and McCracken continued singing the various verses that they had learnt by heart from early childhood, the rest of the men slowly began joining in the chorus:

> *So I'll cherish the old rugged cross,*
> *Till my trophies at last I lay down;*
> *I will cling to the old rugged cross*
> *And exchange it some day for a crown.*

By the time the fourth chorus came along, every single man in the West Mine was belting it out with heart-felt passion. Andy Houston likened the communal rendition to that of a well-trained male voice choir. As the tears rolled down his cheeks, the Oversman wound the handle on the telephone and waited until he heard a distant 'hello'. He said nothing, not a word, and neither did the voice on the other end of the line.

The words of 'The Old Rugged Cross 'were saying all that needed to be said. It was a truly magical moment that no person above or below ground would ever forget. John Robertson's initial shyness had been overtaken by his undying faith:

> 'They asked if I could sing to them, and the only thing I could sing was a hymn, and the only hymn I could sing was 'The Old Rugged Cross', because I was a believer of him that died on the cross. The Lord Jesus Christ is my saviour. When I sang it, all the men joined in the chorus, and they could hear it up on the surface.'

At eighteen years of age, Gibb McAughtrie was the youngest of the trapped miners. Gibb was a 'Bevin Boy'. The introduction, by conscription, of Bevin Boys to British coalmines had been the brainchild of Ernest Bevin, the former wartime Minister of Labour and National Service, who had earlier earned the respect of the working classes for his formidable performance as a feisty trade union official. A few years back, Bevin had realised that wartime Britain's coal mines were in desperate need of more men, in order to replace those miners who had been conscripted to the war effort. And so Gibb McAughtrie, just like thousands of other young lads of his age, had ended up toiling in his local pit, like it or lump it.

And as if that wasn't bad enough, Gibb had now found himself buried alive underneath the village in which his wife of the same age and baby son were now suddenly left to their own terrifying devices. One can only imagine the horrors that were whizzing around in the poor lad's mind at the time.

'Mister Jess?' Gibb asked Dave Jess in a mildly embarrassed whisper, as the latter stretched his legs.

'Whit is it, son?' Jess replied.

'Mister Jess, dae you think we'll ever get oot o' here alive?'

'Christ aye, son!' retorted Jess, beaming a huge grin and slapping the young lad on the shoulder. 'The rescue brigades are already on the ither side o' that coal barrier doon Watterheid Dook, an' they'll be diggin' their way through tae us afore much longer. We'll be oot in nae time! Nae time at a', son! You'll be back wipin' yer wee boy's erse by the morn's mornin'!'

At that, the young Bevin Boy smiled for the very first time since the news of his entombment had blasted into his youthful face. As he turned and started strolling back towards the main body of the miners, Dave Jess gulped hard. A dreadful thought started to seep into his mind, not unlike the sludge that was still edging its way menacingly towards the West Mine. The words formed on his parched lips, and he was powerless to stop them.

'I'll never see my own wife an' weans again.'

Tears attempted to form in a pair of sorry eyes reddened by coal dust, but the big hardy coalminer just wiped them away with utter contempt. Tears were for cowards, not for real men like Dave Jess.

12.00 Noon

The telephone rang again in the West Mine, this time at noon precisely. Right on the button for once, Andy Houston muttered to himself. It was Halliday.

'Right Andy, I'm about to give you a message. It is of such importance that you must write it down very carefully, and word-for-word. The message is from the General Manager. Straight from Mister McCardel himself, Andy.'

Halliday's voice sounded even more distant than on any previous occasion. No doubt about it, the telephone signal was weakening. Houston signalled for Andy McKnight to fetch his trusty notebook and pencil, then spoke again into the receiver.

'Right Willie, read the message out to me very slowly, and I'll repeat it word-for-word to Doch, then he'll write it down in the book. But Willie, you'll need to speak up. Do you understand?'

A moment's silence, then the penny dropped for Halliday. He had already noticed the fading phone connection and now he knew that Houston had too, only the Oversman didn't want his men to know, for fear of adding to their alarm.

'Right Andy, understood.'

McKnight sharpened his pencil, then opened his blue-covered NCB notebook and stood by, in order to home into his Oversman's words. As Halliday delivered McCardel's message over the phone, Houston read it back to him slowly and deliberately while facing McKnight, who proceeded to record it in his own inimitable handwriting. By that time, it wasn't only McKnight who was hanging onto Houston's every word, but each of the other 114 miners, as they held their collective breath in eager anticipation of something positive happening at last.

McKnight's written message was this, absolutely verbatim as McCardel himself had dictated it:

Tell the men that the gas is on the move and the rescue team has already been past the place where the bore is. The bore is 24' thick and it is hoped to give me definite instructions in one hrs time. The oversman will proceed accompanied by a volunteer to the bore hole place now and return to report by phone that there is nothing keeping them from getting there from the Castle side. No operations to start until definite word is passed on. When word is given to start commence on the middle leaf for about 16' and then rise up to the top leaf for holing through because the pavement is hoving on the other side. When nearly getting through keep a bore hole in advance and when the drill goes through test that the air is drawn through the hole to Bank. If the air is coming to us <u>stop</u> the bore hole. The rescue team cannot see the exact position of the bore hole but when they hear the Castle men working they will also start on the coal. The Bank men will try and have the gas out but the first men the Castle men will meet will be rescue brigade men. The oversman must control his men carefully and if the gas is out he will be given the OK for the men to travel. If the gas is not out he must control the men in his own side until instructions. The oversman must arrange that the men take short spells and husband their strength.

The mood among the men changed dramatically. At long, long last something was happening, and suddenly everything was beginning to look a hell of a lot rosier. Houston had now been instructed to go and check out the condition of the road to the borehole, but since Waterhead Dook was very close to a working area of the pit, surely this was just a formality? Furthermore, the miners would dig through 24 feet of coal in no time at all, especially if the rescue brigades could somehow start digging from the Bank side as well. There was now only one problem remaining.

The gas on the other side. That bloody gas.

12.20 p.m.

The Coal Board's definite decision to attempt a rescue from Bank Six was initially received by the trapped miners with much enthusiasm. However, as the chit-chat began to grow arms and legs, the doubters gradually became more vocal.

Aye, a resigned voice was first to opine from the half-light, there's no hope of us getting anywhere near the Castle pit shaft, so the old Bank Mine is our only hope … Aye, dead right, a number of others agreed … But how the hell will the rescue brigades manage to get us through yon huge barrier of coal between Knockshinnoch and Bank? … Jesus Christ, it's over 200 feet thick down there … No, not at the old borehole it isn't, it's only 24 feet deep at the foot of the tunnel where the borehole is … Aye, and we could blast that away in no time with Polar Ajax … Oh, you bloody think so? … The old Bank workings will be in a hell of a state after all these years … Aye that's right … And into the bargain, they'll be so full of firedamp that even firing one single shot could 'blaw up the hale o' New Cumnock' … Well, we'll just have to hack through the barrier from our side with picks and shovels, and even our bare hands if necessary! … Away and don't be so bloody daft, and then how would we get through all that gas in Bank Six? … The brigades will get the firedamp out of the workings in no time with extractor fans … And just how the hell are they going to carry extractor fans nearly two miles down a derelict mine? … Away and don't talk rubbish! …

And so it went on, until Houston eventually held up his hands and reminded them that he had been given a clear instruction, one he had to carry out immediately, and that was to check out the condition of Waterhead Dook 'from our side'. So off he set, leaving the men to continue their rambling debate on the wisdom of the Coal Board chiefs' big decision, but not before he had chosen his own 'volunteer'. Unsurprisingly, it was the highly-experienced and unfailingly reliable Sam Capstick.

As Houston and Capstick left the West Mine telephone station and began marching along the relatively flat road towards the 'Mech', the rabble of anxious men's hugely differing opinions slowly receded behind them into the distance. Less than 100 yards along, they took a sharp right turn into the much steeper Waterhead Dook and continued walking down in the general direction of the massive coal barrier that separated Knockshinnoch from the even greater depths of Bank Six.

The two men were soon approaching a relatively remote area of the pit, which ever since the days of private ownership had traditionally been out of bounds to the Knockshinnoch miners, for fear of having them transgress upon a rival coal company's precious pickings. The obedient miners had always willingly complied, while the more resourceful among them had spotted their mischievous opportunity and filled their boots, not to mention their tubs.

From memory, Houston knew that the next dook he would encounter – a much narrower 'slope road' tailing backwards at an angle of about forty-five degrees to his right - was the very one which had much earlier been driven to facilitate the drilling of the borehole itself. On bowing his head as he entered the cramped tunnel, the Oversman looked towards his trusty lieutenant and took a sharp intake of breath. This was the moment of truth, the road that would be the trapped miners' sole remaining lifeline. Houston knew without a shadow of a doubt that its physical condition would only be the first of many potential obstacles that would determine whether his men would ever see their families again. He prayed a silent prayer, and marched on.

The narrow slope road could hardly have been described as being in great condition, but considering its lack of use and remoteness from the main working areas of Knockshinnoch, it wasn't all that bad either. The road was pitch black, humid and wet. So wet in fact, that countless tiny beads of water trickled down the walls and onto the pit floor, before disappearing like magic into the natural drainage beneath. There they would join up with their thousands of companion trickles, before feeding themselves into the pipeline that would eventually pass through the borehole itself and into the gloomy depths of Bank Number Six Mine, to be pumped away harmlessly to God-knows-where. As Houston and Capstick scrambled on down the steep incline of the slope road, the sound of running water grew more and more distinct, and they knew that they were now nearing the pipeline that would take them straight to the old borehole.

Neither of the two seasoned coalminers had ever experienced anything quite like it. For lesser mortals, this would have been the perfect setting for a screaming, hysterical attack of claustrophobia. Blackness blinding and silence deafening, the former was punctuated by the long ghostly shadows that their cap-lamps cast on the pit floor, while the latter was split only by the eerie trickles of tiny streams that echoed in their ears like giant waterfalls. Whenever one of the two men opened his mouth to speak, the other jumped. A spooky place, and one which every single trapped miner would have to negotiate for himself, if he was ever to escape from this hellhole.

Another hundred yards or so further down, Houston and Capstick reached a sudden dead-end. It was the coal barrier itself, through which the drainage pipeline disappeared, no doubt to reappear some 24 feet further along on the other side. The big question was this. Would Houston and his men ever reappear on the other side with it?

The two men paused to take a breather. Good God, it was a bloody creepy place right enough, even for battle-hardened men of their years and experience of life. All around them, the blackness and silence still ruled supreme, save for the unearthly shadows and the sound of laboured breathing trying to compete with trickling water. Sam Capstick held up his Glennie lamp for the umpteenth time, noted the wonderful sight of its tiny blue flame, and reassured his Oversman once more that the firedamp levels were remarkably low and the air quality reassuringly safe.

The scouting party had finally made it to the old borehole and without any obstacles worthy of note, save for the occasional dislodged roof chock here and minor rock fall there. The half-mile walking route had taken them only about fourteen minutes and had been quite arduous, but Waterhead Dook and its companion slope road that led directly to the locus of the borehole were eminently passable and blissfully gas-free. At least for now.

Houston and Capstick stared once more at the coal barrier, then turned to face each other. One thing was for sure, and no words were needed to confirm it. On this side of the barrier was certain death, and on the other a very slight chance of freedom.

A fighting chance, all the same.

12.30 p.m.

Andy Houston and Sam Capstick quickly retraced their steps from the coal barrier.

They made their way up through the slippery, slithering pitch-blackness of the steep and narrow slope road, then onto the lower reaches of Waterhead Dook and on upwards, before turning left into the Mech, and finally back to the West Mine telephone station. The miners immediately began filing over to hear what the Oversman had to say. Before he spoke, Houston checked his pocket watch.

'The road to the borehole isn't great, boys, but you'll manage it fine. Fourteen minutes down, fifteen back up.'

'Whit aboot gas?' a nervous voice piped up.

'Nane worth talkin' aboot,' was Capstick's quick reply. 'The air's fine, right doon tae the barrier itsel.'

Houston picked up the telephone and wound the handle, his heartbeat rising again. Answer the phone, Willie. Answer the bloody phone.

This time it was a gruff, staccato voice that was unmistakably recognisable. Local Agent Johnny Bone was a man with a wonderful economy of words and a striking propensity to bark them out at whoever happened to be on the other end of the conversation, and his brusque and businesslike style was legion. In the words of Dan Park, 'they used to say that Johnny Bone could write a letter, make a telephone call and conduct an interview all at the same time!'

'Okay, whit's the position?' Bone snapped.

'Oh, it's yourself Johnny,' Houston remarked, a wry smile attempting to form on his coal-black face, but just failing. 'The road to the borehole is fine, eminently passable. Really narrow, very steep, a wee bit wet and slippery underfoot, and as black as the Earl of Hell's waistcoat, but it should be no real problem for the men.'

'Firedamp levels?'

'Less than two per cent. You can tell Mister McCardel that we're ready to go whenever he gives the word. We'd all like to be home by tea-time, Johnny.'

Bone slammed the phone down and stubbed the smouldering remnants of his Players' Navy Cut cigarette into the wet tea leaves lying on the bottom of his teacup. Notebook in hand, he opened the door and made his way across Colliery Square to where General Manager David McCardel had once again found himself surrounded by newspaper reporters from all corners of Great Britain and beyond. Standing there in the glare of the early afternoon sunshine and immaculately dressed in one of the superb hand-made suits he had ordered from Davie Gillies, New Cumnock's famous master tailor, McCardel was at his eloquent best.

'Preparations are continuing,' he announced confidently, straightening his dark blue necktie as pencils scraped on notepads and camera bulbs flashed continuously. 'The rescue brigades are trying to clear the gas from Bank Six Mine, and we remain in direct telephone contact with the trapped miners in Knockshinnoch. We are still hopeful of making a rescue.'

A barrage of questions began exploding in McCardel's face. He spotted Johnny Bone gesticulating towards him, and that was all the excuse he needed to terminate the impromptu press conference.

'Excuse me gentlemen,' McCardel said, raising both hands in apology. 'I really have to go now, but I promise to let you know what's happening the very moment I know myself.'

The Colliery Agent inhaled deeply as the General Manager approached him. Very few people unnerved Johnny Bone, but David McCardel was definitely one of them.

'Houston and Capstick got to the borehole and back, no real problem Mister McCardel,' Bone informed his boss eagerly. 'A quarter-of-an-hour walk, a bit rough here and there, but nothing to worry them. Houston says the men are rarin' to go, as soon as we give them the nod.'

'They'll be going nowhere!' McCardel snapped back. 'Not until we get rid of that bloody gas.'

12.55 p.m.

Down in Bank Six, the gas was proving impossible to shift, a real bastard. This exasperating state of affairs was confirmed to a newspaper reporter by one of the brigade men emerging black-faced and exhausted from the dook.

'If it wasn't for the bloody gas, we'd simply eat our way through that coal.'

The bosses had taken a huge risk by continuing to use an extractor fan powered by an open motor, and in an atmosphere in which the methane-to-air concentration was fluctuating wildly. The firedamp, which at one stage had been cleared almost a quarter of a mile up the roadway towards the coal barrier, was now returning with a vengeance, as it oozed silently and invisibly from the complex maze of old workings and exposed coal seams.

The same *Proto*-clad rescue brigade men who had succeeded in extending the canvas tubing section-by-section for almost 95 yards into the contaminated roadway, were now finding themselves removing the last few sections again, in order to consolidate progress. And still the displaced gas came wafting back down the return roadway, straight into the path of the perplexed volunteers at the Fresh Air Base and towards the extractor fan itself.

'This just isn't going to work,' sighed Alex McDonald to Willie Dick. 'Is it, Willie?'

'No, nae chance, Alex,' the rescue brigades' big cheese nodded in despondent resignation. 'We need far greater capacity than one single fan can possibly provide, nae question aboot it.'

And thus began another physically exhausting and horrendously backbreaking exercise, which would again test the mettle of seasoned rescue brigades and willing volunteers alike, and to the very limit. Their brief was this.

Install a total of three extractor fans, and have them fully operational within the hour. Start by getting rid of Fan No. 1, and replace it with a much more powerful unit, one with a capacity of 12,000 cubic feet per minute. Next, install two more units, Fan No. 2 and Fan No. 3, each of 8,000 cubic feet per minute capacity, and connect them up to run 'in series' for maximum efficiency. Then, erect a number of 'stoppings' at strategic locations along the way, in order to direct all the air available from Bank Number Six Mine's surface fan into the underground Fresh Air Base and all the way up to the coal barrier itself.

It was a task that sounded straightforward enough in theory. Perhaps it was just as well that McDonald, Dick and their troops didn't realise the stark practical reality of what was being demanded of them. By the time the whole operation had been completed, four whole hours would have elapsed and dozens of men would be lying exhausted on the pit floor, most of them spewing their guts up.

It was probably just as well that those same men didn't know the extent of what that gruesome torture session would have achieved.

Absolutely nothing.

2.15 p.m.

As David McCardel sat in his makeshift Headquarters' office on The Castle pit-head, the awful reality of the situation was really beginning to hit home.

Having just wiped his spectacles for the umpteenth time with the silk handkerchief that he normally kept for fashionable display in the 'hanky-pooch' of his hand-tailored suit jacket, McCardel's normal attention to aesthetic detail was temporarily on hold. Once more, he ran his sweaty fingers through his hitherto immaculate wavy-grey hair.

The rescue brigades were working their guts out to clear the firedamp in Bank Six, but their laudable efforts were proving futile, and the men were already nearing exhaustion. Likewise, the ever-increasing masses of courageous volunteers were out on their feet, and becoming demoralised at the lack of progress. Sure, the operation to install three new fans was well under way, but this would take time and there was absolutely no guarantee of success.

And talking of time, the 116 trapped miners had now been down there for 24 hours. A whole day buried alive, and without food to line their aching bellies or water to wet their parched lips. Stuck down there like anguished prisoners of war in some far-off black hole, fretting about their poor distraught wives and children.

Meanwhile, almost exactly one mile away in 'Gold's building' situated in New Cumnock's main street, Jean McMurdo's ears were again welded to her favourite little radio set, as she hung onto every word and syllable of the latest BBC *Light Service* broadcast. This time, the message was being issued from the Coal Board's Scottish Headquarters in Edinburgh. It was brief and businesslike as usual:

> Reasonable hope for the trapped men is held, and there is no reason to suppose that any of them were injured. They are still in communication by telephone with the pit-head, and the Oversman in charge reports that they are in good spirits.

Right on cue, master-tailor Davie Gillies knocked on his daughter Jean's big wooden front door and walked into the hall.

'It's only me, Jean,' he shouted. Taking one look at the young mother nursing her baby son in a woollen plaid, he immediately burst into tears:

> 'I'd never seen my dad crying before,' Jean remarked. 'Not even when my younger sister Nan was hospitalised with Diphtheria when she was only six-years-old and almost died. My dad had always been strong for us, but that afternoon the whole thing was just too much for him. When I asked him why he was so upset, he wouldn't tell me, although I found out later from my Uncle Sammy Shearer that some of the old miners had told him that the trapped men were doomed. "They havenae a hope in hell o' gettin' oot o' that place alive!" was what the men had said to him. Mind you, nobody ever told me that. You see, the men always protected the women in those days, and everybody just rallied around to give us moral support. I also knew that I wasn't alone. John's sister Agnes was in the same boat, because her husband Jim was trapped as well, and her daughter Isobel was only a baby too.'

So what official information or advice did she receive that from the Coal Board, or from any of the emergency services?

'Nothing, absolutely nothing at all. Nobody from the Coal Board ever came near us, and anything we heard was by word of mouth. However, there was a general understanding that the plan was to try to get the men out through Bank Six, but that the place was so full of gas that one spark could have caused a disastrous explosion. My instinct was to go up to the pit-head, but there was a baby to look after and I didn't want anybody to take him away from me. And anyway, I was certain that John would just walk in the front door any minute, and I had to be there for him. You see, he would be ready for his dinner.'

Meanwhile, the other womenfolk of the village paced their own kitchen floors continuously, faces strained with anxiety and hands wringing in awful contemplation of how this hellish situation might eventually turn out. Begging for news, any news at all. Anything other than this dreadful waiting and wondering. Anything just to stop hyperactive minds and galloping imaginations from spiralling completely out of control.

May Robertson sitting on the settee in her husband John's parents' house, being tempted continuously with tea and biscuits, in the full and horrifying knowledge that it was John who needed such sustenance, not her. Jenny Walker returning from her twelve-hour shift in The Castle canteen to find her house full of distraught relatives, some of whom had just come all the way from Dundee. The focus of Jessie Lopez's horrific thoughts oscillating between her beloved father and her new husband, both stuck down that terrible place. And, of course, Mary Walker agonising over the desperate plight of her three wonderful sons buried below in the bowels of the earth, while her other three sons and husband Pup continued toiling tirelessly on the surface, trying to do anything they could that might possibly contribute to the trapped miners' eventual salvation.

For the hardened men entombed half-a-mile below the ground, they were now living their worst nightmare. For the helpless wives, mothers, sisters and daughters up above, their world had just become a slow, lingering hell. When would this ever end? And how would it end?

In tears of joy, or tears of heartbreak?

2.45 p.m.

As Oversman Andy Houston lay down below with his thoughts, Area General Manager David McCardel sat up above with his own.

Houston was becoming more concerned by the minute, and for very good reason. His men had been trapped in the depths of the West Mine for almost a full day now, totally bereft of food and water, and either pacing up and down along the pit floor or merely lying around on the old coal sacks that they had found lying in a pile in an abandoned roadway. And, of course, bellies rumbling with hunger and lips parched by the searing humidity of the enclosed pit bottom. Every last pair of lungs was now continuously inhaling the steadily deteriorating, dust-filled underground atmosphere, absorbing precious life-sustaining oxygen and converting it into the potentially asphyxiating 'black damp', the miners' term for the notorious mixture of nitrogen, carbon dioxide and water vapour that is left behind when oxygen is removed from the air supply.

The men's spirits were still remarkably positive considering their desperate predicament, but some of the younger lads were already showing the first signs of real anxiety. Houston knew that if even one of them should suddenly fly into a panic, the whole mood amongst the men could well start to change very quickly, and an already dangerous situation could soon disintegrate into a perilous crisis.

It was the waiting that was the real problem. This bloody waiting.

And then there was the sludge, that pernicious river of death out there. Still creeping along the floor of the West Mine roadway and oozing down from the return airways above the trapped miners' heads, Houston knew that one more calamitous inrush from another section of Wilson's field and the stuff would soon be chasing them down the dooks of Garrowscairn, Lanemark and Waterhead, until it eventually swept them up like a giant tsunami.

However, what was really troubling the Oversman was something even more immediate. It was the telephone connection itself. At every successive fifteen-minute call, the signal had been becoming progressively weaker. Even the bell was now struggling to make itself heard whenever it attempted to ring in the near-silence of the West Mine. If one of those times the connection should fail altogether, then they would all be completely cut off from the decision-makers on the pit-head, and left to flounder in splendid isolation from whatever rescue operation was being planned on the other side.

Come on McCardel, Houston muttered through clenched teeth, make your mind up and give us the nod to start digging our way out, before this whole thing goes completely tits-up. Sure, the men are very tired now and they could certainly use a good feed, but they've still got the strength to dig a hole through the barrier. Furthermore, it would give them something to do, rather than hanging around listening to their own spiralling imaginations.

The General Manager's earlier edict was still ringing irritatingly in Houston's ears. *The Oversman must control his men carefully* .... Fine words, McCardel, so make a decision and let me do my job. Make a bloody decision, man!

Meanwhile up on the surface, David McCardel brought the latest meeting of the Coal Board's big chiefs to a brief 'pee-break' recess, instructing that everyone must be back in their seats in ten minutes' time, no exceptions. He then decided to escape from the choking tobacco reek of the Headquarters base and take a stroll out into the clean fresh air, all alone for once. He opened the wooden gate of Colliery Square that led him down into an adjacent cattle field, and stood there for a few minutes, taking in the seemingly never-ending panorama of miners' rows, all the way from the Leggate to his right, and as far as he could see to Burnside on his left. Smoke billowed from every single chimney. Knockshinnoch may well have 'fell in', but the coal fires were still burning.

A lump formed in his throat, and he swallowed hard as he contemplated the situation for the umpteenth time. Each and every miner stuck down this hellhole has a house full of despairing relatives somewhere in this village. We need to get those poor bastards out of there, and back to their families. Somehow, and no matter what it takes, we need to get them out. McCardel raised his face towards the heavens, closed his weary eyes and uttered an extremely rare oath.

'What a mess. What a f - - - ing mess.'

His dilemma was this. The miners have now been trapped down there for the best part of a full day, with neither food nor water to sustain them, and in a rapidly deteriorating atmosphere. Houston is a calm and tough old bugger, sure enough, and he's doing a grand job just keeping up the men's morale, but it's only a matter of time before desperation sets in, and possibly panic too, especially amongst the younger lads. If I now give him the nod to start digging through the coal barrier, that alone will give the men something to do and possibly help him to keep them calm. However, when the barrier is holed through, the more headstrong among them might see this as an opportunity not to be missed, and make a run for it. A completely suicidal run.

Not only that, but we're fighting a losing battle against the gas on the other side, so what happens to the gas itself when Houston's men break through the barrier? What happens if the stuff starts surging into Knockshinnoch? Will the men keep their discipline and plug it up again, or will some of them just make a dash for it?

And then there's the sludge, that bloody sludge. If another big section of Wilson's field breaks away, the sludge will burst in again and overpower them. Then they'll be lost for good, while we all bugger about and dither up here, instead of giving them a fighting chance to escape.

And then there's the telephone. That phone is going to fail. Sooner or later, the signal is going to pack in. And then where will that leave us? He cursed again.

Damned if I do, and damned if I don't.

McCardel marched straight back into the HQ Base, knowing that he was about to make the most important decision of his life. As he took his seat again at the head of the table, the telephone rang as feebly as a toddler's imitation toy set. It was Johnny Bone who picked it up. After a few irritated mutterings into the mouthpiece, the look of sheer annoyance on the Agent's face was unmistakeable.

'It's Andy Houston, Mister McCardel. He wants to talk to you. And he says he won't talk to anyone else.'

McCardel grabbed the phone and welded it to his ear. Houston's voice seemed a million miles away, but his message was as clear as it was unambiguous.

'Mister McCardel, I think we should start digging the hole. And right now, before it's too late.'

'I agree, Mister Houston,' the Area General Manager replied instantly. 'But there are conditions, and you must follow my instructions to the letter. Agreed, Mister Houston?'

'Agreed, Mister McCardel.'

3.30 p.m.

'Right boys, things are starting to move. We've now got clearance to start digging the hole.'

Andy Houston's tone suddenly had a new bounce to it, one of confident authority. There was no cheering as such among the men, only huge sighs of relief. Relief that at long last, they were now going to get the chance to do something to help themselves get out of this bloody place, out of this bloody tomb. By that stage, any activity at all would have been welcomed with open arms, but the prospect of actually digging a hole to freedom was therapeutic beyond description.

The miners all knew to a man that their Oversman had played this situation perfectly. His dogged insistence that they must sit tight until he got permission from the gaffers had been bloody frustrating, but they all realised that it was for their own good. Now Houston had forced McCardel's hand, and got his own way as usual, the wily old fox that he was.

Soon they would be hacking away at the coal barrier that separated eternal imprisonment from glorious freedom. Houston surveyed the scene as best he could in the dim glow of a handful of cap-lamps' emergency beams. As far as he could tell, every last man was already up on his feet and absolutely raring to go.

And therein lay his latest dilemma. How the hell do I strike a balance between getting the men primed for hard labour on empty stomachs, and keeping their expectations of an imminent escape totally realistic? Uppermost in his mind were the 'conditions' that David McCardel, in his recent telephone call, had placed on the digging operation.

'Your men will work in squads of five maximum and in rotation, every squad to be relieved after fifteen minutes, in order to husband their strength. Each squad will be supervised by a Deputy or a Fireman, and the men must work strictly to the instructions given to you earlier by telephone. Very importantly, the men must stop working when instructed to do so. Finally, Mister Houston, the success of this operation will depend on your ability to keep the men under control, and working strictly to instructions at all times.'

No pressure there, then, Houston smiled wryly to himself.

'Where's that notebook, Doch?' he nudged McKnight. A few seconds later it was in the electrician's hand, already opened at the page containing the detailed operational plan for digging the hole through the barrier.

'I'm going to need some volunteers!' the Oversman shouted loud enough to ensure that everyone could hear him. A sea of hands shot up, in fact every pair of hands in the whole West Mine as far as he could make out from the long shadows.

'That's more like it, boys!' the Oversman smiled, unashamedly proud of his men for such a courageous display of enthusiasm. There again, perhaps it wasn't only courage and enthusiasm, perhaps it was just about them finally being given the opportunity to take their salvation into their own hands.

Houston thanked the men for their willingness to step forward, but explained that because of the very cramped conditions down at the coal barrier, the work could only be done by using a few men at a time, and so he would need around 40 volunteers at most. However, he thought that it was best to explain the plan to everyone, thereby keeping them all in the loop.

'We're going to start putting some of you into five-man squads, each squad to be led by a Deputy or a Fireman. Those of you selected will be led from Waterhead Dook down to the coal barrier, where you will work for fifteen minutes. Fifteen minutes and no more, boys, got that? Your squad leader will supervise the digging operation. When he tells you to stop, you must do so immediately. No arguments and no exceptions. We can't use Polar Ajax to blast our way through because of the gas on the other side, so it's picks and shovels, boys, … and hand-bore rickety drills of course, not electric. One man will use the drill, and one will start digging with his pick. Two others will shovel the coal away, and the last man will keep checking the Glennie for gas. After your fifteen minute stint, you will return here to the telephone station. It'll be very hard work, boys. Remember that you've had damn-all to eat or drink for nearly a whole day, so you're going to tire very quickly.'

'Aye, I could murder a big plate o' mince an' tatties!' shouted Dave Jess, to a wave of laughter. No doubt about it, the men's spirits had been lifted considerably by the decision to set them to work.

'Well, you might get your mince an' tatties sooner than you think, Dave,' Houston replied, 'but only if you all work strictly to instructions. And for those of you I don't pick for action, you can be sure I'll find something else for you to do! Everybody understand?'

Willing heads nodded and mumbling utterances sounded in compliance. Houston immediately set about choosing his squad leaders, eight of them in total, who in turn helped him to pick their own squads. He then gathered the troops together and began a more detailed briefing, conscious of the fact that the rest of the men would be harbouring a whole range of emotions, from great relief to bitter disappointment about who had been picked for the digging operation, and who had not. However, this was no time for sentiment, this was a time for clear heads and unfailing discipline.

Very slowly and very deliberately, Houston started reading out the text in Andy McKnight's notebook to the selected volunteers, stopping only occasionally to expand on those parts which he felt required a wee bit more clarification:

When word is given to start commence on the middle leaf for about 16' and then rise up to the top leaf for holing through because the pavement is hoving on the other side.

The Oversman felt that he should take a few minutes to explain why the holing-through trajectory needed to start off level, then rise upwards, making the whole procedure considerably more tricky. This was on account of the pavement 'hoving' on the Bank side. Every miner in the pit knew that the literal translation of this present participle was 'heaving', a very common phenomenon in underground roadways where the enormous weight of the pit roofs was unavoidably transmitted onto the 'seat-earths' below, which were composed of soft ancient soils that were much weaker than the coal itself. In underground roadways at considerable depths, the lithostatic pressure from the overlying rock formations would easily overcome the strength of the exposed seat-earths, which would then be squeezed upwards into the void spaces of the pit roadways, not unlike toothpaste from a modern day tube. This phenomenon was called 'floor heave', in those days occasionally dubbed 'floor hove', and it was typically counteracted by the process of 'dinting', which involved industrial 'dinting machines' to trim the squeezed seat-earths away. The dinters could never have stopped the pavements from heaving, indeed nothing could, but at least their use kept them clear for the miners to travel along.

Of course, the big problem now was that the pavements on the Bank side would have been heaving for anything up to seven years by then, with not a single dinter in sight, and so some of them would be in one hell of a mess. Therefore, since the process of digging through the coal barrier might increase floor-heave even further as the rescue hole approached the other side, the escaping miners could very well find themselves terribly squeezed in the refuge area. Hence the decision to start digging the hole on the level, before rising upwards, in order that when the rescue operation began, the men would emerge above – rather than straight into – the damaged pavements.

'In other words,' the Oversman explained, 'you start by digging through the breast coal. Hand-bore rickety, picks, shovels and bare hands, boys. The hole should be about four feet square – high enough and wide enough for big Wull Gray to get through, but no more than that! And remember, you need to keep a much smaller borehole ahead of you at all times, one that you can plug up again if the gas on the other side starts playing silly buggers. As for the sixteen feet, it'll be some time before we get anywhere near that far, and I'll give you further instructions when we do. At that point, we'll need to start digging at a rise, right up towards the head coal, so that when we do eventually break through, we end up on the level on the Bank side, rather than coming out straight into the old heaved pavements. All clear, boys?'

Heads nodding. Houston began reading out another extract from McKnight's written record:

> When nearly getting through keep a bore hole in advance and when
> the drill goes through test that the air is being drawn through to Bank.
> If the air is coming to us <u>stop</u> the bore hole.

'Now, boys,' Houston continued, 'I cannot over-emphasise just how important this is. When you do get through – and remember, it could be any one of you who makes the final breakthrough – test the direction of the airflow right away. My bet is that it will be from Castle to Bank, because of the air pressure on our side being very high due to the sludge having blocked up the roads and return airways, but we won't know that for sure until we've actually holed through. Hopefully, we'll be fine, but if it turns out to be from Bank to Castle, plug the hole up immediately. Immediately, boys, okay?'

Heads nodding again, although faces looking a bit more anxious this time. Houston ploughed on:

> The rescue team cannot see the exact position of the bore hole but
> when they hear the Castle men working they will also start on the coal.

'So there you have it, boys,' Houston said. 'When they hear us digging, they'll start digging too, and we'll be through in no time. I'll show the first squad exactly where to begin holing. After they've made a start on the hole, it will be pretty bloody obvious to the rest of you. And remember, boys, fifteen minutes, then out. Not even fifteen-and-a-half … fifteen! Any questions?'

'Aye,' asked Eck Clapperton. 'Who goes first, Andy?'

'You do, Eck,' Houston replied. 'You and your men in the Mech section probably know that area of the pit better than anyone. You boys will be squad number one. I'll lead you from Waterhead Dook down to the barrier, and show you precisely where to start digging, then you can take it from there. Okay?'

The big Fireman nodded eagerly, clearly desperate just to get on with it. Houston then set about numbering the other squads from two to eight, instructing them that they'd be expected to work fifteen minutes at a time in rota formation, but that if fatigue should set in, he would simply call in some new faces from the men left behind at the telephone station. Finally, he emphasised how important it was for each successive squad to be stationed a few yards back from the coal barrier and ready for action the very moment the previous squad had been told to down tools. This was a battle against time, and any delay could be disastrous.

Houston gave the nod for Clapperton and his men to collect their graith, and off they all marched into the shadows. Meanwhile the others said their own silent prayers.

3.55 p.m.

Eck Clapperton and his men knew the 'Mech' section of the pit like their own navels, particularly the 'endless rope' district where they routinely toiled their guts out for a living, eight hours a day and five days a week, or often six if a wee bit of overtime was on offer.

Down on the right, the steep slope road that led off Waterhead Dook was a bit less familiar, although some of them had earlier chanced their arms to get at the forbidden riches that lay enticingly in wait in 'no man's land'. This was the vast 200 foot thick wall of coal that separated Knockshinnoch from Bank Six. And now here they were, slithering and sliding down the very same forbidden slope road, only this time under official instruction to do so. Instruction to dig themselves and their neebors out of the blackness of their tomb, and into the blinding light of glorious freedom. The stakes could not have been higher.

'This is it, boys,' Houston whispered so quietly that he could have been in a church service. Somehow his whisper seemed to reverberate around the claustrophobic chamber like a big bass drum, almost but not quite drowning out the constant trickles of running water. A creepy place right enough, Houston reminded himself, so let's get these pickaxes and shovels going.

Taking a lump of chalk from his trouser pocket, he marked a large 'X' on a section of the breast coal, about three and a half feet above ground level and a couple of yards to the right of where the drainage pipeline disappeared from view. The beams from the cap-lamps immediately homed in on Houston's 'X'. For a fleeting moment, they reminded the war veteran of ground-based searchlights trying to get a fix on an overhead enemy aircraft.

Eck Clapperton was struck by the crude simplicity of the digging operation:

'There was no way we could use explosives, due to the build-up of gas on the other side. Even an electric borer was just too big a risk. So the men had to use a hand-bore rickety, picks and shovels. Compared to the rate we would normally work, it was gey slow going.'

The first thump of the pickaxe actually made Houston jump. The noise when it walloped into the breast coal could have wakened the dead. For some reason, it just sounded 'wrong' in such a still and silent place, almost sacrilegious in fact. Then the hand-bore rickety drill began screeching its way into the centre of the middle leaf, followed again by a few more thumps of the pick. Next, the two shovels got to work as they started scraping the loosened coal off the pit floor, cranking up the volume by another couple of notches. Very soon, it all began to sound like a normal pit shift at a normal pit coalface. However, Houston and his charges knew that nowhere could possibly have been further from normal than this awful place.

The Oversman then headed back up the dook to supervise the squad rotation operation, leaving Clapperton and his men down at the coal barrier. After a good ten minutes, the singlet vests were being hauled off as the diggers and shovellers continued toiling at the coalface, stripped to the waist in the oppressive humidity of the cramped black tunnel, rivers of sweat pouring down their faces. Christ, it was hard work, especially on empty stomachs and parched lips.

'How's the Glennie, Tam?' the Fireman enquired.

'Fine, Eck,' came the welcome reply. 'Still below two per cent, so nae problem here.'

Five minutes more, and Clapperton made the call. 'Right boys, down tools.'

Another couple of thumps with the pickaxe, the shovels still swishing.

'Now boys, I said! Tools down, right this minute!'

The foot of the dook returned once more to its former silent ambiance, save for the continuing dribbles of water and the deep, heavy panting of three sweat-saturated miners, all of whom immediately slumped to the floor in sheer exhaustion. The next sound was of one of the men doing his best to retch up anything that had managed to remain in his aching guts.

'Sorry boys,' said Clapperton, 'no time for rest, the next squad's arriving already, so we need to get out of here to give them room to work. You've done a great job, boys, a really great job.'

'Here comes the cavalry!' It was the unmistakeable voice of big Dave Jess, as the cap-lamps from the second squad flickered down from the gloom of the dook. 'Leave it a' tae us, an' we'll be through in nae time!'

He could just make out the figure of a burly coalminer scrambling back to his feet. His body was so drenched in perspiration that Jess was sure he had been dragged out of a pool of flood water. The man gasped back in response.

'Well, son … the best … the best … o' luck tae ye!'

Willie Lopez was surprised at how quickly his squad reached the coal barrier:

> 'The road down to the borehole was in fairly good condition, no problem at all. Since we weren't the first squad down, it was easy to see where we had to start digging. It was one of these situations where if conditions had been normal, we would just have blasted our way through in no time at all. We knew there was gas on the other side, though, so we just had to hack through the coal with our picks, shovels and bare hands. It was quite hard work, you know.'

And so for the next few hours, some forty-odd men who hadn't eaten or drunk a single thing for a full day would hack away at a 24 foot thick barrier of coal until they were literally dropping from exhaustion. The fate of every man in the West Mine depended on them breaking through to the other side, and as fast as their bursting lungs and aching limbs could manage. The only thing that mattered for now was holing through to Bank Six.

The gas on the other side? They would worry about that later.

5.20 p.m.

From the gloom of the West Mine, the men could just make out the beams of five cap-lamps slowly approaching. It was the latest squad returning from their self-imposed hard-labour sentence at the coal barrier. Sam Capstick and his four erstwhile cronies, this time.

'How's it goin', Sam?' an anxious voice enquired from the shadows, as the squad re-joined the others.

Capstick and his men just slumped to the ground with amazing synchronicity, all of them still panting heavily.

'You nearly through yet, Sam?'

'Leave it!' Andy Houston snapped. 'Leave it, man! For God's sake, let them have a breather!'

Not another word was spoken. If the men hadn't really appreciated the sheer effort required by the volunteers in digging that hole and then trekking their way back up the dook, they certainly did now, as the sweat-drenched bodies lay prostrate on the pit pavement, chests still heaving from their exertions. The men's silence was also a clear sign that Houston was still very much in charge, so critically important in such a tense situation.

Meanwhile down at the barrier, it was Wull Gray who heard it first.

'Wheesht, Boys!' he said, dropping his pickaxe onto the floor. A shovel continued scraping.

'Wheesht, Jim, for Christ's sake!'

'Whit is it, Wull?'

'Just shut up an' listen!'

Silence. Complete silence, save of course for the ever-gurgling underground streams, and the rapid, heavy breathing of the diggers themselves.

'You hear that, boys?' Gray whispered.

The same aural recipe again. Near silence, split only by running water and men gasping for dusty air. And that … that other noise. That strange, faraway noise. What the hell is it?

'You hear it noo, boys?'

A distant 'clunk', then two more, then another one. A short period of silence, then five-six-seven clunks more.

'It's the men on the other side!' Gray shouted. 'It's the brigades, lads!'

The men immediately grabbed their tools and began hacking at the coal again, somehow mustering up renewed vigour and enthusiasm from the pits of their empty stomachs. A few minutes later, the Fireman reluctantly informed them that their fifteen minute stint was up.

'As quiet as possible for a wee minute, boys,' he added. 'Just let me listen tae this.'

Clunk-clunk-clunk, the pickaxes on the Bank side continued, easily the most reassuring sound the Knockshinnoch men had heard in a very long time. As they turned to face the squad leader, their cap-lamp beams illuminated the strangely puzzled look on his face.

'Whit's wrang?' came the inevitable question.

The Fireman just held up his right arm, to signal for an extended period of silence. Clunk-clunk-clunk-clunk-clunk.

'Somebody point tae where they're diggin', will you?' he asked.

A long pause, then, 'ower there', followed by, 'aye, that's right enough, ower aboot there'.

The five men turned in the general direction of where the distant clunks were coming from. Then they turned back and stared at the hole they had been making in the coal barrier. The two points were about twenty feet apart.

'For Christ's sake,' said the Fireman, shaking his head. 'We're diggin' twae parallel tunnels.'

6.05 p.m.

By the time Andy Houston had returned to the West Mine, Dave Jess was already in full flow.

The ultimate 'Master of Ceremonies', Dave had been regaling the troops for the past fifteen minutes with his seemingly never-ending repertoire of bawdy jokes and increasingly outrageous one-liners. If only around half of his audience was already in howling fits, then the other half was slowly but surely getting there. Even the more reserved, religious ones in the pit – and there were a good few of them – had by then found it quite impossible to prevent themselves chortling at his irrepressible and decidedly risqué wisecracks.

Absolutely perfect, thought Houston, a captive audience with its attention focused elsewhere. He wound the handle on the telephone. A click, a crackle, then a faint voice which he soon recognised belonged to Johnny Bone. This phone line wasn't getting any better.

Seizing his opportunity as quietly and discreetly as possible, the Oversman informed the Agent that the rescue brigades on the Bank side of the coal barrier were digging about twenty feet too far to the Knockshinnoch men's left. In other words, he rephrased it, about twenty feet too far to the brigade men's right. Houston and Bone then double-checked each other's understanding of the situation for the avoidance of doubt, and terminated the conversation instantly, in order to conserve the telephone battery's rapidly-dwindling power.

On the other side of the coal barrier, Jimmy McCreadie cursed when his Whitehill Rescue Brigade received the bad news:

> 'We had been working away at the coal on the Bank side and making quite steady progress, when our Captain got word that we were about twenty feet too far to the right. So there we were, all happed up in our *Proto* gear in the middle of all that bloody gas, and being told that we had just wasted precious time. Well, it didn't go down very well, neither it did. But we just had to get on with it.'

However, for Jimmy and his Brigade neebors, it wouldn't just be a matter of shifting along the barrier and digging a new hole:

> 'By that time our oxygen supplies were nearly exhausted, so we were instructed by the Captain to go back up the dook to the pit-head. Another cigarette, another big bowl of soup from those wonderful Salvation Army folks, an hour's rest, and you had to pass the doctor all over again. Then straight back down, *Proto* gear on again, and back up to the coal barrier to start digging again. Mind you, by that time, another brigade had already started on the new hole, so we were fairly confident we were working in the right place this time.'

Meanwhile back in the West Mine, it was another well-known worthy who had decided to relieve Dave Jess of his one-man show responsibilities. 'Wallace Anderson's party piece was an impression of Ronnie Ronalde,' said Jock McMurdo. 'He was terrific, and his "blackbird" act was unbelievable.' The ever-popular Ronalde, born Ronald Charles Waldron which didn't exactly have the same ring to it, was much loved for his whistling-and-yodelling talents, and therefore quite possibly the only man on earth who enjoyed equal status with connoisseurs of both Alpine and Country 'n' Western music. However, Ronnie was possibly even more famous for his incredibly lifelike birdsong impressions, and it was one of his best-known that the redoubtable Wallace had decided to tackle in the depths of Knockshinnoch Castle Colliery. The bright lights of Glasgow's Empire Theatre and the shadowy gloom of the hopelessly entombed West Mine could hardly have been further removed in terms of ambiance, but that didn't stop the irrepressible Wallace from singing and whistling the glorious song of one of New Cumnock's most endearing indigenous birds:

> *If I were a blackbird, I'd whistle and sing,*
> *And I'd follow the ship that my true love sails in.*
> *And on the top riggings, I'd there build my nest,*
> *And I'd pillow my head on her lily-white breast.*

As Wallace's elegant crooning and melodious whistling blended together in perfect harmony, his captivated audience clapped and roared in approval, the decorum punctuated only occasionally by the odd carnally-suggestive cat-call from the would-be 'stalls' of the pit bottom.

Having done his bit for the time being, Andy Houston found himself joining enthusiastically in the applause, whilst praying silently that some day very soon, every home and hostelry in the village of New Cumnock would be rejoicing in gratitude through the glorious strains of *If I Were A Blackbird*.

One 'music hall act' followed another. The hymns sung in unison by a group of church-going men were interspersed by a few rather coarser songs from some of the more raucous individuals, with the mood constantly oscillating between calm contemplation and belly-laughing bawdiness. A few poignant poems were remembered from yesteryear, and recited with heartfelt passion. Stories galore were narrated to the assembled audience, some so close to the bone that they were well into the marrow itself. Joke-after-joke was delivered, many recalled from the annals of New Cumnock's celebrated 'Burns Suppers', and few of which would ever have lent themselves to telling in more refined company. 'Everybody just got in on the act, and very few complained,' was Andrew McDicken's take on the raucous entertainment. 'To me, though, Dave Jess was terrific with all his stories and jokes. I could hardly breathe for laughing!'

Rab Cockburn thought that Jess's unofficial role as MC was critically important in lifting and maintaining the men's morale:

> 'Dave was a right good character, and kept the whole thing going with his tales and jokes. In fact, anything just to stop us from thinking about it.'

That master of the understatement, Willie Lopez, summed up the mood as succinctly as always:

'It was simple. We were all just doing everything we could to keep each others' peckers up.'

However, according to all accounts, the top-of-the-bill spot belonged to the most unlikely double-act imaginable, in the shape of big Dave Jess and little Jim 'Buffer' Carmichael. As the wisecracks and heckling continued, Dave planked his backside on an old wooden toolbox, then grabbed Buffer under the oxters and sat him down on his knee. The act that followed would become the stuff of legend. Andrew McDicken found himself reduced to tears of laughter:

'There they two of them were, Dave sitting on the box with wee Buffer on his knee, and his hand up the back of his vest, working his heid like a ventriloquist's dummy! My ribs were sair laughing!'

As the 'gottles of geer' lines flowed relentlessly, somehow the unlikely duo's impromptu act had contrived to make every man in the pit forget his woes, if only for a relative instant. The empty bellies had stopped rumbling, the parched mouths had ceased gulping and the galloping imaginations had gone into transient hibernation, to be replaced by diaphragms aching with laughter, if only for those few mirthful moments.

The unplanned climax of the performance arrived when Jess accidentally clattered Carmichael on the head with his safety lamp.

'For Goad's sake, Dave!' shouted wee Buffer. 'I get stuck doon here in a cave-in, an' how it a' ends is that you knock me oot wi' your f - - - in' Glennie lamp!'

And so, as the men rolled around the pit floor holding their rib cages in hysterics, the ventriloquist and dummy performance transpired to be the final act in that wonderful, inspirational 'concert'. The whole thing had been incredibly therapeutic, a tonic of incalculable proportions. It had served, albeit temporarily, to release the tension and stress amongst a group of men who were still hoping and praying for the best.

However, when the curtain finally came down, they would once again find themselves fearing the very worst.

One of Oversman Andy Houston's strangest observations down in the bowels of Knockshinnoch had been this. So far, not one single man had ever moaned to him about feeling hungry or thirsty.

And when you consider that all 116 miners had required to go without food and water for such a long time in the intense humidity of the West Mine, and with many of them having undertaken lengthy periods of hard labour at the coal barrier, their reluctance to even mention the pains of hunger and thirst was all the more remarkable.

However, something other than mere sustenance was starting to play a few nasty tricks on the men's physical and psychological well-being, and it was beginning to trouble Houston. That 'something' was the perceived temperature in the West Mine. The problem was that the Oversman had no way of telling for sure how hot or cool it actually was in the damned place, because for all of the assorted bits and pieces of equipment he routinely carried in his toolbag, a thermometer was not one of them.

In evidence of this strange phenomenon, Houston had already begun to notice a few rather contradictory and unnerving signs. Some of the men were now lying about the pit floor stripped to the waist, with beads of sweat trickling down their faces and torsos, while others had begun putting on their jackets. Houston's concern for the former was that their bodies, already seriously dehydrated by lack of drinking water, could ill afford to lose yet more from perspiration. On the other hand, the latter appeared to be feeling the cold, and indeed some of them were now beginning to tremble slightly, a few actually rubbing their hands together in an effort to heat themselves up.

The Oversman was perplexed. Clearly, this compact area of the pit bottom couldn't be both hot and cold at the same time, so what the hell was going on? Please God, don't let this be the beginning of some rapidly-spreading feverish infection. That's all we need now.

Had the following medical analysis been available to Houston at the time, he might have understood more fully what was actually going on. Sadly, no such words of wisdom were available to him. He was alone with his thoughts, alone with his fears:

'The men in Knockshinnoch would have been under enormous strain by that stage. In such circumstances, the body secretes *adrenaline*. Blood is then diverted to the muscles to 'power' this fight-or-flight impulse, which means that very little remains available to aid digestion. In other words, when the body is under severe strain, digestion shuts down and the appetite disappears. Hence the reason that the trapped men wouldn't feel hungry. It gets worse. Hard-working muscles produce heat, which raises the body's temperature, and this heat must be lost to avoid *hyperthermia*. This is a serious, indeed potentially fatal condition, which occurs when the body produces or absorbs more heat than it can dissipate, leading to elevated body temperature. When the body becomes too hot, the main way it gets rid of the excess heat is by sweating. Sweat evaporates from the skin and takes its latent heat of evaporation from the body, and the temperature drops. However, when a person is 'dripping with sweat', this is doing absolutely nothing to help the process, since plainly the sweat is not evaporating. All that excess sweating achieves is to lose fluid, and a surprising amount of fluid at that. By way of example, just one hour's hard graft in hot conditions can result in the loss of an astonishing two litres of fluid. The big problem, though, is that even if plentiful supplies of drinking water are available, the body can only absorb just over half of that amount in the same period of time, and so body temperature starts rising rapidly. Therefore, for the Knockshinnoch men who had been labouring in hot conditions and with next to no drinking water available to replace those lost fluids, big trouble was already brewing. In short, their bodies each now faced a terrible dilemma. Either stop sweating altogether and suffer a dangerously rising body temperature, or continue sweating profusely and suffer equally dangerous dehydration. It gets worse still. Eventually, lack of fluid in the body determines the issue. Sweat dries up completely and body temperature rises from its norm of 37 degrees, to 39 or even 40 degrees. When this happens, the body stops feeling hot. Instead, it feels that the surrounding conditions are cold, and tries to get warmer by working the muscles to start shivering. By this time, the body is in a really confused and dangerous condition. As the temperature continues to climb to above 40 degrees, it can become a real threat to life. The heart and kidneys begin to fail. The brain, which is extremely sensitive to temperature change, soon becomes confused, resulting in disorientation, stupor, coma and eventually death. It would be difficult to tell how long the Knockshinnoch miners actually had left before the end-game approached, but already their symptoms were exceedingly worrying.'

Unfortunately, the luckless Andy Houston had no such informed medical advice to hand at the time, so all he could do was watch, wait and pray to the heavens above.

Meanwhile, the masses assembled on the Bank pit-head were currently experiencing no such difficulty in establishing the ambient temperature. Dusk was fast approaching as the September skies closed in, and it was cold. Extremely cold, in fact.

As the latest rescue brigade - this one from Muirkirk's Kames Colliery - emerged in singlet vests from Bank Number Six dook into the New Cumnock evening air, they all felt to a man as if someone had just flung a pail of ice-cold water over them. Scattered all over the hillside to their right, more than two-hundred anxious relatives stood shivering in their flannels-and-jackets and skirts-and blouses, their flat-caps, head-squares and woollen scarves hauled down over nipping ears and dripping nostrils. Ashen-white faces adorned with blue lips slowly receded into the bitter darkness of the worst Friday night in the villagers' living memory.

'Any news?' shouted an anxious wife-and-mother, as the crowds pushed forward.

'Any word when they'll be gettin' oot?' beseeched another.

'Naebody's tellin' us a thing!' a young twenty-something female voice yelled in pent-up frustration, 'no' a bloody thing!'

'Aye, no' a single word!' another called out in exasperation. 'For God's sake, tell us whit's happenin'!'

'Somebody ... somebody, please!' an elderly lady begged the brigade men. Then her tears came.

Grim-faced and stoically as ever, the rescue workers marched along the police cordon and straight past the waiting crowd without saying a word, before climbing up the hill into the pit baths for their well-earned cigarettes and soup. Orders were orders, and this was no time for soft sentiment.

And so, as 116 entombed men lay variously perspiring and shivering down below at the West Mine telephone station, an army of frustrated volunteers and distraught relatives stood freezing in the gathering gloom on the surface.

For those above and below ground, their second sleepless night now beckoned. This living, terrifying nightmare knew no end.

10.10 p.m.

Andy Houston awoke with a jolt.

For the first time since climbing wearily into his own cosy bed almost two nights ago, he had allowed himself the dubious luxury of nodding off. Houston was furious with himself, absolutely furious. Until now, as the trapped men's so-called leader, he had somehow managed to beat back the suffocating veils of sleep like his favourite cowboy, big John Wayne, fighting off a marauding Comanche Indian war party.

Until now, that was. Now, he had let sleep get the better of him. Now, he had let his men down. Houston attempted to rebuke himself sternly, but a little voice in his head had other ideas.

You're getting far too old for this, Andy, it said. If we ever get out of here, I'll never go back down another pit as long as I live. I'm going to set up my own wee business. Sewing garments, that's what I'll do, because that's what I'm good at, and it's what I've always wanted to do for a living. And the miners can bloody-well laugh at me if they like. Bugger this coalmining lark. Yes, that's what I'll do. Sewing ... and stitching. 'Hand-stitched by Andrew Houston', that's what the labels will say. And soon they'll be coming from all over the country just to get hold of a 'Hand-stitched by Andrew Houston' garment. Yes, that's what I'll do. Sewing and stitching. And bugger this coalmining lark.

If ... if ... if we ever get out of here.

It was the distinctive sound of pit boots crunching on the pit floor that snapped the Oversman out of his uneasy half-slumbers, that and the blink-blink-blinking of the advancing cap-lamps.

'We're nearly through, Andy,' a breathless voice wheezed, before its carrier slumped over the railtrack in exhaustion. Another four lamps dropped downwards in perfect unison. The poor bastards were out on their feet.

'Right,' said the Oversman, scrambling unsteadily to his own, the creaking of knee-joints rather unforgivingly reminding him of his advancing years. 'I'll go down now and supervise the holing-through myself. Well done boys, that's a pint I owe you when we get out.'

Andy Houston wasn't much of a drinker, but right now he could have murdered a pint of McEwan's 'heavy'. He took a long deep breath to steady his nerves. Houston was well-used to the taste of coal dust in his mouth, but this time he could feel it coating his windpipe as he inhaled, just as his beloved Mary's baking flour stuck to her soda scones before she threw them onto the girdle.

'You come with me too, Sam,' he ushered to the ever-dependable Capstick.

The Fireman's cap-lamp nodded like an obedient firefly on a sultry summer's evening. This was it, make-or-break time. The moment of truth.

Meantime, in Cumnock Town Hall some five miles away, it was American crooner Nat King Cole's number-one hit Mona Lisa that was belting out of the overworked little PA system, as the amorous lads and lasses of the locale shuffled and smooched over the wooden dance floor. And that was when a pair of burly New Cumnockian miners arrived on the scene, on a serious recruitment mission. Every available pair of youthful hands was needed, and needed right now.

Less than half an hour later, a dozen young lads clad in their very best clobber had found themselves at the Bank Auld Pit, being briefed on their tasks as they prepared to join the other volunteers underground.

Their Saturday night jigging and snogging session was over, and soon their Saturday best would be in tatters.

10.45 p.m.

As Andy Houston marched through the Mech towards Waterhead Dook with his trusty lieutenant Sam Capstick by his side, he knew that they'd soon be returning with sensational news.

Would it be sensationally good or sensationally bad, though, that was the big question? The answer would depend on one thing, and one thing alone. The direction of airflow the moment the men holed through. Simple as that.

Houston was fairly confident that the outcome would be good news for the trapped men, and that when the coal barrier was finally breached, the air would immediately rush from the Knockshinnoch side into the Bank Mine, thereby pushing back the lethal firedamp on the other side. After all, the men had been cooped up in what was essentially a pressure cooker for well over a day now, and so the moment the breach was made, the air would surely flow in the 'right' direction.

Wouldn't it?

Yes, Houston was fairly confident. However, he was far from certain. You see, one of the pit's engineers, a great character called Jim Walker, had earlier provided Houston with an excellent analogy of the situation. Jim - or 'Pud' as he was much better known to his neebors - was renowned for many things, but probably two in particular.

First was his determination to do things the 'old-fashioned way', rather than bother with the modern-day accoutrements that the younger engineers were now carrying around in their toolbags. In the words of Dan Park, 'Pud Walker didn't bother his arse with all those fancy new tools that the Coal Board had introduced. There was nothing that he couldn't sort with his hammer and chisel. They used to say that Pud could have carried all his tools in a skip bunnet!'

Secondly, Pud was an ardent horse-racing fan, and loved 'a wee flutter on the cuddies', as in those days did most of the miners. And now down in the depths of the colliery, it fell to the inimitable Walker to engage his gambling analogy, and inform Andy Houston that the chances of the gas flowing in the direction from Castle-to-Bank were 'an odds-on certainty'. This spirited prediction had initially heartened Houston, until Pud felt the need to deliver his coup-de-grace.

'Mind you, Andy, the last odds-on certainty I backed was a big grey horse called Mighty Max at Ayr Races. It was a dozen lengths clear, an' fell on its erse at the last fence!'

By the time Houston and Capstick had slithered their way back down to the coal barrier, the men digging the hole were nowhere to be seen. Like the other teams before them, they had been digging exactly as the Oversman had instructed. By then about four and a half feet high by four feet wide, the hole had been hewn straight through the breast coal for the prescribed distance of sixteen feet, and then upwards in a gradual rise into the head coal. Now, Houston had been informed, they had almost reached the cavity that had been excavated by the rescue workers on the Bank side. In other words, they were nearly through. Houston found himself catching his breath.

How did they know for sure, he asked the men at the coal-face? Because, they replied, they could hear the Brigade men working on the other side, 'as plain as your next-door neebor chappin' through the wa' o' the hoose'. Quite enough analogies for one day, Houston told himself.

He crouched down, and scrambled into the hole and up to what remained of the barrier, without any difficulty. The men will have no problem getting through here, he assured Capstick as the Fireman followed him to the coal face.

There, two men were hacking away at the last few inches of the barrier, both stripped to their waists. In the darkness, Houston had no way of telling who the one with the hand-bore rickety was, but he immediately recognised the one with the pickaxe. He was was none other than Dave Jess himself, and it was his deep melodious voice rather than his substantial physical features that gave him away.

And there in the most desolate of underground tombs imaginable, Jess, as gregarious as ever, was singing one of his favourite Robert Burns' ballads, the one with which he would always regale his family and friends every time the bells of Big Ben rang in yet another New Year:

> *With careless step I onward stray'd,*
> *My heart rejoic'd in nature's joy,*
> *When, musing in a lonely glade,*
> *A maiden fair I chanc'd to spy;*
> *Her look was like the morning's eye,*
> *Her air like nature's vernal smile:*
> *Perfection whisper'd, passing by,*
> *"Behold the lass o' Ballochmyle!*

Parched throat or not, Jess's vocal chords were in fine fettle, as he belted out the words of 'The Bonnie Lass o' Ballochmyle', one of the many beautiful love songs written by Scotland's national bard and Ayrshire's favourite son, the incomparable Burns.

The tension was becoming unbearable. Another salvo of thumps from the pickaxe, then another, and yet another still. How long was this final push going to take?

Houston knew that the next few minutes would determine everything. Whether the holes on the Knockshinnoch and Bank sides were lined up properly this time, or whether they would just slip past each other again like passing ships in the night. And if they did actually align, whether the air would flow from Castle-to-Bank, or from Bank-to-Castle, when the final breach was made.

Put another way, whether the trapped men would live or die.

Next it was the turn of the hand-bore rickety to have a go. As the handle was wound rapidly in a clockwise direction, the drill-bit screeched and crunched as it cut its way into the coal, accompanied by Jess's defiant rendition of the bard's famous chorus:

The Bonnie Lass ... The Bonnie, Bonnie Lass ...
The Bonnie Lass o' Ballochmyle!

Suddenly, the drill-bit burst through the coal face like a hot knife through butter, leaving a hole about the size of a saucer. A rush of air belted Jess on the nape of his neck. For the merest fleeting moment, it reminded him of his wife walking in through the back door on a stormy winter's evening, after a session at the local bingo hall. Shut the door, Mattie, will you?

'We're through, Andy!' Jess shouted. 'We're through!'

'You sure, Dave? You sure?'

'Aye, Andy, as sure as a big dug pishes doon your leg! We're through! An' the air's comin' in the right direction! Castle tae Bank, Andy, Castle tae Bank!'

This time the chorus got the full treatment, as every last molecule in his hot breath exploded from the depths of his dust-filled lungs:

The Bonnie Lass ... The Bonnie, Bonnie Lass ...
The Bonnie Lass o' Ballochmyle!

Houston inhaled deeply. Fully realising the critical importance of the next few moments, he took charge of the situation immediately.

'Right boys, well done! A grand job! But now I want you to stop what you're doing, and listen carefully.'

The men downed tools and stared in the direction of the Oversman's cap-lamp, chests heaving from the sheer exertion of their superhuman efforts. Houston continued. He felt like a party pooper at a wild Hogmanay shindig.

'So far so good, boys, but we're not there yet. There's still a hell of a lot that can go wrong. There will be no more digging until I get clearance from the surface, so just rest up for a minute or two then head back up to the telephone station. No more digging, I say! You all got that?'

Noting the nodding of four compliant cap-lamps, Houston then turned his attention to Capstick.

'Right Sam, I'm leaving you in charge down here, because I need to get back to the station and telephone the surface, so that they can let the brigade men on the other side know what's happening. They're bound to have seen something

177

over there, and felt the air coming into them, but they now need to get as accurate a picture as possible.'

As the Oversman began wriggling his way back down the hole, he made one final and forceful announcement.

'And remember, Sam, if the air stops flowing from Knockshinnoch to Bank, plug up that hole immediately. And no hesitation, Sam. Immediately!'

For the very first time since Wilson's field had erupted into the bowels of Knockshinnoch, Andy Houston felt a wave of optimism wash over his psyche. He was already beginning to feel so close to freedom that he could almost smell Mary's perfume.

10.46 p.m.

Suddenly, something flew out of the coal-face like a lead pellet from an airgun. It clattered against Jock Malcolmson's pit boot.

'Whit the hell was that?'

Malcolmson's shocked utterance was completely inaudible from the mouthpiece under his *Proto* helmet, but his knee-jerk reaction conveyed the full story to his neebors, who just gawked in astonishment. A puff of coal dust billowed upwards in the glow of their cap-lamps, like cigarette smoke through the film projector beam in Biddall's, the local picture house. The Knockshinnoch men couldn't be through already, could they?

'Quiet!' signalled Rab Hyatt with a wave of his right arm, his left palm cupping his mouthpiece in symbolic fashion.

Silence reigned for the nine rescue workers in Bank Six, save for the constant click-click-clicking of their *Proto* gear, as rapidly ventilating lungs converted oxygen from the cylinders strapped along their backs into carbon dioxide destined for the *Protosorb* bag on their midriffs. You didn't ever argue with the Captain of Highhouse Rescue Brigade, no siree. Even the Bank Brigade's own boss, Eddie Smith, stood statuesque at Rab's visual command.

Silence. Silence and clicking.

Then, suddenly, something else, something barely audible in the distance. Something far away, yet close enough to make itself heard. What the hell?

A song! Somebody's singing a song!

> *The Bonnie Lass … The Bonnie, Bonnie Lass …*
> *The Bonnie Lass o' Ballochmyle!*

Rescue worker Dan Jess stood transfixed like a scarecrow in a field of swaying barley. His gob would have fallen open, had it not been for the rubber mouthpiece clamping it shut. Not only did Dan recognise the song, but he instantly clocked the identity of the singer as well.

And in that most bizarre of fleeting moments down in the guts of Bank Six, Dan found himself being transported a few months back in time. To January, in fact, and to New Cumnock Burns Club's annual 'Supper', where one of the local amateur crooners was busily belting out the inimitable lyrics of Robert Burns' classic ballad, *The Bonnie Lass o' Ballochmyle*.

The voice belonged to Dan's brother, Dave.

11.10 p.m.

As Andy Houston made his way back up the steep incline of Waterhead Dook, he was suddenly hit by a feeling of *déjà vu*. What the hell was he going to say to his men this time?

On the one hand, he could simply tell them that the lads had now holed through, that the air was flowing in the right direction and that, God willing, it would only be a matter of time now before they could just walk out of this hellhole. And, by Christ, they could certainly use some good news.

However, on the other, he just instinctively knew that their desperate bid for freedom wasn't going to be quite as simple as that. Houston's job was to 'control his men', and if circumstances happened to conspire against them in any number of ways, he could only do so by managing their expectations from the very outset. Keeping those expectations realistic, in other words.

By the time he had reached the telephone station, the men were already on their feet waiting for the big news, good or bad.

'We're through, boys!' the Oversman announced, his huge grin scarcely visible underneath the glow of his safety lamp.

There was no cheering, only murmurs of relieved approval and assorted comments ranging the whole length of the expletives spectrum. Houston proceeded to give them the good news, which was that the airflow had turned out to be in the right direction, from Castle to Bank, at least for the time being. This was then followed by the bad, which was two-fold. Firstly, and as far as he knew, the brigades were still battling to clear the firedamp on the other side. Secondly, there was no way of telling what might happen to the direction of airflow when the pressure between Castle and Bank equalised, as surely it must do very soon.

One step forward and two steps back. Up one minute and down the next. If this was 'managing expectations', Andy Houston didn't much care for it, but he knew it had to be done.

He wound the handle on the telephone. After the customarily lengthy wait, he was through. The line crackled like Ayrshire back-bacon in a sizzling frying pan, but the distant voice on the other end was still distinctive enough to belong to Johnny Bone.

'We're through, Johnny!', the Oversman announced gleefully to the Agent. 'Holed through at 10.45 p.m. prompt, a hole about the size of a football, maybe a wee bit smaller. The air's flowing from Castle to Bank.'

Silence from the surface.

'Johnny?' Houston continued. A horrific thought hit him. The line's dead. 'Johnny? You get that?'

'Aye, Andy,' the unmistakable voice replied. Houston's sigh of relief sounded like a hurricane in his own ears.

'I've left Sam Capstick down at the barrier with a four-man squad,' the Oversman went on. 'Told them to keep checking the direction of flow, and also the Glennie for signs of gas. Also told them not to widen the hole, and to plug it up if the air starts changing. What happens now, Johnny?'

Silence again, most disconcerting. Bloody annoying, actually.

'Johnny, for God's sake?'

'Sorry, Andy … right … right … tell the men they can start widening the hole, but only a wee bit at a time … and they must be ready to plug the thing up the moment the air starts flowing back from Bank to Castle. Got that, Andy?'

'Aye, got it.' Houston felt a wave of nausea flowing into the pit of his stomach. 'What's wrong, Johnny? What are you not telling me?'

More silence.

'Johnny?'

'We're having an awful job trying to clear the gas in Bank Six, Andy. A hell of a job. This is going tae take a wee while. You'd best prepare the men for a bit of a wait.'

'How long, Johnny? My men have been down here a long time. A bloody long time.'

'Aye, Andy, I know fine. It'll still be quite a few hours at least before we can get rid of all that gas … possibly even … even running into … into days.'

I knew it, I just bloody-well knew it, cursed Houston. He looked at his men, all of them now energised by optimism for the first time in ages, many clearly elated. Good God, some of them even with their jackets back on, lining up to walk out as if they were leaving a church service. David McCardel's words rang again in his ears. 'You must control your men ....'

You try controlling them, McCardel. Sitting up there on your big fat arse, in your pin-striped suit, drinking tea and eating bloody scones. You bloody try it.

'Right, Johnny,' the Oversman continued, mustering up every ounce of self-discipline that he could wring out of his wiry frame. 'If that's the way it is, then so be it. However, any chance of getting a couple of brigade men through here with some food and water? We'll need it if we're going to be here for a wee while.'

'That's what we're working on now, Andy.' And at that, the line went dead.

Andy Houston turned to address the troops once more. This wasn't going to be easy.

Meanwhile, up on the surface, a deafening din split the ghastly silence of the night. It was the pit-horn, and it made many of the anxious souls gathered on the hillside jump out of their skins.

On and on and on it went, signalling God-knows-what, other than that something really big had just happened, and it certainly wasn't just the miners' piece-break. The waiting crowds soon began to swell further, as bewildered faces left makeshift offices and off-duty rescue workers came out of the pit canteen holding rolls-and-sausage in their burly mitts, accompanied by worried-looking catering ladies clad in pristine overalls.

At first, there was much confusion. The pit horn? Why was the pit horn going off? Was something wrong? Oh my God, surely not another section of Wilson's field? A firedamp explosion, that must be it, someone opined. The terror gradually began to crank up, fuelled by reckless rumour, itself inflamed further by abject misinformation and hysterical speculation. Slowly but surely, the anxious grey faces of New Cumnock's desperate womenfolk grew bulging eyes so steeped in horror that tears became impossible. As some wrung their hands in impending grief, others held onto each other for dear life.

Suddenly, someone shouted from their midst:

'They're through! They're through!'

The crowd surged towards the source of the cry, a man in his early fifties wearing a dark suit covered by a white 'shortie' raincoat. At first, there was a low communal babble, quickly building to a more fractious rabble which steadily increased in volume as various individuals started to scream questions in the suit's direction, all of them demanding clarification about his feverish outburst. And in the ensuing mayhem, aided and abetted by the constant ear-splitting hoot-hoot-hoot of the steam-generated pit horn, it was mass hysteria that gradually began to rule supreme.

People started hugging each other like long-lost lovers. One elderly lady sank to her knees on the sodden grassy hillside, her grey hair covered by a scarlet head-square and her shiny plastic boots caked in mud. 'They're saved! They're saved!' she cried, her old wrinkled hands clasped together so tightly that they might later have had to be separated by a surgical scalpel.

Within a matter of seconds, the mood had changed from doom-and-gloom to tears-and-laughter, then to laughter-and-tears. Very soon, the word had reached every corner of the waiting crowds.

The Knockshinnoch men had been saved. Saved!

A few minutes later, the Coal Board's big cheeses emerged from their makeshift HQ to address the masses. Even before its Chairman, the decidedly lofty Lord Balfour, had made his way through the crowd to the minion carrying the hand-held loudhailer, flanked on either side by his Area General Manager, David McCardel, and NUM boss, William 'Wull' Pearson, everyone was already applauding wildly. When Balfour then announced that the Knockshinnoch men had succeeded in holing through the barrier to Bank Six, the applause turned to roars of joy.

However, when the Chairman then informed them that the gas in the Bank side was proving extremely difficult to remove, the same roars began receding rapidly. When he next added that it was likely to be 'some considerable time' before the rescue brigades could start attempting to bring the trapped miners out, silence once more reigned over the barren hillside, save for the eerie whistling of the chilly autumnal wind.

One step forward, and two back. Up one minute, and down the next.

Meantime, down below in the depths of the West Mine, Oversman Andy Houston would have given his right arm for silence. Instead, he was facing a barrage of increasingly hostile questions.

The natives were becoming restless. Worryingly restless.

11.18 p.m.

When the unsuspecting missile had popped out of the coalface and clattered Jock Malcolmson's pit boot, the first reaction of the Highhouse Rescue Brigade men was one of bemused shock. The second was to grab their tools and start assaulting the small aperture in the coal barrier with all their might.

A swift, assertive wave of Rab Hyatt's hand, straight across the front of his chest, soon put paid to that idea. Down tools immediately, his hand-signal commanded the troops. No way was the Captain prepared to start widening the width of the hole without clearance from the surface. The evil gas swirling around the heads of the rescue men was being denied access to their lungs by virtue of a highly technical arrangement of strategically-positioned mouthpieces, noseclips, oxygen cylinders, breathing bags and valves galore. However, if any rash action now allowed that same gas to start seeping through the hole in the barrier, the guys on the other side would have no such protection.

By this time, the old derelict Bank Number Six Mine was more populated than it had ever been, even in its most productive heyday. 'It's like Sauchiehall Street doon here', one startled observer had remarked when he reached the foot of the dook. In addition to the two brigades up at the coal barrier, a whole army of rescue workers and volunteers now busily beavered away at something or other, the latter's access to the mine restricted to no further than the Fresh Air Base.

The volunteers' tasks were wide and varied, but each and every one of them was absolutely crucial to the rescue plan. Some of the younger ones, like eighteen year old Dan Park, simply found themselves scarpering around the main dook in relay fashion, carrying fully-refreshed rescue equipment down to the brigades, and the spent stuff back up again to the surface:

'I actually wore out a good pair of pit boots just running up and down that dook,' said Dan. 'Wore them out in a single day, I did. They were in tatters by the time I was finished!'

You name it, and the volunteers just got on with it, always under the strict supervision of the brigades, of course, whose own various actions continued to be masterminded by Kilmarnock Rescue Station's high supremo, Willie Dick. However, of all the assorted operations taking place in the guts of the old decrepit mine workings, arguably the most important was the mission to get rid of the dreaded firedamp, in order to clear a passage from the hole in the coal barrier to the Fresh Air Base through which the Knockshinnoch men might eventually make their desperate escape.

Essentially, two separate but mutually-dependent operations were required to bring the underground atmosphere under some kind of reasonable control. Those were the ventilation of breathable air from the surface to the working areas below, and the dispersal of unbreathable underground air contaminated by firedamp to other areas of the mine.

The first procedure involved the continuous use of the three giant industrial fans that had already been hauled into position, this under the watchful eyes of both Alex McDonald and Alex Stewart, together with the erection of 'stoppings' at various strategic locations. Stoppings were normally constructed of wood or brick, and their function was to block off sections of the pit in order to direct the ventilation flow down from and back up to the surface. In the Bank Mine, it was makeshift wooden and cloth stoppings that were used to do the job, the latter made of material not unlike carpet underlay, and coated by black tar.

The second procedure was attempted through the positioning of a number of 'brattices', or partitions. Their normal function was to regulate airflow, for example by splitting a shaft or roadway in two, then directing air down one side and the exhausted gas up the other. Down in the gas-contaminated recesses of the old Bank Mine, one of the rescue brigades' key challenges was to position a network of brattices to try to control the flow of clean air and firedamp, in such a way as to clear a safe walking route for the trapped men when they were eventually given the nod to attempt an escape.

Meantime, through the barrier, one of Andy Houston's five-man squads had already set to work again on widening the hole from the Castle side, as directed by General Manager McCardel himself. 'Steady as you go' had been the Oversman's instruction, as the hand-bore rickety and pickaxe started chewing away at the coal, albeit a good deal more cautiously this time.

Still the air flowed steadily from Castle to Bank, but for how much longer, Houston wondered? If it stopped, or God forbid actually changed direction, he would have no alternative but to give the call for the hole to be plugged up again. He shuddered when he thought of the devastating effect that such a course of action would have on the trapped men's already seriously-battered spirits.

Some twenty minutes later, a message was passed from the surface to the telephone at the Fresh Air Base in Bank Six, and onwards 'up the line' to Rab Hyatt at the coal barrier. It informed him that Houston and his men on the

Castle side were now attempting to widen the hole, but very stealthily indeed, and with one eye very much on the direction of airflow. Hyatt and his fellow Brigade Captain, Eddie Smith of the Bank team, carefully examined the small aperture that had been left when the lump of coal had blown out of the face. Air still flowing towards us, they both agreed by virtue of a reciprocal 'thumbs-up' gesture. So far, so good.

Within minutes, the Knockshinnoch men's rickety drill and pickaxes seemed so close to Jock Malcolmson that he was sure he could have stuck his big hand through the hole and grabbed them. And it was that very thought which gave the Highhouse man an idea. A really inspirational idea.

As his neebors watched on, Malcolmson began scribbling something on the back of his shovel with a piece of chalk, and waited until the aperture had been widened to a diameter of about one-foot. Then he stuck his shovel through the hole, right to the top of its wooden shaft, and hung onto the handle. On the Knockshinnoch side, it was the scraping of metal on coal that made the men crawling on their bellies stop digging.

What the hell .... ?

And there in the flickering beams of their safety lamps, they saw it. A shovel. A bloody pit shovel. And with something scribbled on the back of it, something in white chalk. The Knockshinnoch men screwed up their eyes, as the writing slowly came into focus. Two words, only two words:

Highhouse Brigade

Big Jock Malcolmson stood on the Bank side, still grasping the wooden handle, waiting for a response. Any response at all would do.

He certainly got one. Suddenly without warning, he felt a terrific pressure in his right fist, and before he knew what was happening his whole arm had been hauled into the hole, right up to the oxter.

The Castle men were trying to pull him through the barrier.

SATURDAY, 9 SEPTEMBER

12.20 a.m.

The job of being first to crawl through the hole in the coal barrier fell to Willie Jolly and his Whitehill Brigade.

It really was a poisoned chalice, a daunting task strewn with almost every possible danger and obstacle imaginable, but one which Jolly and his men accepted not just as an instruction, but as an honour and a privilege. Getting their neebors out of perilous predicaments was what they had been trained to do, and getting the trapped men out of that tomb was what they were bloody-well going to do. Come hell or high water, or die trying.

Suddenly, the whole situation changed:

> 'When the Knockshinnoch men first holed through, the air started flowing from their side towards us, which was just what we needed to happen,' said Jimmy McCreadie. 'Then a wee while later, the pressure slowly began to equalise, and the air just stopped moving.'

However, to experienced miners like Jolly and McCreadie, this new development was hardly surprising. After all, the Knockshinnoch side had been a pressurised 'cabin' for well over a day by then, so when the breach was eventually made in the barrier, it was well-nigh inevitable that the air would rush through towards Bank. However, only until the pressure equalised on both sides, that was, and when it did, the airflow would surely subside and then stop altogether. Quite how it would then behave was anybody's guess. The likelihood was that the air on both sides of the barrier would simply start ebbing and flowing through the hole, first from one side then the other.

Within minutes, this rather sobering news had reached the pit-head, by dint of the temporary telephone connection from the Fresh Air Base. The gaffers quickly realised what was happening. The air pressure on the Castle and Bank sides had balanced out, and the airflow had run its course. However, they were also acutely aware that equalisation of pressure did not mean that the air would remain completely still, since umpteen other factors would now come into play and cause it to move around continuously. Those included, for example, pockets of air being released from the sludge on The Castle side, stoppings and brattices getting shoved around, and even human movement itself.

Soon afterwards and exactly as had been feared, the rescue brigades down in Bank Six began to detect a sort of 'in-out, in-out' flow of air through the hole in the coal barrier. Back and forth it moved, and very slowly, not unlike a gentle summer's breeze. However, there was one huge problem. Every time the air current decided to drift back in the direction of Knockshinnoch, it would carry its constituent proportion of the deadly firedamp with it.

The atmosphere for the trapped men on the Castle side had been warm and humid, indeed becoming increasingly stifling the longer the 116 souls had been cooped up together at the West Mine telephone station. However, for some reason that none of the men could really understand, the air supply itself had been plentiful, as Jock McMurdo noticed with some confusion:

'It was remarkable how much fresh air was available. Nobody knew where it was coming from, but at one point during our wait we felt a rush of air, probably a pocket that was trapped in the liquid peat and released by some movement.'

The moment the men had holed through the barrier, the pressurised air had 'wooshed' through towards Bank, similar to the cap being released from a bottle of the locally-produced Curries lemonade. Not only did this action allow some of Knockshinnoch's precious air supply to escape through the hole, but it also significantly reduced the air pressure on the Castle side. And, of course, everyone knew what happens on 'low-pressure days' down a colliery. Naturally-occurring methane gas is released from the coal seams, that's what.

In other words, and inevitably, The Castle would now start producing its own firedamp, in addition to the stuff that was already seeping through from Bank.

1.35 a.m.

The Coal Board's top brass were acutely aware of the dangers involved in sending the Whitehill Brigade through the hole in the barrier. And not just to the rescue men themselves.

They knew that the moment the brigade men pulled back the screen-cloth that covered the hole, some of the firedamp on the Bank side would inevitably start wafting through towards Knockshinnoch. However, having weighed up the pros and cons of the situation, the decision to press ahead had been taken on the basis that the appearance of the rescue services would be very uplifting for the trapped miners' morale.

Unlike their next decision, that was. The bosses knew full well that the men in the West Mine really needed food and water, and very soon. However, first and foremost, McCardel and his senior officials simply had to piece together a much more accurate picture of the current status underground. Therefore, the job of the first brigade would be to 'reconnoitre and report back'. Nothing more, and nothing less.

Assuming all went well, only then could consideration be given to sending the next brigade through with some sandwiches and tea. For the trapped miners, the arrival of the Whitehill Brigade would be a sight for sore eyes. At least, until they realised that the men in *Proto* were coming in empty-handed.

Andy Houston mumbled something about going back down to check the conditions at the barrier, and set off again into the darkness. The men just looked at each other quizzically, but thought little of it.

Perhaps he just needed a bit of time on his own. Time away from that telephone, with its demoralising 'nothing to report' bulletins, all of which were becoming despairingly weaker by the minute. And of course, time away from all the men themselves, with their incessantly tiresome questions and pathetic pleas for reassurance, hardly any of which he was in any position to answer or provide.

Houston himself, though, had other thoughts entirely, as he marched purposefully back through the Mech in the direction of Waterhead Dook. They were of his own men, those poor souls, some as young as eighteen and others nearly four times that. Oh yes, and of sandwiches. Glorious mouth-watering sandwiches, lovingly hand-cut and meticulously prepared by Mary and the other wives fretting up above.

As always, Houston kept his highly disciplined mind in check, only this time allowing his senses to drift, particularly those directing his gastronomic juices. Oblivious to the 'reconnoitre and report back' decision that had been taken on the pit-head, he began wondering what kind of 'pieces' the women had made up. Jam probably, to boost the men's energy levels. Or maybe even cheese. Please God, let them be cold meat, hand-sliced from the big ham machine in Scoular's grocery shop. And tea, Lipton's tea. He could almost taste the moist sandwiches slipping over his throat, washed down by a big gulp of glorious sweet tea. The Oversman's stomach rumbled in approval, as he turned sharp right to begin his steep descent down the slope road towards the coal barrier.

The brief given to Jimmy McCreadie and his Whitehill Brigade neebors that early morning was as business-like as it was unequivocal:

'Reconnoitre and report back. That was it, no more and no less. Our job was to get through to the men in Knockshinnoch, assess the situation in as much detail as possible, then report back to the surface. And that was Willie Jolly's job. The Brigade Captain was in charge. He was the only man we could take our instructions from, and he was the only one who could report back. Willie was 'the man', simple as that.'

The Whitehill Brigade's mission would be an absolutely critical one. The 'reconnoitre and report back' brief would provide the gaffers with vital information to assist them in planning the rescue operation, particularly with regard to the condition of the designated escape route and the trapped men's physical and psychological well-being.

McCreadie's account of the Whitehill Brigade's journey through the hole in the coal barrier made it all sound like a Sunday School picnic. However, in reality, the very thought of crawling through such a dark, sinister claustrophobic tunnel would undoubtedly have reduced lesser mortals to gibbering wrecks:

'It was nae bother, nae bother at all. We just pulled back the screen-cloth, and climbed into the hole, one at a time. Then it was just a matter of crawling on our hands and knees until we got through to the other side. The hole itself was about four feet wide by four and a half high, so there was plenty of room. We just had to be a wee bit careful with our *Proto* gear on. We were all through in no time. Nae bother, nae bother at all.'

No bother? Five unbelievably courageous men, crawling on all fours through 24 feet of eerie blackness with 56 pounds of breathing gear strapped to their backs. Dust-filled nasal passages blocked with nose-clips, parched lips biting on rubber mouthpieces, respiration and mortality resting entirely in the hands of a lump of machinery. No bother, Jimmy?

'I can't remember all that much about the road up from the coal barrier, but as soon as we saw the rail tracks and the engines in the Mechanised Section, we knew we were in the right place. We just left chalk marks every now and again, so that we could find our way back out and the other Brigades could find their way in. It was nae bother. We could see the miners all sitting there, away in the distance. Some of them had their cap-lamps switched on, but they were gey dim, turned down to the lowest setting, like. So we just walked up to them, and the Oversman came over and spoke to us. Houston, I think his name was.'

It was a burly coalminer who asked the first question, one which had nothing to do with food or drink, or even the rescue operation itself.

'Have you any chowin' tobacco?'

1.55 a.m.

The Whitehill Brigade didn't hang around in Knockshinnoch's West Mine. Their brief had been crystal clear and non-negotiable. In Willie Jolly's own inimitable words, 'we go straight in, assess the situation as quickly as possible, then get ourselves out of there and report back to the pit-heid'.

Unfortunately, there are conflicting accounts of the detail of the liaison between the brigade men and the trapped miners, if indeed there was any verbal communication at all. Jimmy McCreadie's recollection was that some discussion certainly did take place between both parties, as evidenced by his 'chowin' tobacco' reference:

'We had to keep our breathing apparatus on until we reached the top of the dook that led to the Mechanised Section, then when the Glennie indicated that the air was fine, we took it off. With our mouthpieces off, there would be no reason why we wouldn't have spoken to the men when we met them.'

There again, Jock McMurdo's take on the matter was rather different:

'The worst part was when the rescue team entered the escape hole for the first time. In they came, took a good look at us and left again. Never even took their breathing apparatus off. It was very unnerving. We were stuck, yet they could just walk out. This didn't help the morale amongst the men. At that point, I felt totally helpless.'

What is certain, though, is that both parties were operating under an almighty burden of duress that mere mortals could only ever imagine in their worst dreams. On the one hand, the miners had been buried alive for over 30 hours by that stage. They were parched, starving, overheating and dehydrated, some quite possibly even near-hallucinating as a consequence of their rapidly deteriorating physiological state. When the first rescue brigade men eventually arrived, they would have been greeted like saviours from the heavens above. The end of their nightmare, the answer to their prayers. Blessed shepherds sent to lead them from the bowels of hell to glorious reunification with their beloved families on the surface.

On the other, though, the brigade men had a job to do, and a brutally clinical brief instructing them how to do it. Reconnoitre and report back. Go in, assess, then get your backsides out of there. No room for interpretation or soft sentiment, only action for the greater good. There was only one thing that mattered to the Mines Rescue Service - getting those poor devils out of that pit alive. And if it meant that they might have to suffer a little longer in order to achieve that goal, then so be it.

Little did anyone realise that their suffering had only just begun.

3.05 a.m.

It was now a good hour since the Whitehill Brigade had left the West Mine, and the trapped men's morale had hit rock bottom.

Well gone were the sterling hymns, the riotous jokes and the ventriloquist-dummy performances. In their place was now silence, a deep and heavy silence, punctuated only occasionally by the odd mumble of dissatisfaction and moan of disapproval.

However, simply bursting to escape from assorted pairs of dust-filled lungs were the first helpless cries of embryonic despair. None had been heard, at least so far, but Oversman Andy Houston knew they weren't all that far away. He could see the developing panic in a few youthful eyes faintly illuminated by the dull rays of the cap-lamps, and corroborated by fingernails being bitten to the quick.

Down below, this wasn't a good situation, not a good situation at all. Up above, the latest official Coal Board bulletin was hardly any more encouraging:

'Just when the rescue squads begin to think that the air is clearing enough to attempt to bring the men up to the pit-head, the gas comes seeping back in again. At 2.00 a.m., the gas returned with a vengeance, and the rescue squads had to abandon the idea of bringing the 116 men up the pit.'

The West Mine telephone's latest ring sounded as if it was coming from the bottom of the engineers' water barrel. Houston answered the thing again, this time with a heavy heart rather than his customary nervous stomach. It was Willie Halliday on the other end, his voice scarcely audible.

'How are the men, Andy?' he asked apologetically.

'How do you think, Willie?' Houston snapped back, most uncharacteristically. 'They've just watched the brigade men march in, then march straight back out again complete with breathing apparatus, while we're all left down here in this hell hole. They're getting really anxious, Willie.'

'We're sending in some food and drink,' the Pit Manager announced a bit more cheerily. 'I wouldn't say anything to the men for the time being. Just make your way to the escape hole so that you can meet the next brigade. It'll be the Kames boys this time.'

Houston hung up the receiver and sat there for a few moments, not knowing whether to laugh or cry. He knew that the arrival of food and drink would be a massive boost for the men, but by this time the seriously disillusioned Oversman had become so used to things going arse-over-tit that he was sure something or other would conspire to intervene and stop the precious supplies reaching his men. As sure as hell, the latest in a long, long line of unbelievable setbacks was lurking menacingly somewhere around the corner. He stumbled wearily to his feet, and yawned. Andy Houston was tired, very tired indeed.

'Where are you aff tae, Andy?' Sam Capstick enquired, somewhat half-heartedly.

'I'm just going back down to the barrier to see what's happening,' the Oversman replied. 'You stay here with the men, and I'll be back within the hour.'

Capstick just nodded and leant back on his elbows on an old cloth sack, watching Houston as he made his way yet again towards Lanemark. The next thing the Fireman knew, a whole hour had elapsed. It was the increasingly agitated babble from amongst the body of men that had roused him from his restless, bad-dream-infested slumbers. Where the hell are you, Andy?

As discreetly as possible, Capstick then set off under cover of darkness in his Oversman's footsteps. Although Houston had now walked the route to the barrier several times, it was nevertheless a very tricky path to negotiate, one strewn with many a potential hazard, particularly for someone of his advancing years. The very thought of Houston having come a cropper filled Capstick's mind with dread. That's all we need now, for Christ's sake.

No sooner had he started down Waterhead Dook, than he saw a faint glow about 200 yards further down the slope. It was a miner's cap-lamp coming towards him. As he screwed up his eyes, another light came into view, then a few more.

'That you, Andy?' he shouted.

'Aye, Sam, it's me!' came the welcome reply, as many years of collegiate familiarity facilitated the process of voice recognition, with no need at all for visual confirmation. 'And I've got the Kames Brigade with me.'

'Jesus Christ, Andy!' Capstick exclaimed more angrily than he had intended. 'I thought somethin' had happened to you. You've been away for bloody ages!'

When Houston and the rescue men reached the top of the dook, Capstick could see that the Oversman was breathing very heavily and carrying a big cardboard box, which he immediately took from his grasp. In the collective glow of the lamps, he could just make out that three of the others were similarly burdened, two carrying big glass bottles and the other hauling what looked like a large urn. If McKnight had initially felt the need for explanation of the men's strange cargo, then his curiosity was fully satisfied the moment the glorious smell of fresh sandwiches hit his nostrils.

The purvey had arrived at last.

3.10 a.m.

It was Alex Stewart who eventually decided to voice what everyone else on the Bank side of the barrier had been thinking anyway.

'We're fighting a losing battle here,' were the Sub-Area Production Manager's sobering words, as the rising yellow flame snaked its way up inside the Glennie lamp to corroborate his worst fears.

Stewart had never been a man to lose heart easily, but the brutal reality was now staring him in the face. The firedamp was returning yet again, only this time with absolutely lethal intent.

A quick confab on the telephone between Stewart and his boss Alex McDonald, who by that stage had returned to the Knockshinnoch pit-head, prompted the latter to dump the gloomy news on McCardel and his assorted minions gathered in the temporary HQ. McDonald didn't pull his punches.

The battle against the gas in Number Six was being fought, and fought hard. Tragically, it was being fought and lost. Time was now running out fast. One final option remained. Immediate consideration should now be given to devising a plan to bring the trapped men out through the gas-contaminated area wearing breathing apparatus.

The initial reaction of the Coal Board's senior officials was one of bemused outrage. Bring the men out in breathing apparatus? You must be joking? Bring them out wearing *Proto*? Are you out of your mind, Alex? Only fully-fledged rescue brigade personnel have been properly trained in the use of *Proto*! And it's an eight-week training programme, for God's sake! Out of the question, absolutely out of the question.

McDonald eventually got a word in.

'I'm not talking about *Proto*, gentlemen. I'm talking about *Salvus*.'

Blank stares, weary heads spinning on strained necks. *Salvus*? What the hell is *Salvus*? McDonald now had their undivided attention.

He waded straight in, giving them a brief overview of the apparatus itself. Essentially, the 'Salvus Self-Contained Compressed Oxygen Breathing Apparatus' was a 'light oxygen rebreather' for industrial use, which was mainly deployed in firefighting situations, and in underwater scenarios such as submarine rescue. *Salvus* had been used extensively during the Second World War, its compact size being ideally suited to allowing divers to enter the cockpits of ditched aircraft, for example. Its downside was a relatively limited 'breathing time' of around 30 minutes on a full oxygen cylinder, stretching to 40 minutes at best, dependent on each individual's metabolism. The *Salvus* apparatus was always worn on the front of the body, its total weight when fully loaded with pressurised oxygen being 18 pounds, all supported from a collar harness and neck strap. It had a pair of eye goggles, a nose-clip and a mouthpiece, each contained under a protective 'gas mask'. Its respiratory mechanism involved a pressurised oxygen cylinder, breathing bag, cooling canister and carbon dioxide absorbent, all regulated by two main valves.

Basically, the rationale for any decision to deploy *Salvus* in the Knockshinnoch scenario would all boil down to assessing the balance between its one big advantage and one huge disadvantage. On the upside, it was very compact in size and much simpler to use than the more cumbersome and technically complex *Proto*, which could only be used by fully-trained rescue brigade men. However, on the downside, its breathing capacity was less than 25-percent of that of *Proto*.

However, to compound matters, a couple of additional factors had to be taken into account as well. Firstly, *Salvus* had never been deployed in mines rescue before. Indeed, no provision in British law existed to permit its use, and so any such decision would require a 'Special Exemption' by His Majesty's Inspectors of Mines. Secondly, not a single one of the 116 trapped miners had ever clapped eyes on a *Salvus* before, far less received any training on its use.

Therefore, any decision to attempt to bring the trapped men out wearing *Salvus* could not be taken lightly, although the increasing likelihood that the brigade men were never, ever going to get rid of the gas in time to save their lives was also a rather poignant consideration.

Once more, it was Hobson's choice for the big chiefs. Miners' lives are going to be lost if we do nothing, and miners' lives might still be lost if we use *Salvus* as a last resort.

In the event, McDonald got his way. After much discussion, it was agreed - 'in principle only' – that consideration might have to be given to bringing the trapped men out wearing *Salvus*, and that a draft operational plan for their evacuation should be developed accordingly. However, under no circumstances was any such plan to be set in motion until the General Manager himself had given his personal approval. In the meantime, every effort would continue to be made to clear the gas from the escape route.

From the entombed miners below, right up to the top brass of the mighty National Coal Board, every single person involved was now entering completely uncharted territory.

3.15 a.m.

It was quarter past three in the morning, and David Walker Park paced the floor of the makeshift Headquarters at Knockshinnoch Castle Colliery like a caged lion in a city centre zoo. He had been in that same room for five hours now, and his frustration at the lack of progress was as obvious as a suppurating boil on the nose.

Nowadays rubbing shoulders with the great and the good of the coalmining industry, Park's surge to prominence within the National Coal Board had been simply astronomical. However, no matter where that illustrious career might ultimately take him, he would always be a New Cumnock man through-and-through.

From humble beginnings as a bright schoolboy raised in the village's miners' rows, he had followed the well-worn path of his peers and found himself down the pit, aged only fourteen. David Park had never once objected to the cards he had been dealt, because they had come from the very same pack that had been dealt to every other male school-leaver in the village. However, what had distinguished Park from most of his contemporaries was his burning ambition to progress to the very top. One day soon I'll be a Fireman, he had promised himself. Then an Oversman, then a Pit Manager, then an Agent, and then … who knows?

The mighty National Coal Board was the biggest employer in the world, and now that world was Park's oyster. Not only had he achieved his first two career goals before even reaching his thirtieth birthday, but he had then shot up the greasy pole of corporate management with consummate ease and blistering speed. Today, Park was a veritable bigwig, a 'high-heid-yin' as the miners would say. Depute Labour Director of the Coal Board's Scottish Division, no less, and his hometown was very proud of him.

Never once, though, did Park forget his roots, nor indeed his former coalmining mates with whom he would always share a few pints of beer and tales of derring-do every time he returned to New Cumnock to visit his family. Yes, Park was now one of the Coal Board's big cheeses, but to his neebors grafting away at the coalface he was still 'Davie', and always would be.

Park was a man of strict discipline and impeccable routine. The previous morning - Friday 8 September to be precise - his steam train had pulled into Edinburgh's Haymarket Station as usual. There at the newspaper kiosk, he had purchased his customary copy of the *Scottish Daily Express*, and stuck it under his oxter while he strode purposefully towards the Coal Board's Scottish Division Headquarters' buildings at 14-16 Grosvenor Street. It was a thoroughly well-rehearsed routine.

'Would you like a cup of tea, Mister Park?' enquired a grey-haired lady peering at him through a pair of horn-rimmed glasses perched on a little upturned nose. 'The men from the planning department haven't arrived yet.'

'That would be lovely, Janet. And one of your wee shortbread biscuits too, if you've got any left. You bake the best shortbread in Edinburgh!'

Janet skipped away as if she had just been awarded a 50% pay rise, returning a few moments later with a white china teapot and a matching cup and saucer. The former pit-boy from New Cumnock had all but perfected his considerable social skills, aided and abetted by a smile warm enough to charm the birds down from the trees.

As soon as the quaint little secretary had closed the door behind her, Park immediately let down his guard and sighed heavily. This was his life now, the one he had chosen. Another bloody meeting in another bloody drab city-centre office. Another ordinary day. He loved his job, really, but how he longed at times for some genuine banter with the 'real' mining folk, the great characters like Dave Jess at the coalface and Toe Melvin in the engineers' shop. Those were the days, he smiled to himself, they really were.

Taking the first sip from his teacup, Park lifted up his broadsheet newspaper and shook it open to look at the morning headlines. His eyeballs exploded from their sockets:

129 MINERS ENTOMBED IN PIT DISASTER!

Normally calm and studied to a fault, Park's gaze began shooting in a haphazard frenzy from paragraph to paragraph, like a bluebottle darting over a summer picnic.

One hundred and twenty nine men buried alive in a pit cave-in! Where for God's sake, where? Oh Jesus, it's ... it's New Cumnock! It says here that it's ... no it can't be ... it's Knockshinnoch! Please God, no! No, not The Castle! I've got family ... family and neebors in The Castle! Oh my God, it is ... it is The Castle!

The office door creaked open again.

'Here's your shortbread, Mister Park ...'

Janet's innate intuition and long experience had taught her when to speak and when to shut up. And if by any chance the raised hand in her direction hadn't been sufficient to counsel her to choose the latter option, then Park's ashen-faced expression would have done the trick all by itself. He looked as if he had seen a ghost.

Friday had turned out to be a day dominated by seemingly never-ending high-profile meetings, each and every one of which demanded Dave Park's undivided concentration. Noted for his unfailing professionalism and legendary attention to detail, his concentration that day would be anything but undivided, as vivid mental images of the horrors unfolding at Knockshinnoch flashed constantly through his mind.

Park's last meeting had finished at 5.45 p.m. precisely, and by 5.55 p.m. his feverish sprint had taken him back to Haymarket Station, where he purchased a ticket to Glasgow. From the city's St Enoch station, he would catch the 8.05 p.m. service that would whisk him to his native village of New Cumnock, but not before he had run every single possible disaster scenario through his mind at least twenty times over.

How the hell had this happened? This … accident, this … terrible disaster? A cave-in, a bloody cave-in? This is 1950, and things like that just don't happen these days. And certainly not in Knockshinnoch of all places. Good God, The Castle is one of the most modern pits in the British Isles, with a productivity and safety record second to none. We even hold it up as a beacon of excellence for all-comers to see for themselves, for God's sake! And now what? Over one hundred men trapped, and thirteen of them reported 'missing' … and we all know what that means! Oh my God Almighty! This is no pit accident, Dave. This is … this is… a catastrophe!

It had been many years since Park had last worked in the New Cumnock Coalfield, but as former pit-boy who had made his way quickly through the ranks to join and ultimately captain the rescue brigade 'elite', he still remembered the general layout fairly well. He was particularly familiar with the Bank Auld Pit complex, and also with its much more modern and illustrious neighbour, Knockshinnoch. He felt sure that the majority of the men on the ill-fated backshift would have been working in the West Mine area of Knockshinnoch, more or less adjacent to the old derelict Bank Six Mine. But the thirteen missing men? They must have been working in a different section altogether, and got cut off by the inrush, poor bastards.

Suddenly, the penny dropped. The new heading that they had been driving to the south-east of the shaft to chase the main coal seam, that was it! What was it called again? Number Five Heading, that's what they called it! That was the one the boys were complaining about in Bridgend Bar, the last time I was back home. Number Five! Number Bloody Five!

Shuffling around uncomfortably in his British Railways steam train carriage, Park had then attempted to piece together a mental reconstruction of the underground layout of The Castle. The main shaft lay about a couple of hundred yards to the east of Knockshinnoch farm. From the bottom of the shaft and in the opposite direction ran the West Mine Turn, where the great majority of the men would have been working at the coal seams, so that was probably where they would now be lying trapped. That was nearly a mile from the main shaft, a whole bloody mile! And now they were obviously cut off from the shaft itself. Good God Almighty!

The train began to slow down as it puff-puffed its way into Kilmarnock station, finally stopping with a judder. It wasn't the shrill blast of the steam whistle that made him jump. It was the Station Guard opening the carriage door.

'Make yourself comfortable, madam,' the blue-uniformed little guard had said to the elderly lady as he helped her into the carriage and lifted a light-brown case onto the luggage rack above, before turning to Park himself. 'Good evening, sir.'

Exchanging pleasantries with total strangers normally came very easily to David Park. After all, the art of being polite and respectful was the product of a good coalminers' upbringing. On that particular Friday afternoon, though, Park could have seen the dainty little station guard far enough, and the dear old lady too. The remainder of the journey to New Cumnock was the longest of his life.

A black Austin A40 Devon van was waiting for Park when the big steam train 'toot-tooted' its way into New Cumnock railway station, bang on time at 9.56 p.m. precisely. A few minutes later, the Depute Labour Director was being escorted through a police security cordon and ushered into the temporary Headquarters on the pit-head at Knockshinnoch Castle Colliery.

Dave Park was now back home and there was a job to be done, the most important job of his life. Still he paced the wooden floor, his mesmerised brain registering and despairing at every single precious minute that ticked by. It's now or never, he told himself. He walked over to the conference table and sat down on a wooden seat, staring directly at David McCardel.

'Something on your mind, Mister Park?' the General Manager enquired, a tad impatiently.

Park cleared his throat. He knew that what he was about to say wouldn't go down well, but he was damned sure he was going to say it anyway.

'I want to go down there. I want to speak to the trapped men.'

3.25 a.m.

When Oversman Andy Houston escorted the Kames Rescue Brigade men into the West Mine telephone station, there was the briefest moment of intrigued silence.

'Something to eat and drink boys!' Houston announced, and the cheering began.

Matt Sanderson observed the dynamics with interest, a moment of great excitement, but tinged with just a tad of suspicion:

> 'We saw the lights coming back towards us. A brigade man was carrying a large cardboard box under his arm. There were no tyings around the box, and the flaps were loose. The brigade man could not have carried it up through without a carry handle. It must have been opened at Waterhead Dook for some reason.'

Matt also watched the initial flurry of desperate fervour amongst a group of men whose only sustenance in the past 32 hours had been a handful of blue-moulded crusts off the pit floor, and a couple of licks of oil-infested stagnant water from the engineers' barrel:

> 'The box was full of sandwiches. As the brigade man lowered it to the pavement, four or five men stepped smartly forward wanting to get there first. The brigade man just as smartly lifted the box back up, turning his back to those men. Andy Houston instructed them to sit back down, and told them that the Deputies would collect a sandwich for each man in his District. This prevented any lapse of integrity, and the hand-out went smoothly.'

Willie Lopez summed up the excitement of the moment when the food arrived, and its effect on the mood of the men:

> 'The sandwiches were great! Beef pieces, and "weel-made-up" tae! It gave us all a great lift, it really did.'

No doubt about it, the arrival of the 'purvey' was a tremendous morale-booster for the trapped miners, and the atmosphere changed in an instant. As they tucked into their 'beef pieces' and drank their tea with predictably voracious appetites, the chat soon began to flow again.

'These must be oor Agnes's pieces', Pud Walker piped up. 'Too much butter oan them as usual!'

'Glendinning's breid, an' Scoular's beef!' opined Doch McKnight, whose wife Margaret worked in the grocery store of the latter's name.

'Nope,' argued Dave Jess, 'the Co-op's breid, an' Hunter's beef. An' I should ken, because oor Mattie shops there every Setterday.'

'Och, away you go Dave!' a chirpy voice spluttered through a mouthful of grub. 'How the hell would you ken? You'd eat onythin' that wisnae still leevin'!'

'Aye,' retorted the big man. 'An' you'd drink onythin' that wisnae watter! An' through a shitey cloot, at that!'

The whole ensemble erupted in laughter. Suddenly, the West Mine had become a completely different place. Suddenly, something positive had happened. Clearly, the most important factor was the provision of life-sustaining food and hydration to a group of men who had been deprived of both for such an inordinately long time. However, the calm and controlled handing-over of essential supplies had also provided the men with something else, something equally vital.

The clearest message yet that their families, friends and neebors up on the surface were all working their fingers to the bone to get them out of their subterranean tomb.

It was probably the excitement and relief of the moment that contrived to conceal three rather more sombre faces from the trapped miners' view. Those belonged to Andy Houston and the two Firemen whom he had met about half-way up Waterhead Dook, as he was leading the brigade men towards the West Mine.

They had just witnessed their own 'ghost', but agreed to keep the sighting to themselves to maintain the trapped men's morale, an act of considerable selflessness and great courage. In that moment, the words of one Harold Wilson, an aspiring Labour Member of Parliament who would go on in a few years' time to become British Prime Minister, would have done them proud.

'Courage is the art of being the only one who knows you're scared to death'.

Only a few minutes back, and as Houston and the Brigade men had been carrying the food up Waterhead Dook, they had stumbled upon Firemen Rab Anderson and Ian Stewart, who were in the process of erecting a tar-coated brattice towards the top of the dook. When Houston had asked them what in the hell they were doing, Anderson showed him his Glennie lamp, and the snaking yellow flame had done the rest.

When the hole was driven through the coal barrier, the pressure in Knockshinnoch had suddenly been released, and the vast pit was now producing its own gas.

The killer that was firedamp.

4.05 a.m.

'You've got to be kidding, Dave!'

If Alex McDonald's voice smacked of scorn, then his facial expression was one of incredulity.

'I've never been more serious in my life, Alex,' the Depute Labour Director retorted sharply to the Area Production Manager.

General Manager David McCardel ran his fingers through his wavy grey hair, and blew a huge sigh. The top page of his notepad rippled from his breath.

'Okay chaps, there is no such thing as a daft idea at this stage. We're really up against it, and we must consider all options. Let's hear it, Mister Park.'

David Park leaned forward in his chair, put both elbows on the table and clasped his hands beneath his chin.

'Okay, this is the way I see it, gentlemen. Those men have been down in the West Mine for almost a day-and-a-half now, and their nerves will have been tested to the very limit. Sure, the sandwiches and tea have probably helped a great deal, but Houston's last phone call indicated that their spirits are now flagging badly, mainly because of the continued delays. We know that these delays are unavoidable because of the problems we're having with the gas in Bank Six. And we also know the huge efforts being made by the brigades. However, the men don't.'

Park paused momentarily, before continuing.

'Put yourselves in their position, gentlemen. Stuck down there like kittens in a sack. Nobody really telling them anything, apart from the odd phone call down a crackly line. And one bloody cheese sandwich apiece after all that time. There are boys down there as young as eighteen and older men well into their sixties, almost every single one of them thinking about his wife and children on the surface. Somebody needs to get in there and explain the situation to them, eyeball-to-eyeball, and reassure them that everything that can possibly be done is actually being done.'

The comments and questions came fast and furious.

'But Dave, we've been phoning Houston every fifteen minutes to keep him informed, so that he can update his men.'

'And the brigade men have been talking to them too, Dave.'

'What difference would it really make if you went in, Dave? What could you tell them that we've not told them already?'

'And why you, Dave? I know you've had a lot of experience down the pit, but I'm sorry, that was in your younger days when you were much fitter. You've spent the last few years sitting in an office, pushing a pen. If we let you go in now, you could end up being a liability to us. Just think about it, Dave.'

For two peas, Park could have lost the rag right there and then. He looked around the table at all the suits sitting knowingly in their wisdom. What the hell did they know about Knockshinnoch? Or even about the nuts and bolts of coalmining for that matter? At least I've been there and done it, a lot more than can be said for these pen-pushing bureaucrats.

Deploying the mellow diplomacy that he had nurtured from hard-won experience, Park took a deep breath and decided that discretion was the better part of valour. His deep-rooted New Cumnockian street-fighting tendencies would wait for another day.

He smiled politely.

'I can well understand your reservations, gentlemen, believe me I can. Every single one of you in this room just wants the same as I do, which is to get these men out of that pit and back to their families as soon as possible.'

The heads all began nodding. Park sensed the moment was now right, and waded straight in.

'What I'm asking you, gentlemen, is to put yourselves in the men's shoes. They've been down there for a very long time now, and no matter how this whole thing might pan out, they'll still be down there for a hell of a lot longer. Sure, they've had bulletins over the phone and some of the brigade men have spoken to them. And, yes, they've even had a sandwich now, a whole bloody sandwich. But ask yourselves this. What is actually going through their minds at the moment? What are they thinking? Do they really trust us to get them out of there? What horrors are being brewed up in their imaginations?'

Park paused again, and observed the dynamics for a couple of seconds. To a man, his colleagues were shuffling restlessly in their seats as they reluctantly began to put themselves in the trapped men's shoes.

'I think you all know, don't you? They'll be tired, exhausted in fact, still very hungry and very thirsty. And worried, very worried indeed. Worried about their wives and kids, worried about whether they're ever going to get out of that place alive, and worried about who's going to put bread on the table if they don't. And frustrated – no, absolutely bloody exasperated – about how long this whole damned rescue mission is going to take ... or whether it will ever happen at all. Perhaps some of them are even beginning to panic, especially the younger lads. And all of them furious at the thought of us sitting up here in our offices, dipping our biscuits into our teacups, and dithering while they suffer. Somebody needs to go in and speak to them ... and right now! Not another brigade man ... a manager, one of the senior officials, one of the men actually making the decisions. Somebody needs to get in there and talk to the men face-to-face, to explain what we're doing to get them out. Somebody who is prepared to stay with them, reassure them, keep them calm.'

'Okay Dave,' came the expected interruption, 'a fair point ... but why you? For example, when was the last time you were down a pit? What qualifies you to go in?'

Park was ready for that one.

'Well, gentlemen, several reasons. First of all, I've worked in both Bank and Knockshinnoch, admittedly a long time ago, but I know the layout very well. I was also Brigade Captain here for a few years, so I understand the territory ... and the mechanics of the job that needs to be done. I'm also very familiar with the *Proto* breathing gear, and I've probably had more experience of using it than anyone else down there. But there's another reason too. Andy Houston and I go back a long way, and I think he'd appreciate a bit of company. I also know a lot of the other boys down there too, so that gives me a head start.'

Much scratching of heads and shuffling of feet. Suddenly, the telephone rang, and Johnny Bone answered the damned thing. It was Houston.

Silence reigned in the emergency room, as Bone absorbed the Oversman's latest bulletin from the depths of the pit. His facial expression alone was enough to tell the officials that they weren't about to become the recipients of good news.

Bone put down the receiver, and turned to face his captive audience.

'We've now got gas in Waterhead Dook. Two and a half percent - and rising.'

The shoulders slumped in admirable synchronicity. McCardel just stared straight across the table at Park.

'Right Mister Park, come with me. We're going to speak to the Chairman.'

4.20 a.m.

As the rumour factory moved into top gear, the mood on the pit-head began deepening even further. The rumours themselves came thick and fast, and whooshed through the waiting crowds like an electric firestorm, each one belting terrified relatives with yet another hefty thump in the guts.

Rumour Number One. The firedamp was proving impossible to control. Not only had Alex Stewart and his men been unable to get the lethal gas out of Bank Six using suction pumps, but now their efforts to blast it out with compressed air had also proved equally futile. When the Kirkconnel Rescue Brigade then emerged from the Bank dook sporting glum and exhausted faces, that was all the confirmation required by the doom-and-gloom merchants, especially when brigade man Simon Grant was carried out on a stretcher, having been overcome by the gas itself. If experienced rescue workers equipped with *Proto* breathing gear were now dropping like flies, what chance would over one hundred unprotected trapped miners have?

Rumour Number Two. There had been a disastrous fall in the depths of Bank Six, where one of the old derelict roofs had just given way. Nobody really knew how bad it was, or whether any of the rescue men had been injured in the fall, but what was absolutely certain was that the underground road from Bank to Knockshinnoch was now completely cut off.

Rumour Number Three. Another huge section of Wilson's field had now given way, no doubt assisted by this latest downpour of freezing-cold autumnal rain, and the sludge was again rushing along the West Mine Turn towards the trapped men. Surely it would only be a matter of time now before they would be drowned where they sat?

Acutely aware of the pernicious rumours flying around, it fell once more to the hard-pressed General Manager, David McCardle, to attempt to disabuse despairing relatives and eager journalists alike of the pure nonsense that was circulating. Yes, the rescue brigades were having one hell of a job trying to get rid of the gas in the old mine, but in no way had they given up the ghost. And yes, there had been a roof fall in one of the old Bank Six roadways, but no one had been injured, and they were now using an alternative roadway as a diversion. This would make the trapped men's escape route a wee bit longer, but not unduly so. And yes again, Wilson's field was still moving, but Wimpey's men were now securing the sides of the crater to prevent any further inrush of sludge into The Castle's workings.

So why have all the ambulances and other emergency vehicles been stood down then, enquired one perplexed onlooker? They haven't been stood down at all, came the answer, all they've done is turn their engines off. What would be the point of having them all sitting there with their engines running and blue lights flashing when we're nowhere near ready to bring the men out to safety? And just take a look at all the activity still taking place here on the pit-head, with successive rescue brigades going down to the coal barrier, dozens of volunteers carrying wooden props, fans, gate-end-boxes, breathing apparatus and God-knows-what-else up and down the dook, and every kind of emergency vehicle you can think of scurrying around Wilson's field over yonder.

McCardel's attempts to convince the anxious onlookers might have been delivered with heart-felt commitment, but his influence on the collective mood was only peripheral at best. These were despairing times, and no words, however honest and well-meaning, could ever have provided the reassurance that the distraught relatives so desperately craved. Only the glorious sight of their own menfolk emerging from the mine could ever achieve that.

And right now, standing shivering on the rain-swept hillside in the dead of the darkest night in living memory, very few really believed it was a sight they would ever witness again.

4.40 a.m.

'Sit doon, son, an' gie yer face a rest! You're talkin' a load o' shite!'

It was the booming voice of Wull Gray. For some time now, the tension in the West Mine had been escalating, and some of the younger lads were now huddled in a corner of the roadway, mumbling and muttering away to each other. Oversman Andy Houston decided to keep his counsel for the time being, reckoning that his direct intervention would have greatest effect when it was most needed. In the meantime he would let the battle-hardened miners like Gray handle the more reactionary rookies.

Houston wouldn't have long to wait. It was his trusty lieutenant, Sam Capstick, who first clocked what appeared to be a worrying new development. Apparently, some of the younger lads were now losing patience, and talking about 'making a run for it', as Jock McMurdo recalled:

'Everybody became more tense and nervous the longer we were stuck down there. The majority of the men stayed calm, but of course some did panic. Some stayed silent and some complained, while others just clowned around, but that didn't last long.'

The Oversman eventually hauled his skinny big frame onto its weary pins and wandered over towards the group in question.

'What's up, boys?' he enquired, knowingly.

Silence, not a squeak, only a semi-circle of furtive glances in the diffuse light of the pit bottom. Houston had another go at flushing out the embryonic mutiny.

'Just try to be patient, boys, the brigades on the other side ...'

'Whit aboot the brigades on the other side?' one of them suddenly snapped. 'Whit are they gonnae dae? F - - - all, that's whit!'

'Aye, that's right enough, Mister Houston,' opined another. 'I mean, whit have they done for us sae far? Waltzed in wi' a' their breathin' apparatus on, had a guid look at us withoot even openin' their mooths, then waltzed straight back oot again.'

Another concordant, dissenting voice.

'An' they'll a' be up there noo, wolfin' intae Jenny Walker's soup, an' no' givin' a damn aboot us bein' stuck doon here.'

'Shut your faces!' came an exasperated shout from the main body of men, as the youths' shaking voices grew louder and louder. 'You don't ken whit you're talkin' aboot. These brigade men will be breakin' their backs tryin' tae get us oot o' here. So shut your faces, or I'll come ower there an' shut them for you!'

'Right lads!' Houston interjected. 'Stop it now, and listen to me! We have to be patient! We have to wait until we get the signal that it's safe to travel. If you lose your heads now ...'

'If we don't get oot o' here noo, we're a' gonnae die!' screamed one of the youngsters. 'We're a' gonnae sterve, or die o' thirst, or the gas is goin' tae get us, an' suffocate us! We've got tae get oot o' this place noo, Mister Houston!'

'Aye, Mister Houston!' bawled another, thrusting his finger in the direction of the miners lying on the pit floor. 'And if you lot want tae stay here, that's fine, but we've decided tae make a run for it. If we soak some sackcloth in the barrel watter an' cover oor faces, we can get through the hole an' up tae the surface. We're no' stayin' here only longer, no' anither minute!'

'You won't get far in all that gas, boys,' the Oversman replied calmly, as the group of intrigued onlookers grew in size and moved closer to observe the developing drama. The scene reminded Houston of a fight in the school playground. 'In fact, you won't get ten bloody yards! The gas on the other side is fifty percent! Fifty percent, boys! You'll be dead in minutes!'

At that, one of the young lads lost it.

'If we don't get oot o' here … I'm gonnae … I'm gonnae lose ma f - - - in' mind!'

Houston could clearly see that the poor boy was now hurtling headlong towards real panic, as he began grabbing at his own hair. There were tears in his reddening, staring eyes. This was not a good situation, indeed one which if the developing unrest were to spread, could very quickly escalate until it was out of control. After all, he had seen it several times before in the trenches. He didn't ever want to see it again.

'Come on, boys, we'll be oot o' here in nae time!'

It was the voice of the inimitable Jim 'Pud' Walker. 'We'll have tae be, because the St Leger starts at quarter past three, an' I've got five-boab on Asterios!'

As the engineer wrapped his big muscular arm around the lad's shoulder, he started sobbing. A few seconds later, Pud had him laughing bravely through the tears. Yes indeed, this was the early morning of Saturday 8 September, and the starter's flag for the St Leger – the final 'classic' of the 1950 flat horseracing season – was due to be raised that very afternoon. And come hell or high water, Pud Walker would find out at the earliest opportunity if his financial investment had come up trumps at the tasty odds of 12-1. Come on Asterios!

For a moment, Andy Houston thought that his enigmatic engineer's timely intervention had saved the day. Only for a moment, though. Suddenly, another one of the younger brigade sprang to his feet.

'F - - - this, you lot, I'm for oot o' this place right noo!' He began marching past the main body of men in the direction of Lanemark, arms pumping and eyes bulging, pit boots crunching along the pit floor.

'Try it son, an' I'll knock you oot!'

Silence descended in the West Mine, as the pit-boy stopped dead in his tracks. A burly figure stepped forward. It was Dave Jess, and nobody messed with Dave Jess. This time, he rephrased his statement to the youth, in order that there could be no room for misinterpretation.

'Try it, son, an' I'll drap you where you staun'!'

208

The lad took one look at Jess, decided much the better of it, and began trudging back in the direction from whence he had come. The tension in the place was by now electric, and defined by intense negative polarity. Houston prayed silently that the intervention of three of the pit's most endearing and respected characters – Gray, Walker and Jess - might have defused a potentially perilous situation.

Alas, it hadn't, as Matt Sanderson recalled.:

'I heard a man maintaining he could walk through to Bank Six with a wet scarf around his face. When he was told he was talking foolishly, he persisted in his view, but when he was then challenged to go alone and prove it, he stayed where he was. He was known as an erratic man who was easily roused, and when someone told him to sit down as he was causing extra "stoor", he took off his jacket and flapped it like a housewife shaking the fireside rug, and shouting, "I'll give you so-and-so stoor!" He then sat back down.'

Remarkably, that was the final act of would-be mutiny, the jacket-waver having been called a 'mad bastard' the moment his backside hit the wet pit pavement. The final act for now at least, as peace returned to the West Mine.

The question was, how long would it last?

4.55 a.m.

A blunt butter-knife could have cut the tension in the room. It was David McCardel who broke the uneasy silence.

'Mister Park has a suggestion, Your Lordship.'

Dave Park took a deep breath, and cleared his throat. On his climb up the slippery pole of senior management, he had stumbled across most of the Coal Board's high-and-mighty at one stage or another, but this was the very first time he had actually met Lord Balfour in person.

'Okay Mister Park, the floor is yours.'

Park inhaled again, to calm himself.

'Thank you, Mister Chairman,' he began. 'I believe … or should I say, we believe … that the time is now right for someone in authority to go down into the West Mine and explain the situation directly to the trapped men. Not over the telephone, and not relayed through the rescue brigades, but face-to-face.'

He paused momentarily to get a reaction from the chairman, but none was forthcoming, only an impatient hurry-up wave of the hand.

'I'm listening, Mister Park.'

'Well, Mister Chairman, we've all had an in-depth discussion about this, and my suggestion is that I should go in personally.'

Again Park paused, but wished he hadn't. Another brusque get-a-bloody-move-on wave of the same hand.

'I've worked in both Bank and Knockshinnoch, I've been Brigade Captain, I know the layout well, and I know a lot of the men, particularly Andrew Houston who could probably do with a bit of moral support. I'm also very familiar with the *Proto* breathing apparatus. I think I'm the man for the job.'

This time, he did get a reaction. Lord Balfour's eyes lit up.

'All well and good, Mister Park,' a dissenting voice interjected. It came from the pouted gob of a rather posh-looking chap clad in an expensive three-piece suit, who was sitting by the chairman's side, obviously one of his closest henchmen. 'So you claim you know everything about both collieries, and about *Proto*, is that right Mister Park?'

'Certainly not everything, Sir,' Park responded quietly but confidently, mustering every ounce of self-restraint to prevent himself telling this odious little shit where to stick the gold-plated fountain pen that he was waving around to all and sundry. 'Yes, I am very familiar with both collieries, and very experienced in the use of *Proto*. However, if you can find someone else who is better qualified to do the job … '

The chairman's eyes twinkled, and McCardel stifled a chuckle. Still the suit continued, as if unaware that he had just been put in his place by a relative minion.

'Okay Mister Park, pit layout fine, *Proto* fine. But now we're talking about using something else entirely, something other than *Proto*. What's it called again?'

'*Salvus*, Sir,' Park continued, ready to move in for the kill. 'It's called *Salvus*. Or more correctly, the *Siebe Gorman Salvus Self-Contained Breathing Apparatus*. It's a light oxygen re-breather, normally deployed by firefighters and in undersea operations. *Salvus* was used extensively during the war, mainly because it is compact in size and much easier to use than the *Proto*. But there again, Sir, I'm sure you're aware of that.'

That certainly shut up the suit. Clearly impressed by Park's knowledge and tenacity, the Chairman took over the reins once more.

'Mister Park,' he enquired, rubbing his chin. 'Have you any experience of using *Salvus* itself?'

'Yes indeed, Mister Chairman,' Park responded, seizing his big opportunity. 'When I worked for a time in the north-east of England we used it on a number of occasions, mainly when tackling fires. It is very light compared to the *Proto*, and much easier to use. It also requires less training than *Proto*, but we have to remember that these men have had absolutely no training in either apparatus. Furthermore, *Salvus* has never been used in mines rescue operations before. Most of the brigade men themselves will never even have been trained in its use. Therefore, if you do make the decision to use *Salvus*, it will be vitally important to have someone down there who actually knows how to use it. Someone checking each and every set of apparatus, someone showing the men how to put it on, someone telling them what to do and what not to do. Someone giving them confidence and keeping them calm.'

Game, set and match.

Lord Balfour's telephone rang for the umpteenth time. His personal secretary, who had been well warned not to disturb him unless it was materially relevant and critical to the unfolding events at Knockshinnoch, lifted the receiver. Standing with the phone in her hand, she waited until her boss returned her gaze.

'What is it, Audrey?'

'Your Lordship, Mister Halliday has just been informed by Mister Houston that some of the miners are becoming very restless.'

Lord Balfour looked over at David McCardel and nodded. McCardel nodded back, then turned to face Park himself.

'Okay Mister Park, we'll do it your way,' the General Manager decreed. 'Get yourself back over to the Bank Pit, and pass the doctor. If he says you're fit enough to do it, you can go in with the next brigade.'

Dave Park nodded back, smiled politely and took the biggest, deepest breath of his life.

What the hell had he just let himself in for?

5.05 a.m.

Within minutes, neighbouring Cumnock's Hearth Road telephone exchange had become a hive of frenetic activity, as the Coal Board's administrators set about contacting every fire station and naval base all the way from Yorkshire to the north of Scotland.

Their mission was to get hold of as many sets of *Salvus* breathing kits as humanly possible, and as quickly as humanly possible. The decision was described as a 'precautionary measure', but everyone knew it was now do or die for the trapped miners. Their last chance saloon.

Former mines rescue veteran Matt Burns recognised the 'impossible dilemma' that now faced his beleaguered brigade colleagues:

'We heard that there was a telephone discussion in the early hours of Saturday morning, from the Home Office in London to Superintendent Willie Dick. The civil servants were requesting an update for the British Government on the progress of the rescue mission. Willie informed them that all efforts to clear the gas from Bank Six had so far proved futile, and that the trapped miners' last hope of escape was for the brigades to attempt an evacuation by equipping them with self-contained breathing apparatus – *Salvus* - for which they had never been trained. He also reminded the Home Office that there was no current provision in law for the use of *Salvus* in such circumstances. Apparently, a senior Government official then asked Willie, "are you telling me that the only thing preventing you from getting these men out of there wearing gas masks is the rule book?" to which he replied that the brigades were clearly under an obligation to conform to the laws of the land. The story went that the guy then shouted at Willie down the phone, "well throw the bloody rule book away, and get these men out of there!"'

Matt clearly recognised the nature and intensity of the dilemma that now faced Dick and his men. Essentially, they were in the classical 'no-win situation', principally because of where the legal responsibility for deploying *Salvus* now lay. Sure, it was the Coal Board's high-ranking officials who had taken the 'in principle' decision, but it was the Mines Rescue Service that would ultimately be held legally accountable for its implementation.

And so the dilemma was this. The brigades were now facing two nightmare scenarios.

Scenario One. They refuse to break the law, and so deny the use of *Salvus* to the trapped miners. The men all perish. Headlines in the newspapers the following morning? 'Rescue brigades protect their own backs, and allow 116 miners to die!'

Scenario Two. The brigades decide to 'throw the rule book away', and attempt to bring the trapped men out wearing *Salvus*. Some or all of them don't make it. Next morning's headlines? 'Rescue brigades use illegal breathing apparatus, and 116 miners die!'

A dilemma indeed, and one which left a huge rhetorical question hanging in the air. While it was easy to see where the credit would have been heading if the rescue mission should end successfully, who would be left carrying the can if it went terribly wrong?

I think we all know the answer to that one.

7.35 a.m.

Daylight was breaking on the Bank pit-head, as the Depute Labour Director of the National Coal Board's Scottish Division manoeuvred his substantial middle-aged backside into the fourth bogie of the man-riding haulage.

Customarily welcomed by sycophantic greetings and sweaty handshakes alike wherever he set foot these days, David Park was as anonymous as any one of the two-hundred-plus bleary-eyed onlookers shivering beneath their flat-caps and headscarves amid the rain-soaked crowds on the hillside. Numbed by biting cold and bitter despondency, nobody could really have given a damn that Saturday morning about who, in the hutches, was who. All they really cared about was when they would see their loved ones again. Very few thought they ever would.

'Everybody in?' shouted the rake-runner, and off the man-riding haulage trundled down the dook of Bank Six, leaving greyish skies and despairing relatives behind. Dave Park wondered briefly if his own family and friends were about to join the ranks of the broken-hearted. Silently, he called himself a crazy old bastard, then gritted his teeth in anticipation of the job he knew he simply had to do. If it worked, it worked, and if it didn't, it didn't. However, he could never have forgiven himself for not trying.

As the rake rumbled further and further down the dook, he thought of the trapped men – some of them distant relatives and others close friends – sitting around on the wet pit floor of Knockshinnoch, craving food and water, gasping for fresh air and aching to see their beloved families again.

He also thought of the scene he had just witnessed at the giant crater that once was Bill Wilson's farm field. Public works contractors trying valiantly to shore up the crumbling sides of the enormous ravine, but clearly struggling to do so. An armada of fire engines pumping hundreds of thousands of gallons of flood water into the Afton Water, which was now bursting its banks onto the low-lying town centre of his much-loved hometown, New Cumnock. Dozens of utterly exhausted volunteers of all ages chucking everything under the sun down into the cavernous hole beneath their feet - wooden pallets, steel hutches, old fences, whole mature trees, and even one dismantled timber garage – only to see the bloody things twist and turn for a few seconds before plummeting hopelessly into the void, into the vaults of hell itself.

Yes Dave, he told himself, you've done well to climb up the slippery pole of success, but now your place is with your 'ain folks', not sitting in some posh city-centre office wallowing in tea and shortbread. He knew without a shadow of a doubt that this was something he must do, even if it meant he would perish trying. The alternative was doing nothing, sweet bugger-all, and living the rest of his life in shame wishing he had.

It wasn't the pitch-blackness of the mine that took Dave Park by surprise, nor was it the clank-clanking of the rake's metallic wheels as it bounced over the old rusty rail track. He had seen and heard it all many times before.

It was the awful stench. Twelve years it had been since Dave Park last descended Bank Six, and he clearly remembered the distinctive smell of coal dust sweeping over humid, damp pit pavements, a smell that only hardened coalminers would ever recognise. In fact, even on occasion when he was sitting in his plush office these days, chairing one of those interminable meetings, the smell of the pit bottom would somehow contrive to assault his nostrils from out of nowhere. It was a smell that rather oddly seemed to both reassure and energise him for the day ahead.

However, today was different. Today, the place reeked of something else entirely. Yes, the coal dust and the dampness were still very much in evidence, but so too was the awful stink of rotting timber. It was the stench of dereliction, the stench of things gone terribly wrong.

What had earlier been a place ringing with the glorious sounds of thumping picks and swishing shovels, and tough men singing crude songs and almost choking on their 'chowin' tobacco' at bawdy jokes, was now almost funereal in character, despite the army of rescue workers and willing conscripts shuffling around in all directions. Bank Six had once been a hive of harmonious hard labour. Now it was a silent, sombre mausoleum.

Dan Park – no relation to namesake, Dave – vividly remembers the adrenaline rush of the whole thing. An eighteen-year-old pit-head apprentice at the time, Dan readily accepted the brief that he and umpteen other young volunteers had been given that Saturday morning. It was to deliver *Salvus* breathing apparatus down to the Fresh Air Base, whenever the various sets became available from assorted fire stations around the land.

Carrying them two at a time, one under each oxter, Dan and his mates would make their way carefully down the Bank dook, hitching a lift in a bogie of the man-riding haulage whenever one happened to become available. From the foot of the dook, they would then scramble their way over the sodden, treacherous underfoot conditions for the remaining mile or so to the Fresh Air Base, before returning empty-handed to the pit-head and repeating the whole procedure all over again:

> 'Bank Six was a very serious place that morning, but to young boys like myself, the whole thing was actually quite exhilarating! "Mind your feet, boys, and watch out for old rail tracks and other obstacles!" That was what the brigade men told us. It was hard graft, but really exciting, because we felt we were doing something really important!'

They were indeed. The official decision to deploy *Salvus* may not yet have been formally approved, but the strange-looking contraptions would certainly be lying there in plentiful supply whenever the big call came.

By the time the Depute Labour Director had reached the Fresh Air Base, his oak-panelled office walls and the glorious aroma of freshly-percolated coffee had become a very distant memory. In their place now were dark, wet coal seams glistening in cap-lamp beams, and the stenches of rotting timber and choking coal dust competing feverishly for the upper hand.

This was certainly not the Bank Six that Dave Park remembered, the one that once reverberated with raucous camaraderie and jovial congeniality. This was a different Bank Six altogether, one still characterised by constant, frenetic activity, but now sadly defined by gloom and despair. The gas – that hellish firedamp – was now really beginning to get everyone down. Hour after hour everyone had worked their fingers to the bone trying to get rid of the bloody stuff, but still it ruled supreme in front of them, all the way from the Base to the barrier, grinning a huge, invisible grin of malevolent contempt.

Park had now arrived at the Fresh Air Base, the final outpost for all but the trained rescue brigade men. Ahead of him lay a quarter of a mile of gas-contaminated roadway. Next, a 24 foot long tunnel to haul his backside through, the one that had been widened considerably by sitting on office chairs instead of doing a proper job of work. Then after that, who knows?

A curly-haired lad walked forward carrying a *Proto* apparatus. The boy looked as if he should still be in school. Park took it from him with a 'thank you, son', and a warm smile which completely belied the dread building up in the pit of his stomach.

It was now or never.

8.15 a.m.

If David McCardel and his minions in the Knockshinnoch Castle HQ office had somehow contrived to avoid the backbreaking hardship and near-intolerable conditions presently being suffered by the rescue brigades and volunteers down below, then they had a completely different demon to contend with up above.

The waiting. The never-ending, gut-wrenching waiting.

And, of course, if the waiting was bad enough for the men in suits, then for those standing shivering on the muddy slopes of the Bank pit-head it was absolutely hellish.

By now, the activities of the rescue teams had become predictably repetitive, almost farcically so. Down they would go, half-a-dozen of them at a time in the man-riding haulage of the Bank dook, their serious faces invisible beneath pit helmets and cap-lamps, to the odd frantic yell of 'good luck, boys!' Then after yet another interminable wait, up would come another team, always looking exhausted and demoralised, some of them absolutely out on their feet and being oxtered up the slope to the pit baths, the occasional poor chap being carried on a stretcher.

For the brigades, it was a dreadful task that required superhuman effort and incredible courage. For the trapped miners' loved ones observing the dynamics, it was one continuous nightmare.

And so, when the Coal Board's Depute Labour Director had slipped down the dook under cover of semi-darkness and standard pit clobber, not a single soul on the hillside had the foggiest idea that New Cumnock's prodigal son was about to return to the fold. Now here he stood, almost one mile underground at the Fresh Air Base in Bank Six, being helped into the *Proto* gear that he had never even clapped eyes upon for the best part of a decade.

No sooner had Park congratulated himself on reaching the very limit of the fresh-air zone, than a vaguely familiar figure approached him. It was Eric Richford, HM District Inspector of Mines, and from what Park could make out, his facial expression was anything but welcoming. There then followed a rather protracted three-way spat between Richford, Park and the Brigade Captain, with the Mines Inspector protesting most vehemently about Park's very presence. Park himself then insisted that high-level clearance for his involvement had been given by none other than Lord Balfour and David McCardel themselves, only for the Brigade Captain to decree that it was he who was in charge of this particular foray into Knockshinnoch, and he alone who would decide who was going and who was staying. After several minutes of an increasingly acrimonious verbal tug-of-war, Richford eventually relented and agreed to Park's participation, but on one clear and incontrovertible condition.

He must come back out with the same brigade men on their return to the Fresh Air Base. Park nodded, but said nothing. Not a single word.

'Right, Mister Park,' snapped the Captain, clearly irritated by the time-wasting distraction. 'You remember the set-up, I hope? Breathin' bag an' *Protosorb* doon there, oxygen cylinder ower yer back. Helmet oan. Hooter at your side, just in case you get intae bother. Noo, put oan your moothpiece an' then your nose clip. All clear?'

Park nodded, and breathed in an almighty last gasp of fresh air. It smelled anything but fresh. He pushed his rubber mouthpiece into place and bit on it, then snapped the steel clips over his nostrils and inhaled. It had been a long time since he last breathed pure oxygen, but it tasted good. A lot better than the stench-laden atmosphere of Bank Six, that was for sure. Within a matter of seconds, the old familiar click-clicking of the *Proto* valves opening and shutting came back to him. Soon it seemed as if he had never been away from the subterranean travails that had made him the man he now was.

Today, though, there would be one big difference. Today, he would be tested like never before.

Park had been authorised to go in as the sixth and additional member of the hitherto five-man rescue brigade. The journey from the Fresh Air Base to the coal barrier was only 400 yards in distance, but it would take almost half an hour to negotiate and it was fraught with danger all along the way. The underfoot conditions were horrendous, the old mine's long-abandoned pavements having heaved in numerous locations over the years, leaving behind a perilous trail of piles of rubble and deep potholes full of water. Within a matter of minutes, Park's borrowed pit boots were absolutely saturated, but his feet, freezing cold at first, soon heated up as the temperature equalised. However, one daft stumble and he'd be flat on his face, his breathing bag no doubt bursting open as he bit the dust, a particularly ignominious way to go.

His next thought was hardly a particularly hopeful one either. Just how the hell are we going to lead 116 starving, parched and exhausted miners through this maze, wearing breathing apparatus that they've no idea how to use? They'll never make it, never in a month of Sundays.

As Park trudged along the old roadway, his heavy breathing reverberating in his own ears, he could scarcely believe just how badly the mine's old workings had deteriorated. In the faint glow of the team's assorted cap-lamps, all around him lay crumbling coal walls and bent, rotting wooden props that were attempting laughably to hold sagging pit ceilings in place. If even one of those pit props should collapse, he reflected in horror, they'll still be trying to dig our corpses out in ten years' time.

By the time the team reached the coal barrier, Dave Park's heartbeat was thumping in valiant competition with his respiratory rate, and neither of them was winning. Too much time sitting in too many offices, Dave, he scolded himself, and eating too many buttered scones into the bargain. I'm getting far too old for this.

Out of the blue, he thought of a very old friend whom he knew was among the men trapped on the other side of the barrier. He was one Juan Carracedo, a Spanish immigrant much better known to his neebors as 'Auld Whang', and at 68 years of age the oldest man on the ill-fated backshift. For the briefest moment, Park found himself wondering how the old boy would be coping with all of this. If Auld Whang can do it, I can bloody do it, he mouthed silently through gritted teeth.

At long last, the Brigade Captain gave two 'toots' on his hooter, signalling for his men to take a well-earned breather. The Vice Captain, bringing up the rear, reciprocated with two of his own to ensure that all six men understood the 'stop' command. Park rested his hands on his knees for a few moments, relishing the pause. He knew it would be brief, and it was.

Suddenly there was a tap on his shoulder. The Brigade Captain was giving him the thumbs-up, but in a questioning way, clearly asking Park if he was ready to go again. The Depute Labour Director nodded breathlessly. He knew that time was of the essence. The *Proto* had two hours of oxygen, and at least thirty minutes' worth had gone already.

When the Captain pulled back the tarred screen-cloth, the hole in the coal barrier was a good bit larger than Park had expected. From what he could make out in the diffuse light, it looked about four feet wide by about the same high, maybe even four and a half. Those hardy buggers on The Castle side had certainly given it 'laldy' with their picks and shovels, and their determination to hole through.

The entrance to the hole was about waist-high from the old pavement, and the Captain was the first to clamber his way into it, followed by a pair of his crew. Park got the signal to go in next, with the remaining two brigade men making sure that his back was being protected. He knew fine well that the hole was 24 feet long, and he had counselled himself that the journey, no matter how long it might take and how enormously claustrophobic it might turn out to be, would end eventually.

However, in the pitch-blackness of the tunnel, it was a journey that seemed to take an eternity. Shuffling along in the dark with his head bowed and doing everything humanly possible to protect his *Proto* gear from a potentially catastrophic mishap, it was his elbows and knees that were left to take the strain of his body weight and the friction from their constant rubbing along the coal floor. Again, Park wondered, just how in hell will those poor exhausted miners fare on this nightmarish journey, especially if they have to attempt it wearing *Salvus* gear that could be ripped apart at the slightest stumble.

Suddenly, the Captain and his two accompanying Brigade colleagues were through, each of them clambering down onto the wet, glistening pit floor. Park gratefully followed suit, followed by the last two brigade men. It had been a very long time since he had last visited the depths of Knockshinnoch Castle Colliery, but now he was back 'home' again.

This time, though, the circumstances were somewhat different.

8.35am

If peace had broken out in the West Mine, then it sure as hell didn't last long.

'These bastards up there are daein' absolutely nothin' tae get us oot o' here! Sweet f - - - all!'

It was another vocal doubter up on his feet, waving his fists furiously in the general direction of the pit roof. This time it was the Oversman who lost the rag.

'Shut your mouth, you stupid man!' shouted Houston, most uncharacteristically. 'And sit down, for God's sake!'

The protagonist responded immediately. 'Aye Houston, trust you tae side wae the gaffers, instead o' your ain men. Always lickin' the gaffers' arses, that's you!'

As Houston took two steps forward, Sam Capstick took three. He placed the palm of one hand on his boss's chest, and turned to face the dissenting voice. 'The Oversman has telt you tae sit doon an' shut up. So sit doon an' shut up!'

'An' whit are you goin' tae dae aboot it, Capstick?' came a different voice from the depths, as the tension escalated from deep to profound.

Houston knew he had to seize back command at once, or this little verbal spat really could escalate into a full-blown mutiny.

'Right boys!' he snapped. 'Now listen to me! Hear me out, please!'

No one spoke. First bit done, thought Houston, at least I've got their attention. He continued, his hands shaking, but somehow keeping his voice from doing likewise.

'I know we've been down here a long time, boys, a bloody long time. And we're all feeling the pressure. We're all hungry and thirsty, and we've all got families to feed up there. Even me too, if you can believe that. And we've all done well, boys, very well indeed. But we need to keep our nerve and rely on the brigades to get us out. They are our only hope, boys, our only hope. And I for one believe that they'll be bursting their guts to get us out as soon as they can. But we need to keep calm, boys. We need to keep the heid!'

'Aye, that's a' right for you tae say, Andy,' another voice replied. 'But just remember, you're the only man in here that really kens whit's happenin' up there. You're the man that's been talkin' tae the Brigade Captains, an' you're the man that's been hoggin' the phone. I ken you've been tellin' us things, Andy, but how are we supposed tae ken whit they're actually sayin' tae you? How are we supposed tae ken if you've been tellin' us the fu' story, or maybe just the things you want us tae hear?'

Just as the Oversman prepared to respond, the telephone bell tinkled again. It sounded pathetic. When he walked over to answer the thing, a small group of youngsters began following in his wake.

'Hello!' said Houston. This time, it was Bone on the other end, but whatever he was saying was being drowned out by the men's frantic yells in the direction of the receiver.

'Right, c'mon, whit's happenin' up there?'

'C'mon you bastards, when are you goin' tae get us oot o' here?'

'Dae somethin', you buggers, dae somethin' tae help us!'

Houston placed the palm of his left hand over the mouthpiece on the listening tube he was holding with his right, and pressed his ear to the earpiece. Still he couldn't make out what Bone was saying, because of the shouting. Something about the brigades? Something about a ... a visitor? A visitor? What?

'Shut up, you bloody clowns!' he rasped, as half a dozen of the more seasoned men moved forward to restrain the rowdy few. A scuffle threatened to break out, but the younger guys took a long hard look at their more senior and muscular neebors, and immediately thought the better of it.

To Houston's consternation, the phone went dead. Suddenly, as he prepared to launch his verbal wrath at the mutinous upstarts who had interrupted a critically important communication, Andy McKnight began pointing along the dark roadway in the direction of Lanemark.

'What is it, Doch?' Houston barked. 'What are you pointing at, man?'

'Lights, Andy,' came the electrician's reply. 'Lights. It's another brigade, I think.'

The Oversman strained his weary eyes. McKnight was dead right, some cap-lamps were approaching. Four or five, in fact, ... no, it could even be six. The number six struck him as a very unusual number indeed. There were seldom, if ever, more than five in a rescue brigade.

Houston began walking along the roadway to greet the latest team. My God, but how opportune is this? Another welcome distraction to quell the dissenters. Oh yes, and some more sandwiches wouldn't go amiss either.

'Great to see you lads!' he said, as their paths converged then merged. Houston did well to conceal his disappointment that this latest squad had arrived empty-handed. Or had it?

'We've brought you a visitor, Mister Houston,' the Captain added. 'We thought you could dae wae a wee bit o' company! A different face, you ken?'

A stocky figure stepped forward. 'Andy Houston!'

The Oversman recognised the voice immediately. For the first time in almost a day and a half, his heart filled with hope.

'David Park?' he gasped, scarcely able to believe it. 'Christ, Dave, are you a sight for sore eyes!'

The two old friends immediately exchanged vice-like handshakes.

Andy Houston had been the loneliest man in the entire pit. Now he was only half as lonely.

8.55 a.m.

This time around, it was Alex McDonald's turn to pace the office floor.

'Sit down, Alex, for God's sake!' General Manager David McCardel beseeched his Production Manager. 'And let's go through the whole damn thing again.'

McDonald reluctantly slumped down on his chair, and sat back rolling his eyes skywards, expelling a sigh so loud that his breath could be felt by those sitting straight across the table.

'Right, here goes … again!' he began. 'And forgive me if I sound like a stuck gramophone record. The latest position is this. We have to assume … or rather, we have to hope … that David Park will make it through to the West Mine. And, of course, we won't know that until Houston phones the surface, which we expect he will do the moment Dave arrives. When he does arrive, he will talk to the men, inform them that we're all doing everything possible to get them out of there, and try his damnedest to reassure them and keep them calm. Dave will then have a good look around, and assess the situation and the men's condition as best he can in the circumstances. However, he won't be able to give us a detailed briefing until he returns with the brigade to the Fresh Air Base in Bank Six, which he has been instructed to do. As soon as Dave and the brigade men get back to Bank Six, another team then goes straight in with more food and drink for the men. Therefore, gentlemen, our hope is that Dave Park's arrival and words of encouragement, followed swiftly by the provision of more food and drink, will be sufficient to keep the men's spirits up. Quite simply, we need to buy ourselves as much time as possible … but I'm afraid that time is running out, and running out fast. It's the gas that's the problem, and it's getting worse by the minute.'

Communal sighs this time, shoulders slumping in unison, speechless mouths on strained faces, bleary eyes staring at the paper-strewn conference table. It was McCardel who broke the silence.

'Tell us about the gas, Alex. Warts and all, please.'

'We're going around in circles,' McDonald conceded, throwing up his arms in resignation. 'We've tried everything to get rid of the bloody stuff. We've had a real go using suction, but the more of the gas we withdraw from the evacuation route, the more it just seems to come pouring back in from somewhere else. Fifty percent it is now in some of the roadways around the evacuation route, fifty bloody percent! We've even tried reversing the fans and blasting the stuff out, but all that has achieved is to shift it along a bit, then every time we do, it just comes racing back in from another direction. And the most worrying thing of all is the time we've lost trying to get rid of the gas. There must be hundreds of thousands of cubic metres of firedamp down there, maybe even millions.'

'Bottom line, Alex?' asked McCardel, well aware of the inevitable response that was heading his way.

'We're fighting a losing battle,' McDonald conceded, his sombre expression unable to conceal the anguish of a proud and dignified man unaccustomed to failure. 'We now need to think very seriously about using *Salvus*. It's the men's last hope, gentlemen.'

For the next few moments, the silence in the room was deafening. Again, it was the General Manager who broke it.

'Not yet, Alex, not yet. The risks of using *Salvus* on untrained men is too great, at least until we've explored every possible alternative. Keep going with the fans meantime, and let's wait to hear what Park says when he gets back to the Fresh Air Base. Okay, gentlemen?'

McDonald knew that McCardel was right, and that any definitive decision to deploy *Salvus* could only be taken as a very last resort. However, what he didn't know was that Dave Park had no intention of returning to the Fresh Air Base. Absolutely none at all.

At least, not until every last man in Knockshinnoch had gone before him.

9.00 a.m.

The latest bulletin from the Coal Board bosses could hardly have been less encouraging for the miners' anguished relatives standing on the surface in the early morning drizzle.

It confirmed that over one thousand feet of firedamp gas still blocked the trapped miners' escape route, and regretted that it would be 2.00 p.m. at the very earliest before any attempt could be made to bring the first man out. It also confirmed their fears for the thirteen missing men, but stated that no names would be released until every last one of the 116 men trapped in the West Mine had been brought out, 'to enable cross-checks to be made, in order to confirm names via the pit roster'.

Meanwhile, down in the West Mine, Dave Park's arrival had been an enormous shot in the arm for Andy Houston. The hero of the day had burst onto the scene, and here he now was to lead the Oversman and his men to safety.

For a fleeting moment, and as a big 'western' movies fan, Park's dramatic introduction had reminded Houston of the silver screen's depiction of General George Custer leading the 7th Cavalry on horseback to take care of Crazy Horse and his rebellious tribesmen during the Great Sioux War. Unfortunately the euphoria of the moment soon passed when he remembered that General Custer had eventually met a very sticky end, as also had every last one of his cavalrymen.

For Little Bighorn, Andy, read Knockshinnoch's West Mine.

'What are you going to say to the men, Dave?' Houston enquired, deep concern wrestling with cautious optimism as he waited behind to grab a quiet word, while the other five rescue workers walked over towards the miners gathered at the telephone station.

Park replied with a question of his own. 'What do they know already, Andy?'

'More or less everything I know, because I told them I'd keep nothing back from them, and I've been true to my word.'

'Everything?'

'Everything. Well, except …'

'Except what, Andy?'

'Except … except the gas we've now detected in Waterhead Dook. They know all about the gas in Bank Six, and the real difficulties you guys are having trying to get rid of it, but I haven't told them about the gas in here yet … the gas in The Castle side.'

'Probably wise, Andy. They've had an awful lot to contend with already. And anyway, I don't see what good it would do them if we did tell them. Well, for the time being at least. Some of them might start panicking and thinking about making a run for it.'

'A few already have, Dave. It's the younger lads, and we're just managing to keep a lid on it, but I'm worried about how long we can keep them from losing their heads.'

Park nodded ruefully, and scratched his chin. He knew that he would have to choose his words to the men carefully, very carefully indeed. The two old pals then set off towards the West Mine telephone station.

'We've got a visitor!' Andy Houston announced to his men, as cheerily as his heavily sagging spirits could muster.

Park spoke two words. 'Hello boys.'

Many of the miners had no idea who Park was, particularly the younger ones. After all, it had been the best part of a decade since he had last set foot on the New Cumnock Coalfield, and into the bargain very few pit-boys could really have given a damn about who was who among the Coal Board's high and mighty. All they knew was the received wisdom they had been fed by their more cynical peers, which was that the 'suits' were nothing but a shower of lazy, overpaid bastards who sat on their big fat arses at a desk all day long, doing sweet bugger all.

However, many others did know Park well, certainly well enough to recognise that he was a proud New Cumnock man, who despite his fortuitous elevation to the top of the management tree, had at least 'been there and done it' down the pit.

'It cannae be!' shouted big Wull Gray. 'Davie boy! Whit the hell are you daein' doon here?'

'Davie Park?' exclaimed Dave Jess, almost disbelievingly. 'My God, it's good tae see you! You'll hae brought some chowin' tobacco wae you?'

Park just managed to stifle a giggle as he shook the grimy hands of those who shot forward to extend them. This was no place for laughter or frivolity, though. He had a job to do, and very little time left in which to do it. And his reception would be very mixed indeed, as he was about to find out.

To young Willie Lopez, the newcomer was a relative stranger, but a very welcome one:

'I'd never met Dave Park myself, but I'd certainly heard of him. And as a former Bank Pit man, that seemed to lift the men's spirits a good bit.'

Jock McMurdo's reaction to Park's arrival was similarly warm, although Jock had met him personally several years back:

'When Dave Park came in and joined us, that really was a great morale booster.'

Meanwhile, Matt Sanderson observed the developing dynamics with great interest, and was soon less than convinced that the eminent visitor's entrance would be as successful as it was dramatic:

'Dave Park came through to be with us, to reassure and give what assistance he could. It was a brave act on his part, but it had a bad impact on me. He started to tell of the build-up of the rescue services and the concern being shown by the national media. Alex McCracken stopped him talking, saying we did not want this news. We just wanted to know when we were going to get out of here. I thought his answer was a terrible one. He said, "we are still hopeful of making a rescue". I felt a pang of fear in the pit of my belly.'

In truth, Alex 'Eck' McCracken actually felt that Park was treated 'very badly' by some of the trapped miners. After all, here was a man who could have been luxuriating in some cosy metropolitan office that morning, but who had chosen instead to return to his beloved New Cumnock and risk his own life by entering the very vaults of hell itself, in the full knowledge that he might never again escape.

Park began by telling the men, in as much detail as possible, everything that was being done on the surface and in the old Bank mine. He confirmed what they already suspected, namely that it was Bill Wilson's field that had collapsed into Number Five Heading, and God knows how many thousands of tons of sludge with it. He told them about the enormous crater, and the sterling efforts being made by the emergency services to stabilise it and prevent a further inrush of sludge. And, of course, he gave them the lowdown on the operation to get rid of the firedamp from Bank Six, in order to clear an escape route to the surface.

The comments and questions came fast and furious, and with increasing impatience, some bordering on outright hostility. Not enough information, a frustrated voice opined, tell us exactly when we'll be getting out of this hellish place. Too much information, barked another, we don't need to know what the activity on the pit-head looks like, or how these parasites from the press are pestering everyone and taking snapshots of our distraught wives and weans. The coal barrier to Bank Six was holed through ages ago, so why the bloody hell are we still sitting here, why can we not just line up and walk out? On and on it went, as searing questions and increasingly personal insults rained down on the Coal Board's Depute Labour Director.

Park fully understood the reasons for the verbal silos. Essentially, there were two of them. First he was a 'suit', and second he was 'there'. Okay, he had chosen to be there, but there he now was, and he would have to take it all on the chin if he was to stand any chance of getting his message across. Suddenly, the mood changed in the most dramatic fashion.

'To hell with this!' exclaimed one of the pit-boys, springing angrily to his feet. 'I'm for oot o' here! You lot can just hing aroon' in this place for as long as you like, but I've had it. I'm off!'

'You won't last more than a few seconds in that gas,' Park replied, surprisingly calmly. 'So I think you should just sit back down, son.'

Another dissenting voice piped up, then another, and before long there were around half a dozen men on the brink of mutiny, and not all of them youthful rookies. Suddenly, Dave Park abandoned his hard-won diplomatic charm. He lost the rag completely.

'Call yourselves miners!' he rasped at them. 'You're a bloody disgrace to coalmining, and a bloody disgrace to New Cumnock! Look at the men around you! Go on, look at them! They've been stuck down here for as long as you have. They're thirsty and starving like you, and exhausted too. And they've got wives and children waiting for them, just like you. So for God's sake, take a leaf out of their book, and behave like men! Real men!'

The rebellious few fell silent, with heads bowed. Eventually, one of them spoke in an effort to save face. 'Listen, Mister Park ... '

'No, you listen, son!' Park snapped, still seething. 'There are men out there ... literally hundreds of them ... working their guts out to try to get us out of here, so ... '

'Us?' one of the group interrupted, sneering at him. 'Us? Whit dae you mean "us"? You just f - - - in' waltz in here wi' your breathin' gear on, an' in a wee while you'll just f - - - in' waltz straight back oot again, while we're a' left behin' in this shithole tae fend for oorsel's!'

'Aye!' yelled another 'That's right. You come in wi' your bloody oxygen supply, then gie us a' a big lecture on whit we should dae an' shouldnae dae, then you just bugger off again an' leave us stuck doon here!'

Dave Park took a long, deep breath of the rancid Knockshinnoch air, then raised both arms in apparent acquiescence. His actions were about to be anything but acquiescent.

'Okay, boys!' he said, doing his best to eyeball the unruly group in the near darkness of the West Mine. 'Watch this. And watch carefully.'

Very calmly and deliberately, Park began removing his *Proto* apparatus. Having earlier dispensed with his helmet, off now came his breathing tubes, followed by his breathing bag. Finally, he disconnected the oxygen cylinder that lay horizontally along the base of his spine. As everyone watched in astonishment, he then unscrewed the valve, and the oxygen began whooshing out of the cylinder that had been his sole lifeline back to the surface.

Not a single word was spoken, the only sound audible in the whole place being that of the oxygen cylinder spewing its precious contents into the foul atmosphere of the pit bottom. It was only when the hissing eventually stopped that Park broke the dreadful silence.

'There, lads, are you all happy now? I'm going nowhere. I'm staying here with you till the brigade men come and get us, and I'm going to try to stay patient while they do what they need to do. I suggest that you do the same. Now, are there any more questions?'

None were forthcoming, as 116 pairs of eyes stared at the pit floor. Peace had broken out again in the West Mine.

9.45 a.m.

'Still no decision yet on *Salvus*?' asked Alex Stewart, more in hope than expectation.

'Nope,' replied Alex McDonald, glumly. In some strange way, the Production Manager felt more at ease now that he had returned underground. 'McCardel wants us to keep going with the fans for another hour, then report back to him.'

'We're just buggering about down here, Alex,' Stewart replied. 'Somebody needs to make a decision. And fast.'

His boss just nodded, as did Mines Inspector Eric Richford.

'I think we should draw up a contingency plan,' said McDonald. 'On the use of *Salvus*, I mean. And I think we should do it now, just in case McCardel gives the go-ahead earlier than we expect. After all, there's no point in us just standing here scratching our backsides, waiting for a phone call. Everyone agree?'

Stewart and Richford nodded, and the 'brainstorming' session began. Brainstorming was a technique often deployed at the time by those in mine management, particularly during scenario planning, even although those two 21st century terms were still awaiting invention. However, terminology notwithstanding, brainstorming was never at its most effective when those involved had gone 36 hours without any real sleep.

No sooner had their deliberations led to the identification of a range of options, than the options themselves began falling one-by-one, like melting snow off a drystane dyke. Worse still, even those that somehow survived the process of elimination were predicated on a number of assumptions. Rather ambitious assumptions, at that.

Assumption One. McCardel gets his 'Special Exemption' from the national HM Mines Inspectorate to deploy *Salvus*.

Assumption 2. He then gives the green light to authorise an agreed plan to bring the trapped men out wearing *Salvus*.

Assumption 3. Sufficient numbers of *Salvus* sets (estimated to be a minimum of 40) will have been collected and made available by the time the agreed final plan of evacuation is put into operation.

Assumption 4. Given that any rescue attempt is likely to take anything up to two full days, the trapped men will not have been overcome by either a further inrush of sludge, or asphyxiation due to rising firedamp levels.

Assumption 5. The rescue brigades will be able to sustain the men by providing regular supplies of food and drinks.

Assumption 6. There will be no 'casualties' in the West Mine that might require individuals to be stretchered out, thereby causing a further huge delay in the whole process.

Needless to say, confidence was not high that each and every one of those six assumptions could be realised. Indeed, it was nearer rock bottom. And, of course, those same assumptions applied to critically important factors which pertained to the circumstances that would have to prevail <u>before</u> the evacuation process even began. Only then would the tricky bit commence.

Quite remarkably in the circumstances, it took Messrs McDonald, Stewart and Richford less than an hour to decide on the most feasible – or more correctly, the least unfeasible - course of action. Having dispensed with all other options, they came to a unanimous decision on a possible rescue plan. In essence, it was this.

The trapped men, who would have their lives depending on *Salvus* apparatus for which none of them had ever received any training whatsoever, would be evacuated from the West Mine in 'threes'. Each rescue brigade would 'go in as a six and come out as a nine', with two brigade men taking responsibility for one trapped miner apiece on the near two mile long journey. Each pair of rescue workers would escort their allocated evacuee first along Lanemark, then down the slope of Waterhead Dook, then down the precarious slope-road to the coal barrier, then through the coffin-like rescue tunnel, and finally through the gas-contaminated roadway of Bank Six until they reached the Fresh Air Base. There, they would have their near-spent *Salvus* gear removed, and be given a quick medical check-up by one of the many doctors who would be available for duty, before being helped by an army of volunteers the remainder of the way to the foot of the Bank dook, where they would be taken up to the surface in the hutches of the man-riding haulage.

In theory, it looked possible. In practice, it was a ten-thousand-to-one shot. However, it was now the only show in town.

10.30 a.m.

'Haw McCreadie, the beef stew's a' feenished. It'll be corned beef pieces for you Whitehill boys!'

Jimmy McCreadie recognised the voice, but couldn't place the face, even though it had just been scrubbed clean from recent underground travails. It came from the midst of the Kames Colliery Rescue Brigade, whose members were sitting at a table in the far corner of the Knockshinnoch Castle Colliery canteen, tucking into the last remnants of Jenny Walker's wonderful beef-and-onion stew. It might only have been half-ten in the morning, but that day Knockshinnoch knew no set meal times.

Jenny and her apron-clad compatriots had been instructed by the matronly Miss Hyslop to prepare as much hale-and-hearty food as possible, to keep it coming and to hell with what time of day it happened to be requested. There were brigade men to be fed and a whole army of volunteers too, the very men who were the trapped miners' last hope of ever seeing daylight again. Those incredible ladies in the canteen had now been on duty for more than a full day non-stop, save for a couple of ten-minute tea-breaks here and the occasional pee-stop there. By now they were dropping on their feet, one young woman quite literally so when she fainted from exhaustion and had to be given emergency medical treatment by an off-duty ambulance-man who just happened to be in for a cup of tea at the time.

In the event, McCreadie and his Whitehill neebors found themselves washing down their corned beef sandwiches with big plates of newly-made cock-a-leekie soup. Breakfast time or no breakfast time, it tasted magnificent. Even more importantly, it was the very stuff that the Whitehill Brigade would need to fuel them on their next perilous foray into the bowels of the West Mine.

How the hell Jimmy and his neebors had managed to 'pass the doctor' this time was a miracle. Two hours' sleep since their last shift, a mere two hours, and lying on the cold, hard floor of the Bank Pit baths into the bargain. Indeed, if it hadn't been for the good grace of local policeman Sergeant Leslie, they would have had none at all, not a bloody wink.

It was only four hours since they had dragged their weary frames up the Bank dook and past the waiting crowds on the hillside into the pit baths, where they had collapsed on the floor utterly exhausted. No sooner had glorious sleep begun to engulf them, than Sergeant Leslie had waltzed in demanding to know who the hell was dossing on the tiles. When Whitehill Brigade Captain Willie Jolly then lost the rag and told Leslie where to go, the popular local 'bobby' had seen the error of his ways and promised to make amends.

'Sorry boys,' he had said, most embarrassed by his own clumsiness. 'Get your heids back doon, and I'll staun' guard at the door. You'll get twae hours o' guid sleep. No' a single bugger will disturb you.'

And true to the sergeant's word, not a single bugger did. So here they all were now, still bleary-eyed in the canteen after polishing off the soup and sandwiches. It was Willie Jolly who told them to finish off their post-meal Capstan fags, and get their arses back in gear.

The Captain's surname could be a real misnomer at times, it really could.

11.35 a.m.

The telephone rang at the Fresh Air Base in Bank Number Six Mine. It was the General Manager looking for Alex McDonald.

'Hello Mister McCardel,' McDonald grunted wearily, his spirits dropping considerably faster than the firedamp levels that were still swamping the designated escape route.

'Any better, Alex? The gas, I mean?'

'No change, Mister McCardel, just exactly the same. We're getting nowhere. Absolutely nowhere.'

A long pause. McDonald thought the line had gone dead. It hadn't.

'Right, Alex,' said the General Manager. 'We go with *Salvus*. Have your plan ready to put into operation without delay.'

McDonald closed his eyes and took a sharp intake of breath. *Salvus* had been his call all along, at least his and Alex Stewart's, and he knew it. Now 116 miners' lives depended on that call being the right one.

Meanwhile, the Whitehill Brigade had again made it through into the West Mine, armed with a second supply of tea and sandwiches for the trapped men. Their arrival was greeted with predictable enthusiasm, lifting the mood accordingly. However, it was while the brigade men were in the process of handing out the long-awaited supplies to the miners that Oversman Andy Houston made what would ultimately prove to be his one-and-only mistake. And a pretty calamitous mistake at that, as Jimmy McCreadie immediately realised:

'The Oversman – Houston, I think his name was – suddenly started checking for gas. Standing there in the West Mine, he just held up his Glennie. I could see the flame rising myself, and so I had no doubt that some of the men would be able to see it as well. I really don't know why he did that in front of the men, no idea at all, but that was the first the men knew that there was now gas in The Castle side.'

Andy Houston had been almost out on his feet with physical and mental exhaustion, his brain hopelessly numbed by the unimaginable responsibility and stress of the whole situation. In all probability, he had simply lost his concentration and all perspective of where he was actually standing when he checked his Glennie lamp this time. Together with Dave Park, Sam Capstick and Firemen Rab Anderson and Ian Stewart, Houston had thus far managed to conceal from the main body of miners the devastating news that methane gas was now present in the West Mine. However, the cat was now well and truly out of the bag. As the sombre news circulated, the mood quickly plummeted and the frantic chatter intensified as the implications of 'gas in oor side' hit home.

As if we didn't have enough to contend with already, they began muttering to each other. We've been stuck down here for the best part of two days now. We've done everything that's been asked of us, even digging that bloody hole through to Bank Six. And what good has it done us? The hole's through, and we're still stranded down here because those useless bastards up there can't get rid of the gas. What's the point of us sitting here, waiting? Sure, if we make a move now, the gas on the other side might overcome us, but if we just sit here doing nothing, the gas that's now on our own side will get us sooner or later.

Before long, talk of 'making a run for it' was rife again, leaving Andy Houston, Dave Park and a few of the more experienced others with the unenviable task of trying to take the wind out of the recalcitrants' flapping sails. By that stage, Willie Jolly had started gathering his Whitehill squad together again for their long and arduous trek back to Bank Six and onwards to the surface for another extremely well-earned breather. Suddenly, a rather menacing voice piped up.

'I ken you, Wullie Dick' it rasped. 'An' if you try tae go back oot o' here wearin' that *Proto* gear, I'll take it aff you masel'! If it's guid enough for you, it's guid enough for the rest o' us!'

Now, for the avoidance of any misunderstanding, the 'Willie Dick' in question was one of the five-member Whitehill Rescue Brigade, and not to be confused with his considerably loftier namesake, the formidable Superintendent of Kilmarnock Mines Rescue Station. And it was this particular Willie Dick that a furious miner's wrath was being aimed at, and aimed at with clear intent to pull the trigger.

'I'm tellin' you, Wullie,' he continued, 'If you can just walk back oot, then so can I. Take yin mair step, an' I'll rip the *Proto* aff your back an' walk oot in your place!'

Andy Houston made to intervene, but Dave Park got there first. 'Just try it, man, and see what happens! Try it, and you'll get one on the chin!'

Silence, total silence. The tension in the pit resembled a stand-off in a seedy Wild Western saloon bar, as everyone held their breath waiting to see who would make the first move. Sensing that the moment was right, Park decided to take the heat out of the situation.

'Now listen to me, lads!' he barked, doing his best in the near darkness to make some form of eye contact with an exceptionally captive audience. 'Apart from the Whitehill boys and myself, there's not a single man among you who has been trained to use the *Proto*. It's a very complicated piece of equipment, and it takes many weeks of training to learn how to use it. Seven valves it has, you know, seven bloody valves! And you need to know exactly how to operate them. None of you do, and not a single one of you would stand a hope in hell of getting through that gas trying. So enough of this nonsense, and let the brigades do their job. All agree?'

Silence once more. Bleary eyes staring at mud-caked boots.

'I asked you a question, lads!' Park continued. 'And I'll make you a solemn promise. I've already let all the oxygen out of my own *Proto*, so I'll be staying with you right here, right to the very end. I'm going nowhere until every last one of you is out of here. So no more silly talk, and let's leave the brigade men to do their jobs. Agree, I asked?'

Heads nodding wearily this time, as a mumbling chorus of reluctant accord split the uncomfortable silence. Sitting there in the dark, David Park felt strangely proud of himself. He had saved the day, at least for now.

But had his actions just cost him his own life?

11.50 a.m.

'I'll never forget the sight of that poor pit-boy lying there on a stretcher. He wasnae well, no' well at all, and we knew that we had to get him out of there.'

The young lad that rescue brigade man Jimmy McCreadie had witnessed lying in quivering spasms on the pit floor was none other than eighteen year old 'Bevin Boy' Gibb McAughtrie, the youngest of all the 116 trapped miners. As far as McCreadie could ascertain, McAughtrie had suffered some kind of mental breakdown, no doubt brought on by the hellish realisation of his own plight down there in the guts of Knockshinnoch, and that of his young wife and baby son left to fend for themselves up above on terra firma.

The poor unfortunate lad had undoubtedly succumbed to some sort of stress-related incident, and had 'taken ill'. So ill, in fact, that Oversman Andy

Houston had ordered that he be restrained on a makeshift stretcher, and taken away from the main body of the miners into a more remote area of the pit. Houston's explanation to his men was that young Gibb had 'come down with something', and that he felt it best to isolate the lad under supervision 'just in case it's something infectious'.

Houston knew full well what had happened to McAughtrie, and that it was indeed potentially infectious, but not in the strict medical interpretation of the term. The lad had suffered a 'panic attack', plain and simple. No bacteria, no viruses, and hence no need to fear cross-contamination in a purely physiological sense. However, every need to fear a pernicious psychological effect on his troops, who had just witnessed an otherwise perfectly healthy young man being crippled - quite literally - by such a horrifically distressing condition. In short, the lad's panic attack might now grow arms and legs, and spread rapidly throughout the entire workforce, resulting in mass hysteria.

If only Andy Houston could somehow have received informed medical advice on the cause and effects of such a dreadfully distressing condition, he might have been in a much stronger position to understand what was actually happening before his very eyes. Like the following explanation, for example, which came straight from a highly experienced doctor:

'A panic attack is something once seen, never forgotten. I've only seen a full-blown panic attack once, and I never want to see another. The patient resorts to genuine gibbering idiocy for which you can only feel sympathy. Complete physical paralysis, no chance of moving on one's own. One of the classical symptoms is "hyperventilation", or hysterical over-breathing in layman's language. When this happens, too much carbon dioxide is expired from the lungs. The level of carbon dioxide in the blood then falls, as does the blood's natural acidity, and the body generally becomes more alkaline. This is called "metabolic alkalosis", and it gives rise to a condition called "alkalotic tetany" which results in muscular spasms, fitting and eventual unconsciousness. Houston, the Oversman, would almost certainly have seen it all before in the First World War trenches, and he would have recognised the young miner's condition instantly. In all probability, the poor lad would have had to be strapped onto a stretcher for his own safety, given his complete inability to coordinate or even control his own movements. Personally, in all my years as a GP, I've never witnessed a panic attack that actually led to complete unconsciousness. There again, I've never been buried alive for several days down a bloody coal mine! Even for an experienced doctor, the sight of someone suffering a full-blown panic attack is bad enough, very frightening. However, for the miners down that pit, it must have been absolutely hellish to watch.'

Gibb McAughtrie had suffered a full-blown panic attack. He was a mere eighteen-year-old lad at the time, one who had not chosen coalmining as a career, but who had been compelled by law to work down the pit as a 'Bevin Boy', and had then found himself entombed in the bowels of Knockshinnoch, leaving his teenage wife and baby son all alone up above. It is little wonder that after almost two days of being buried alive, he finally 'cracked'. For him to have done so was not a conscious decision on his part. It was an uncontrollable emotional response to an unimaginably horrific situation, and one which led to an overwhelming physiological reaction. That reaction effectively rendered McAughtrie incapable of all rational thought and coordinated movement, to the extent that he had to be secured on a stretcher to save himself and others from serious harm.

There was no shame in what happened to Gibb McAughtrie, absolutely no shame at all. Indeed, one can only hazard a guess at how close a number of his own neebors might actually have come to full-blown panic in the hellhole that was Knockshinnoch. Neither was there any shame in the Coal Board's next decision, which was this. Commence McAughtrie's emergency evacuation immediately, even if it means doing so before the details of the general rescue plan have been finalised. In other words, get him out of there right now, to avoid the awful prospect of mass hysteria.

However, and no matter how laudable that decision might have been in the circumstances, no-one could ever have foreseen the extent to which it would jeopardise the lives of all 116 others.

12.00 noon

The telephone 'hotline' rang again in Knockshinnoch Castle's pit-head HQ. Having just returned to the surface, it was Area Production Manager Alex McDonald who answered it this time. Sensing yet more gloomy news from the Oversman, he took a sharp intake of breath.

'Hello Andy,' he said, hesitantly.

'It's me, Alex,' a distant voice crackled over the perilously tenuous connection.

McDonald recognised the voice immediately. It was David Park.

'How are things down there, Dave?' McDonald asked, dreading the inevitably grim answer.

'Can't say much, Alex,' Park continued, clearly whispering into what was an already hopelessly weak connection. 'Walls have ears, you know what I mean?'

'What is it, Dave?'

'Gas, Alex, that's what it is. And less than a hundred yards from the telephone station. About three and a half percent, and rising. By this time tomorrow, it'll be too late. You understand, Alex?'

McDonald closed his eyes in horror, and sighed the deepest sigh of his entire life. The news was about to get even worse.

'The young lad McAughtrie is in a bad way,' Park went on. 'Panic attack, you know? And a bad one at that. Hellish for the men to witness, very distressing. Both Andy and I agree that we need to get him out of here. And bloody fast, Alex.'

'Leave it with me, Dave. I need to speak to Mister McCardel. Stand by the phone, and don't let anyone else near it. Okay?'

'Okay, Alex. But be quick.'

A full ten minutes elapsed in the West Mine before the little hammer again began tapping feebly on the telephone bell. Park lifted the receiver. It was Alex McDonald again.

'We're sending in the Dailly Brigade. Get the boy ready.'

12.05 p.m.

Young Gibb McAughtrie was in a very bad way. By now secured firmly to a stretcher, his mind was completely out of it, even if his whole body continued convulsing in violent contradiction.

Meanwhile, McAughtrie's dismayed neebors took turns to wipe the sweat away from the boy's burning forehead, wetting his lips with the little that remained of the cold tea reserves, as they prayed silently for the next brigade to appear with more. None of them had ever seen anything like this before, and none of them ever wished to see anything like it again.

The semi-conscious lad's gibbering utterances sounded deliriously confused, save for the odd frantic yell of his wife's or his baby's name, each one accompanied by an incredible tensing of his biceps as he strove to burst his frame free of the restraints that were attempting to save him from injury. For his neebors, the sight of one of their own in such a dire condition was distressing beyond description. For young Gibb himself, it was a living, screaming nightmare.

Andy Houston and David Park decided between them that the time was now right to address the troops. They told them that a plan was being prepared by the bosses, a plan to take the men through into Bank Six and then up to the Bank pit-head. Since firedamp was still a huge problem, the decision had now been taken to equip them all with *Salvus* breathing apparatus. It was likely to be a few hours yet before the plan would be put into operation, but it was as well letting the men know now what it entailed.

Silence reigned once more in the West Mine telephone station, split only by the sound of heavy, anxious breathing and the omnipresent, unearthly creaks and squeals of metal twisting in some faraway sludge-infested heading. Those, and the anguished yells of the poor lad tied to the stretcher. Indeed, anything but silence.

Park continued without breaking his verbal stride. From what he himself understood at this juncture, the men would be put into groups of three, and each group would be 'escorted' by a team of brigade men. Their journey would take them from The Castle, first down the steep contours of Waterhead Dook, and then down the tricky little slope-road to the coal barrier. There they would crawl on their hands and knees through the hole in the barrier, with brigade men in front and at the rear. Once through the hole, they would be led through the old gas-filled Bank Six roadways to what was called a 'Fresh Air Base', where they would be able to remove their *Salvus* masks, and be given a quick check-up by a doctor, before being taken up to the surface.

The first remark was predictably negative, but borne out of deep anxiety rather than bare cynicism. 'You make it sound easy, Dave.'

'I never said it would be easy, son,' Park replied calmly. 'Andy and I just thought you'd like to know what the plan is, that's all.'

Houston waded in. 'It won't be easy at all, boys. The whole journey is fraught with danger, but it's our only chance. I've been down to the barrier several times now, as many of you have too when you dug the hole through. It's fairly straightforward, but remember that when it's your turn to go, you'll be wearing the *Salvus* apparatus. None of you have been trained for *Salvus*, but Dave knows it well, and he'll talk you through the whole procedure. Won't you Dave?'

Park gave an assured nod of his head. Houston ploughed on.

'The hole in the barrier is about four feet square, so plenty of room even for the big arses among you, but it's 24 feet long, and you'll have to crawl on your elbows and knees the full way. Once through the barrier, your brigade escorts will lead you through the old Bank Six workings to the Fresh Air Base, but it will be hard-going because the old mine has lain derelict for the past seven years. After that, it'll be a quick medical examination, then up in the bogies to the surface and home for tea.'

Anxious eyes closing in terror, dust-filled lungs inhaling huge gulps of increasingly foul air.

'That's the general idea, boys,' Park continued, 'but obviously the detail has still to be worked out.'

'How long will it take us to get from here to the Fresh Air Base?' enquired old Jim Haddow.

'It's about half-a-mile,' Houston replied. 'So say half an hour, 40 minutes at most.'

'And how long will our oxygen supply last?' Haddow persisted.

'About half-an-hour, maybe 40 minutes.'

If the men hadn't realised before just how touch-and-go their perilous situation had become, then they sure as hell did now. A 40-minute journey along old, hopelessly derelict mine workings and through a lethal atmosphere, and a 40 minute breathing supply under a big oppressive gas mask. One bloody stumble, and its goodbye and goodnight.

Jock McMurdo quietly observed the verbal free-for-all that followed:

'There was a lot of arguing about who was to go first. It was decided by Andy Houston that the oldest and the youngest should be first out. Since I was 30 at the time, I knew I would be leaving in one of the last groups.'

Dave Park soon brought the shapeless debate to an end.

'Right boys, we've told you everything that we know ourselves. It's now up to the men on the surface to work out the finer details of the rescue plan, and we simply have to trust them to do their jobs. It's our only chance, boys, remember that. In the meantime, the Oversman has been instructed to draw up a list, putting you all into groups of three. As he has told you already, the oldest and the youngest will be going first. That's it, boys.'

Park was certain that his next statement would be met by outrage. Undaunted, he ploughed on.

'The Dailly Rescue Brigade will be coming in shortly to take Gibb McAughtrie out. He needs urgent medical treatment.'

There was no outrage, only relief. Relief that, at long last, some kind of rescue attempt was finally going to be attempted. And relief that young Gibb's suffering would soon be over, as would his hellish yells of anguish.

One big question remained. Would the brigades actually manage to get him out alive?

Because, if they couldn't get Gibb out …

12.06 p.m.

Apparently, the men from the south Ayrshire village of Dailly had been so chuffed at being selected as the first to attempt an evacuation of one of the trapped miners, that in their pent-up enthusiasm to get cracking, they omitted to heed the directions of their Whitehill Brigade colleagues who had just returned from the West Mine.

Jimmy McCreadie was furious:

'The Dailly Brigade thought they knew everything, but they knew nothing! They never listened to a bloody word we told them about the road up to the West Mine, or even the chalk marks we had left for them to follow, so the inevitable happened. They ended up going down the wrong dook, and got bloody lost! So the Muirkirk boys had to go in and get them back out again! Then the Dailly Brigade had to start all over again. They werenae so bloody smart the next time!'

It had been a colossal mistake, and one which further delayed an exceptionally dangerous procedure that had suffered quite enough setbacks already. However, if the Dailly Rescue Brigade had begun their journey as the butt-end of umpteen wisecracks, they would end it as the focus of undying sympathy and gratitude.

McCreadie himself outlined the perilous nature of the Brigade's rescue mission, like a veteran headmaster explaining his school's one-way system to a first-year assembly:

> 'What you have to understand is how complicated the whole thing was. Remember, these men didn't know the pit at all, neither Bank nor Knockshinnoch. Once they had got into The Castle side and reached the boy on the stretcher, they then had to work out for themselves how they were going to get back out, mainly by following the chalk marks we had left for them. Then they had to cover a distance of half a mile. Half a mile, wearing 56 pounds of *Proto* gear, and carrying a grown man on a stretcher. Heavy work, really bloody heavy work.'

After their inauspicious start, the Dailly Brigade eventually arrived in the West Mine telephone station at 12.42 p.m. on that early Saturday afternoon. Precisely three minutes later, young Gibb McAughtrie's evacuation had begun. The five-man team, all of them wearing the more sophisticated *Proto* breathing apparatus, had brought four sets of *Salvus* gear with them. It all added to their already heavy burden, but their reasoning was sound. It would take a hell of a lot longer than the estimated 40 minute walking time to carry a man on a stretcher to the Fresh Air Base in Bank Six. And if four sets of *Salvus* couldn't give young Gibb sufficient breathing time to get there alive, then neither would the brigade men's own *Proto*, and the job of the next rescue team would be to collect six corpses.

At first, there was much arguing about whether Gibb should be restrained by tying him securely onto his stretcher to prevent his arms and legs from flailing around. However, all efforts to do so only added to the lad's state of alarm.

Matt Sanderson received a very firm knock back from the Brigade Captain when he dared to suggest restraining young McAughtrie:

> 'No prior warning that a rescue brigade was on the way had been given to us, and the patient was lying loosely on the stretcher. The Brigade Captain was the only one to remove his mouthpiece. I suggested to him that two or three minutes would secure the patient. The Captain bluntly replied, "I'm in charge now". I felt snubbed. The brigade team put a heavy apparatus on top of him, and lifting the stretcher, they left.'

As the five man team began their marathon trek, it was a hasty decision that would return to haunt them. They headed along Lanemark towards Waterhead Dook, two at the front and two at the back carrying the stretcher. The fifth man's job was to lead the way and keep checking on the patient, while awaiting his turn in the 'cairryin' rota' at one of the four designated positions; ten, two, four and eight o'clock respectively.

As the rescue team's silhouettes began disappearing from the view of the West Mine, the trapped miners' good wishes almost succeeded in disguising their innermost feelings of deep foreboding. If Gibb McAughtrie didn't make it on a stretcher, then neither would they on their feet. Not a snowball's chance in hell.

At first, the brigade men's task was relatively straightforward, if extremely taxing. As they made their way along Lanemark with its relatively level pavement and twelve foot high roof, they could walk quite normally, the young patient's dead-weight fairly evenly distributed among them. However, the very moment they turned down Waterhead Dook, they would no longer be walking. They would be half-walking, half-crawling. And God alone knew how they were then going to carry the stretcher, particularly if the lad started flailing around again. They were about to find out.

As the lower roof levels of Waterhead Dook loomed nigh, the Captain ordered the fifth brigade man to relieve his 'ten o'clock neebor', and they instinctively began stooping to enter the dook. It took less than 30 yards of descent for the stretcher-bearers to realise just how ridiculously punishing this journey was going to be. With heads lowered, backs and knees bent and no longer able to walk straight, their quad and calf muscles soon began to ache from the leaden weight they were carrying. Half-way down the dook, the Captain commanded them to collapse in an orderly heap for a few minutes' rest. He gasped for breath to the rhythm of the rapidly increased click-clicking of his *Proto* gear.

Another rota change, and off they went again, only to collapse again at the entrance to the next dook, where one of the brigade men suddenly started writhing around in agony.

'I've got cramp in ma leg! F - - - in' cramp!' he cursed wordlessly into his hard-bitten rubber mouthpiece, as he continued squirming.

Thirty seconds' rest then off again, following the white chalk marks down the steep contours and four and a half feet height of the slope-road. This time, there would be no lifting-and-carrying. This time, it could only be pushing and pulling.

And so the brigade men began doing just that, pushing-and-pulling with all their might, bare hands scraping along the stony abrasions of the pit floor until they bled freely. As Gibb McAughtrie's limp torso bounced over the ground, he started flapping and yammering again. This is all we need now, the Captain muttered inwardly.

Some twenty minutes later, the Dailly team had somehow managed to drag their patient down to the coal barrier. As they lay exhausted on the wet floor, three flat-out on their backs and the other two contorting in the foetal position, the Captain smiled a wry invisible smile. Now comes the hard bit.

He pulled his portly frame up from the floor, and walked over to McAughtrie, trying his best with hand-signals to persuade the boy to stay calm. Taking another oxygen cylinder from a grey sackcloth, he quickly removed the near-spent apparatus from the young lad's back and replaced it with the full one. A necessary operation – and one that could have gone disastrously wrong - had worked out fine. Perhaps it was an omen of better things to come. There again, perhaps not.

The Captain knew that the task of getting young McAughtrie's stretcher through the hole in the coal barrier would be no walk in the park. A crawl through the gates of hell, more like. He climbed up into the hole and lay down on his stomach, his pit boots pointing in the direction of the sanctity of Bank Six and his helmet facing back towards the tomb that was Knockshinnoch, signalling for another one of his team to do likewise and squeeze in alongside him. Next came Gibb on the stretcher, followed by two other brigade men, both head-first and side-by-side, with the fifth man bringing up the rear.

As the two at the front pulled, the two at the back pushed, and the stretcher began to slide-and-bump its way into the hole. The sheer effort required by the four men was utterly backbreaking. About half-way through the hole, the Captain held up his hand, signalling in the faint glow for his men to take a breather. He felt so exhausted that he could have fallen into a deep comatose sleep. If only.

Without any warning, McAughtrie started writhing around again, only this time trying his best to rip the *Salvus* helmet off his own face. Instinctively, the brigade man at 'two-o'clock' dived forward and grabbed the lad's arm with one hand, securing his *Salvus* in place with the other. As the Captain hauled on the stretcher from the front, the two others at the back shoved it as if there was no tomorrow. Perhaps a prophetic thought.

The Captain felt his feet touch something soft and pliable. It was the tarred screen-cloth covering the entrance to Bank Six. He kicked it aside, and they were through. He lowered his feet onto the ground, and his neebor followed suit, still holding young McCoughtie's breathing mask firmly in place. Out came the stretcher, followed by the three remaining members of the Dailly Brigade.

They had made it through the barrier. The brigade men looked at their Captain, expecting him to return their triumphant thumbs-up signal. He did not.

Instead, his legs suddenly gave way and his head hit the pit floor with a sickening thud.

1.40 p.m.

Willie Dick's brutal training regime in the Kilmarnock 'torture chamber' had taught his rescue brigade graduates many things. Perhaps most important of all was the necessity to avoid panic, to stay calm and to 'always trust your training', no matter the situation.

However, at that precise moment, a sense of deep dread hung heavily in the foul air of Bank Number Six Mine. Half a dozen men being kept alive by an assortment of crude breathing apparatuses, one prostrate in a makeshift stretcher, their esteemed leader either dead or unconscious at best, and the four others absolutely out on their feet with exhaustion. And all six with a fair old distance still to travel, and about 40 minutes' worth of oxygen remaining to aspirate them to safety. Hardly an encouraging situation.

And that was when the physical toughness and mental fortitude of supremo Dick's brutal training regime kicked in. As the lethal firedamp gas swirled invisibly all around the four Dailly Brigade men still standing, it was laced with fear. However, their *Proto* gear would take care of the gas, and their training would deal with the fear. Four spent men on legs trembling with exertion, but four remarkably cool heads.

One immediately took control of the situation, and began hand-signalling a familiar message. He was going on ahead, and he would bring back more brigade men with him. Meantime, the others should stay put, to look after the Captain and the boy. Three heads nodding, three thumbs pointing skywards.

It only took twenty minutes for him to return to the barrier, accompanied by four others clad in *Proto* and carrying another stretcher, while yet another three full rescue brigades lined the route back to the Fresh Air Base. Afraid to remove their Captain's *Proto* helmet for fear of firedamp contamination, the Dailly Brigade had been unable to establish the extent of the head wound he had undoubtedly sustained the moment he hit the deck. As for young McAughtrie himself, the rescue boys had managed to keep him reasonably safe, even if his limbs were still going like the clappers.

After a few quick blasts of pressurised oxygen, the Dailly Captain regained consciousness, but he was clearly much too weak to continue the journey on foot. A succession of knowing hand-signals, a single 'toot' on the hooter, and the extended team began to 'advance' once more in convoy on their do-or-die trek towards the Fresh Air Base.

By this time slightly more familiar with the network of old roadways, the brigade men split themselves into two teams of four, each team taking charge of a stretcher apiece. The Dailly Brigade had voluntarily drawn the short straw. Their Captain was built like an oil tanker, and about twice the weight of the taller and lankier McAughtrie, but he was their Captain after all, and that was all that mattered.

The journey from the coal barrier to the Fresh Air Base resembled some kind of wickedly treacherous army assault course, and very soon all five rescue brigades had to be deployed in rotation. Even then, it was a gut-wrenchingly exhausting procedure for every single man-jack of them. Sure, the stretcher-bearers were now able to walk reasonably normally through the old seven foot high Bank Six roadways. However, such was the condition of the mine roofs at umpteen locations along the way that they found themselves constantly having to duck their heads as they carried the dead-weights of their respective patients, which put tremendous strain on their neck and back muscles. Worse still were the countless knee-deep pools of water through which they had to swish and slither their way, and the waist-high piles of rubble and fallen roof matter over which they had to clamber with their laden stretchers.

It really had been the journey from hell. At 2.15 p.m., a total of 26 brigade men finally stumbled into the Fresh Air Base in Bank Six, where they and their patients were immediately descended upon by the massed ranks of medical personnel and volunteers. Each and every one of them was on his last legs, and completely beyond words. By the time their *Proto* – and Gibb McAughtrie's *Salvus* – apparatus had been ripped off, they all had less than ten minutes of oxygen left in the cylinders strapped to their lumbar regions. The moment the humid, dust-filled atmosphere of the old mine hit their nostrils, half a dozen of the stretcher-bearers immediately began retching their guts up onto the pit floor.

Each brigade man was then given a quick medical check-up by one of the doctors on duty in the Fresh Air Base. All 26 of them were immediately declared unfit for further work and 'stood down indefinitely', a rather nifty term which somehow contrived to disguise the sickening reality of their predicament. They had all been just ten minutes from death.

Some twenty minutes later, the same men were being oxtered - and two of them stretchered - towards the bogies of Bank Six Mine's man-riding haulage. This was the 'Bank rake'. The very same rake which only twelve years back had caused the tragic deaths of five courageous miners.

The rake of death had suddenly become the rake of life.

At precisely 2.45 p.m. on Saturday 9 September, young Gibb McAughtrie was stretchered into the blinding light of a very dark and cloudy September afternoon. As the waiting hundreds surged towards him from the grassy slopes of the Bank pit-head, the cheers that rung out could be heard in New Cumnock's Pathhead, almost two miles away. The pit horn began blaring again, this time in joyous celebration.

At last, the first of the trapped miners had been saved. Surely, now, it would only be a matter of time before the others followed.

Wouldn't it?

3.05 p.m.

Andy Houston broke the long and awkward silence.

'Something's wrong, Dave. Something's far wrong. We should have heard by now.'

David Park took another look at his pocket watch. It was just after three o'clock, some two and a quarter hours since the Dailly Brigade had left the West Mine with their sick patient. Sure, they had faced a momentous task in carrying the boy through all those God-forsaken old roadways to safety, but two and a quarter hours? It should never have taken them that long, and even if it had, they would probably have run out of oxygen long before they even reached the Fresh Air Base. Andy Houston was right. Something has gone wrong. Badly wrong.

246

'Och Andy, it was never going to be an easy journey for the Dailly boys!' Park replied dismissively, almost but not quite concealing his deep anxiety about the inordinately lengthy passage of time since they had last heard a word from anyone in authority. 'Hauling a grown man in a stretcher through all that stuff, and with 56 pounds of *Proto* on their backs? Come on, Andy!'

Houston just nodded, leaned the back of his head against the pit wall and closed his eyes. Within seconds, he had drifted into another dreadfully uncomfortable dreamlike trance. This time, he found himself lying in his bed at home, all alone. Mary was in the house too, but she was far, far away. She was watching him as he slept, as were hundreds and hundreds of other pairs of tearful, reddened eyes. But he wasn't asleep at all. How could he possibly sleep in that brick-hard bed, still dressed in his pit clothes and pit boots, and with all those sad, terrified eyes staring at him? And with that bell ringing in his ears. That bloody annoying bell.

'You going to get that, Andy?' Park's voice made Houston jump with a start.

The Oversman leapt to his feet like a kid hearing the unmistakable jingle of his favourite ice cream van, his body already in overdrive but his brain still half-comatose.

'Houston here.'

'Gibb McAughtrie's out, Andy!' He had never heard Willie Halliday so excited about anything. Never in his life.

'Say that again, Willie?'

'Young Gibb's out! It took us nearly two hours, but we got him out!'

'That's terrific, Willie,' Houston replied, his brain now on high alert as he turned to give Park the thumbs-up. 'What happens now?'

'Well, we've had to stand down quite a few of the brigade men.'

This time, the tone of Halliday's voice had returned to its more pragmatic norm.

'They had a hell of a job getting the boy out, Andy, a hell of a job. So there might be a wee delay. Just an hour or two, though, then we'll be coming to get the rest of you.'

One step forward and two back, thought Houston, every bloody time. Up one minute and down the next. He briefed Park quietly, then gathered his men around, and mustered up every last ounce of upbeat enthusiasm, right from the soles of his pit boots up to the top of his balding cranium.

'Gibb's out, boys! He's on his way to hospital, but he's fine. Soon they'll be coming to get us as well!'

The cheering was more muted than the Oversman had expected, but he ploughed on.

'The plan remains the same. The brigades will come in, fit a *Salvus* on each of you, and lead you through to Bank Six. It might be a wee while yet, though. A good couple of hours at least.'

The cheering faded from muted to silent.

3.15 p.m.

For Alex McDonald and Alex Stewart, Gibb McAughtrie's successful evacuation had initially felt like a personal triumph.

They had proved two things to themselves. Firstly, that it was possible to get a trapped man out of that crypt on the other side. Secondly, that their decidedly risky insistence on resorting to the use of untried *Salvus* apparatus really had worked. On this occasion, at least.

However, there was also a downside, and a bloody big one at that. Now that young McAughtrie was out, the public expectation that the others would follow immediately was immense. But, of course, they would be doing no such thing, and for one very good reason. Gibb's evacuation had taken two full hours, and had led to the near-demise of the Captain of the Dailly team and the indefinite standing-down from duty of five entire rescue brigades.

The blinding reality of the situation was dire, and two-fold. Firstly, half of all currently available rescue brigades were now being rushed to hospital and completely out of action for the foreseeable future. Secondly, the task of getting the remainder of the 116 trapped men out using a similar methodology would take several days, and they probably had less than one full day of breathable air left in their West Mine tomb. This whole thing needed rethinking, and fast.

Meanwhile back at the Bank pit-head, McAughtrie himself was making a rather remarkable recovery as his stretcher got manoeuvred carefully towards a waiting ambulance. As the police battled to keep the swarming crowds away from the vehicle's exit route, the young man was busily chatting away to notepad and pencil wielding newspaper reporters, telling them that all was well with the men down below and that they were 'singin' like linties'. He then informed the ambulance crew that before heading for nearby Ballochmyle Hospital, he would be dropping in home to see his wife and baby son, only to be told in no uncertain terms that he would be doing nothing of the bloody kind. A few moments later, the ambulance screamed away from the pit-head, its bell clanging and blue light flashing in triumph.

It fell to Alex McDonald to persuade General Manager David McCardel that the main rescue mission must now commence without further delay. The plan was a daring one, and bordering on the impossible. Unabashed by his other colleagues' scepticism, McDonald nevertheless continued to press home his heart-felt conviction that this was the right thing to do, indeed the only thing to do. Sometimes, as he counselled his boss, desperate situations call for desperate measures, and nothing could be more desperate than this hellish mess. And, of course, bordering on the impossible did not necessarily mean impossible.

One very important principle had to be established from the outset, though, no matter how difficult that principle might transpire to find conversion into practice. Under no circumstances could another 'stretcher rescue' be attempted from the West Mine. The evacuation of Gibb McAughtrie might well have ended successfully for the lad himself, but it had seriously delayed and profoundly compromised the main rescue mission. Therefore, one brutally clinical message had to be delivered, not only to the rescue brigades directly involved, but to the trapped miners themselves.

Every single man would need to 'walk out under his own steam', since any more attempts to stretcher out casualties could further delay the main rescue operation to the extent that mass fatalities would be inevitable. A subliminal, unspoken message to the miners would then be crystal clear.

Keep walking, and you have a chance of getting out alive. Drop, and you'll be left lying where you fall.

3.25 p.m.

As Alex McDonald had already decreed, sometimes desperate situations call for desperate measures.

It was a harsh message to deliver, but it was for the greater good, and there could be absolutely no compromise. Young Gibb McAughtrie's tortuously protracted evacuation had seen to that.

The essentials of the main rescue plan had already been agreed in principle by the Coal Board's top brass. The six-man rescue brigades would enter the West Mine in pre-determined rotational order, each brigade picking up three of the miners. In other words, and as previously established, they would 'go in as a six and come out as a nine'. The order of evacuation was presently being determined by Oversman Andy Houston, who had allocated the men into groups of three, the general idea being to send out the older ones first, then the younger ones after that, and finally those in their mid-twenties to mid-thirties. Dave Park would check each and every *Salvus* apparatus personally, and assist the brigade men in fitting them onto the miners as they prepared to leave. The six brigade men would then split themselves into 'three twos', each pair taking responsibility for one miner. So far, so good, in theory at least.

However, much more thought now needed to be given to what was without question the most treacherous and hazardous part of the journey; the half-mile trek from the barrier itself, through the gassed-out roadways in Bank Six, to the Fresh Air Base. This was undoubtedly the part of the operation that concerned McDonald most. By that stage, the miners' oxygen supply would be near-exhausted, and in an atmosphere of 50% toxicity they would be physically weakening and feeling enormous psychological stress as their faces and scalps began 'burning' from the inevitable effects of methane gas. Not only that, but one spark from the trailing pit boot of an exhausted miner could blow the whole mine to kingdom come. McDonald, though, had another suggestion, one that might considerably reduce the likelihood of such a disastrous scenario materialising. It was brilliant in its conception, but would it actually work in practice?

His master plan was to line the half-mile-long, gassed-out Bank Six roadway, right from the coal barrier all the way to the Fresh Air Base, with a continuous rotational supply of rescue brigade men stationed at fifteen-to-twenty-yard intervals; a 'human chain', in others words. Each brigade man in the chain would have a two hour supply of oxygen in his *Proto* to sustain him, the newest arrivals in the rota going straight to the head of the chain nearest the barrier, with those whose oxygen supply was fast diminishing dropping back to the foot of the chain at the Fresh Air Base, before heading back up to the surface for a three hour break. When the trapped men came through the hole in the barrier and saw the long line of cap-lamps showing the way, they would then be passed along the chain from one brigade man to the next, until they had reached the safety of the Fresh Air Base. Next, a second 'human chain', this comprising volunteers spaced at similar intervals apart, would then line the full length of the remaining one-mile of the 'breathable' walk-out route, from the Base to the foot of the Bank dook. There, the rake's hutches would be waiting to take the miners up to safety on the Bank pit-head.

McDonald had put his case well, and McCardel was clearly impressed by such an innovative plan having been thought through in such a short time and under such enormous pressure. However, the General Manager still had serious reservations about its practicability in these desperate circumstances. His questions to McDonald were numerous and unrelenting:

How many brigade men will we need in total? A hundred minimum, at least eighteen to twenty full rescue brigades, to service the 'first human chain'.

And just where the hell are we going to get as many as that from? From all over the country. And beyond, if necessary.

Which other personnel do you need to help you put the plan into operation, and how many? We need at least four doctors, the same number of first aiders, about a dozen tradesmen to man the pumps, fans, lights, telephones and so on, plus another 50 or so volunteers to operate the 'second human chain'.

Can you guarantee the safety of the brigades, the medics, the tradesmen and the volunteers? Absolutely not. One single spark from an electrical appliance or a miners' pit boot, and it's curtains. A roof caving in, likewise.

And we'll be breaking the law if we use Salvus, won't we? Yes indeed we will, but we'll be saving lives, not just our own backsides.

McCardel nodded ruefully, and said he would like to think about it. Suddenly, there was a loud knock on the Headquarters office door. In marched Willie Dick, not this time he of the Whitehill Rescue Brigade, but the Superintendent of Kilmarnock Mines Rescue Station, and he had an urgent message from Dave Park in the West Mine. So sensitive was the message that Park had entrusted the Dailly Brigade to convey it personally to the surface, rather than telephone himself and run the risk of having it overheard and spreading panic among the trapped men.

Park's message was this.

'The gas in the West Mine is now four percent and rising steadily, less than fifty yards from the telephone station. If you are still considering a rescue attempt, you really must start now, or I fear it will be too late.'

4.37 p.m.

Dave Park's unequivocally stark message from the depths of Knockshinnoch's West Mine really did work the oracle this time. The Coal Board's high-and-mighty could wait no longer.

At precisely 4.37 p.m. on Saturday 9 September, BBC Radio's *Light Programme* interrupted the latest episode of its highly popular drama series, 'Mrs Dale's Diary', to broadcast the following message to the nation:

> *This is an urgent message for the British Mines Rescue Service. All rescue brigades stationed in Scotland and the North-East of England please make their way immediately to Knockshinnoch Castle Colliery, New Cumnock, Ayrshire. Repeat – all rescue brigades to Knockshinnoch Castle Colliery, New Cumnock, Ayrshire.*

The greatest mines rescue in history was about to begin, and the world held its breath.

4.55 p.m.

By the time the main rescue mission was due to commence, almost all preparations had been completed. Almost, but not quite all. Time was of the essence, and preparatory perfection simply wasn't an option. It was green for go, fingers crossed, and pray to the heavens.

The logistics of the operation had been worked out meticulously, at least insofar as the reliability of extremely limited management information coming from the West Mine and the dwindling capacity of three sleep-deprived brains – those of Messrs McDonald, Stewart and Richford – could possibly achieve.

By 4.55 p.m., a total of 87 sets of *Salvus* respirators and 100 spare cap-lamps had been delivered to the Bank Auld Pit, with countless promises of more to come, a quite remarkable achievement in itself. Those had been despatched from umpteen fire stations and naval bases scattered all around the British Isles, then transported to the village of New Cumnock by a seemingly never-ending armada of motor cars, vans and lorries. Certainly, some would be in better condition than others, and more sets would be needed, but they were now already in sufficient supply to get the mission underway. The Coal Board's contingency plan to fly in an additional consignment of *Salvus* sets from the United States of America could now be put on hold, at least for the time being.

By that stage, a bit of headway had been achieved at last by Alex Stewart and his men in clearing the firedamp from a vitally important stretch of the contaminated roadway nearest to the Fresh Air Base. This terrific breakthrough had been a long time coming, but while it only freed up an additional few hundred yards of 'breathable' roadway, it still allowed Stewart to set up an 'Advanced Fresh Air Base' a bit closer to the coal barrier. This immediately realised two huge advantages. Firstly, it would reduce both the distance and duration of the trapped miners' highly dangerous and stressful walk-out, imprisoned by the suffocating claustrophobia of their hugely oppressive *Salvus* gas masks. Secondly, it would facilitate the bolstering of the 'human chain' of brigade men that was now being positioned to help the miners reach the safety of the main Fresh Air Base.

All along the way, from the foot of the Bank dook to the main Fresh Air Base, and still further beyond to the newly-established Advanced Fresh Air Base, a huge army of willing volunteers now lined the roadways. With doctors and first-aiders stationed at both bases, and electricians, engineers and other assorted pit personnel scattered all along the entire length of the walk-out route, any miners who might be lucky enough to get this far certainly wouldn't be short of company. Having spent more than two full days in the near-pitch blackness of their West Mine catacomb, the sight of such an incredible sea of twinkling cap-lamps would greet them like the village's spectacular Castle Races funfair on a late summer's evening. God willing, it would be a sight to behold. And God willing, every single one of them would survive long enough to behold it.

It was shortly after five o'clock that Alex McDonald made the call which at one stage he had thought he would never make.

'We're ready to go. It's now or never.'

4.57 p.m.

The telephone rang once more in the West Mine. Andy Houston lifted the receiver and took a long, deep breath.

'This is it, Andy!' the voice on the other end announced. It was Willie Halliday, and he sounded as excited as a teenager who had just wedged himself into his first pair of drainpipe trousers. 'The main rescue operation is under way!'

Houston just closed his eyes, and swallowed the deepest swallow of his life.

'You got your list ready, Andy?' Halliday continued. 'Your rota?'

'Aye,' Houston replied, his voice trembling slightly. 'All 117 of us, including Dave and me. Groups of three, the older ones first. I might have to let some of the younger lads jump the queue, though. They're really feeling it, Willie.'

'Okay, Andy. Good luck, old pal. I'll see you on the surface in a few hours' time!'

'I hope so, Willie. I really hope so.'

The phone in the West Mine went dead again. Houston held his blue-covered NCB notebook firmly in the palms of both hands. Clasping his fingers together, he whispered a silent prayer. He then turned to face David Park.

'This is it, Dave. This is it.'

5.00 p.m.

This was indeed 'it'.

Word had reached the miners' loved ones on the Bank pit-head that the main rescue mission was about to begin, and all they could do now was to hold their collective breath and pray. Meanwhile, Cumnock's Hearth Road telephone exchange was in a veritable frenzy of activity, as phone calls and telegrams flew all around the world.

David McCardel demanded the final position statement that would allow him to push green for go. This was the six-point bulletin he received:

One: A total of 87 *Salvus* sets were now lying in wait at the Advanced Fresh Air Base, with more on the way, together with 100 spare fully-charged miners' cap-lamps.

Two: Food, water and hot tea were now in copious supply at both the Advanced Fresh Air Base and the main Fresh Air Base.

Three: A human chain of men was now in position all along the full length of the walk-out road, first between the coal barrier and the Advanced Fresh Air Base, and then onwards to the foot of the Bank dook and the waiting hutches.

Four: A total of four doctors, four first-aiders and 30 volunteer stretcher-bearers were now ready at the main Fresh Air Base, equipped with a dozen stretchers and a full range of medical supplies including respirators and oxygen masks.

Five: Each successive rescue brigade had been instructed, on arrival, to station itself and remain in position at the main Fresh Air Base, until it received a detailed briefing from Coatbridge Rescue Station's 'permanent instructor'. They were not to continue to the Advanced Fresh Air Base until the next brigade had arrived at the main Base.

Six: Once each brigade had been given clearance to progress to the Advanced Fresh Air Base, it was to remain there until it had received a more detailed briefing from another Coatbridge instructor. Only when each and every brigade man fully understood his duties and the next rescue brigade had moved up from the main Base, would they be given permission to advance to the coal barrier then through the hole into the 'operational zone' of Knockshinnoch's West Mine.

The first rescue brigade to be sent into the operational zone was one of Coatbridge Station's 'permanent' teams. Its role would be an absolutely critical one, and its brief was this. Advance to the coal barrier carrying a first cargo of *Salvus* sets and spare cap-lamps. Then crawl through the hole, follow the chalk marks up the slope-road and turn left into Waterhead Dook. Once up Waterhead, you will see the rail tracks of the Mechanised Section of Knockshinnoch. Follow those tracks into Lanemark, and you will soon be able to make out the cap-lamps of the trapped miners lying a few hundred yards inbye at the West Mine telephone station.

Next, though, came the much more sophisticated part of the brief. A few hours back, the Coal Board's bosses had learned a very harsh lesson from the experience of the first few brigades who entered the West Mine, and that was this. The trapped men had not taken kindly to their brigade colleagues failing to communicate directly with them. Indeed, it could even be argued that the brigades' initial brief to 'reconnoitre and report back', and not to remove their mouthpieces, had actually contrived to increase the men's sense of isolation, and in a few cases, to fuel the very embers of panic itself. A lesson taught, a lesson learned. Therefore, this time, the Coatbridge Brigade's brief was blunt and unequivocal.

'As soon as you reach the trapped miners, take your f - - - ing mouthpieces out and talk to them!'

The no-nonsense instruction continued. Remove your *Proto* gear, act as calmly as possible in the circumstances, and whatever you do, keep talking. Do everything you can to build up the men's morale and 'gee up their ginger'. For some of them, this alone could prove to be the difference between life and death, and of course, the last thing we need now is someone else having a panic attack.

Next explain, calmly but firmly, the general nature of the rescue plan and the use of the *Salvus* gear, all the while reminding them that Gibb McAughtrie has already made it out wearing *Salvus*. When the six-man brigades then start arriving to collect their three-man squads, fit a *Salvus* set onto each miner, issue him with clear instructions on its use and build up his confidence, making certain that he knows he'll have two escorts 'watching his arse' at all times.

Then, the really bad news for the Coatbridge team. You should remain in the West Mine operational zone for as long as humanly possible, ideally without any relief at all and until every last one of the trapped miners has gone. Yes, that will mean you will be working for many hours on end without breathing apparatus, and in an atmosphere of deteriorating quality and increasing peril. However, doing so will achieve two critically important strategic objectives. First of all, it will enable reliable, consistent instructions to be relayed to every one of the 116 men, as they prepare themselves physically and mentally for their treacherous journey. Secondly, it will build up their confidence and greatly reduce the likelihood of any of them losing their nerve and flying into a blind panic.

Finally, the Coatbridge team was informed that a succession of other rescue brigades would be forming a human chain through the irrespirable zone between the coal barrier and the Advanced Fresh Air Base. Those brigades' first job would be to pass a continuous supply of additional *Salvus* sets and cap-lamps along the chain, then through into the Knockshinnoch side for the Coatbridge boys to collect and deploy.

The briefing given by the designated instructor to all other rescue brigades followed the same pattern of near-military precision. They were to form a human chain all along the half-mile expanse of the irrespirable zone, right from the Advanced Fresh Air Base and onwards to the coal barrier. The distance between each man had to be progressively reduced as soon as additional Brigade members became available. Each new brigade, equipped with fully-charged oxygen cylinders, was to proceed straight to the head of the chain at the Knockshinnoch end, to allow those with dwindling oxygen reserves to retreat back towards the Advanced Fresh Air Base.

That, they were informed, was the general thrust of the operation. However, if any individual member of a brigade should discover that his oxygen supply was decreasing faster than that of his neebors, then he – and he alone – must seek the permission of his Captain to retire immediately to the Advanced Fresh

Air Base, leaving all other members of his own brigade to remain in position for as long as possible.

Next came the ruthless bit. Under no circumstances, unless clearly and specifically ordered from 'on high', was any attempt to be made to stretcher out any casualties, no matter how dire their physical condition. Furthermore, if any of the escaping miners were to collapse, absolutely nothing should be done to hinder the flow of the general rescue operation. Gibb McAughtrie's earlier evacuation had taught the top brass a very harsh lesson, and their instruction to the brigades was now brutally non-negotiable.

The brigade men had already been advised that it would probably take between 25 and 35 minutes for them to travel from Bank Six's Advanced Fresh Air Base to where the trapped men were assembled on The Castle side. Therefore, each brigade man should personally ensure that he had a plentiful enough supply of oxygen to cover the entire 'return journey'.

Every single piece of the jigsaw had now been brought to the table, and only one big question remained. Would all the pieces fit together in time to save 116 lives?

Nobody knew the answer to that one.

5.05 p.m.

Oversman Andy Houston opened his blue NCB notebook, and in the faint glow of his rapidly-weakening cap-lamp, stared at his pencil-written notes for the umpteenth time. No more changes now, Andy, he commanded himself. This is it, the very final list.

Houston had already explained to his men that they would be going out in 'threes', the oldest men first, then the youngest and finally those in the middle. However, several developments had since conspired make him reconsider the order of evacuation, not least Gibb McAughtrie's illness that had shot him to the very front of the queue. There had then followed a series of incidents, admittedly none quite as spectacular as McAughtrie's full-blown panic attack, but still sufficiently worrying to prompt the Oversman to promote a few of the younger, nervier lads a bit further up the list.

Crucially, at every stage in his deliberations, Houston had run his latest thinking past Dave Park. However, most importantly of all, he had also kept his men fully informed. His evacuation rota was now final, and while it didn't exactly meet with universal approval, it did command both respect and acceptance.

'Right boys,' Houston said calmly, but authoritatively. 'The next brigade will be coming in any minute now, so we need to get ourselves ready. The first three to go will be Juan Carrecedo, Jim Haddow and Tommy Currie. The Coatbridge boys will now get you ready. Good luck, lads. See you on the surface!'

A muffled chorus of 'good lucks' and a few other less refined platitudes rang around the telephone station, as the Coatbridge team approached the three elderly men. 'Auld Whang' Carracedo was the backshift's elder statesman, a man of proud Spanish descent and broken English diction that was a constant source of friendly leg-pulling down the pit. Haddow was a year his junior at 67, and while Currie was three years younger still, he carried the considerable additional burden of being a chronic asthmatic.

Houston's strategy was very clever. Get the oldest guys out first, and the morale of the remainder will shoot up instantly, generating a sort of, 'if the old buggers can do it, we can do it too,' mentality. Willie Halliday had promised to let Houston know the minute they reached the surface. It was now much too late to even think about any alternative outcome.

The Coatbridge team set about briefing the three conscripts on the detail of the journey they would make, and on the use of their *Salvus* breathing apparatus. The brigade men began securing the gear in place on each of them; oxygen cylinders across the lower back, and breathing bags containing the absorbent component over the stomach area. The fitting of the mouthpieces and nose clips would await the arrival of the first rescue brigade, to ensure that the three men's precious supplies of oxygen would not start flowing until the last possible moment. Only then would big oppressive gas masks be hauled down over anxious faces.

'Hold on a minute!' It was the distinctive voice of David Park. The Coal Board's Depute Labour Director shot to his feet. 'That rubber tubing's burst!'

And it was. The black hose on Jim Haddow's *Salvus* apparatus had developed a slight tear, almost certainly as a result of the Coatbridge men's unavoidable contortions when they had been scrambling through the hole in the coal barrier. The tear was so small that the only person who had noticed it was the very experienced *Salvus*-user, Park himself. However, it was still big enough to have caused Haddow an agonising demise from asphyxiation the moment he hit the irrespirable zone of Bank Six.

Park immediately removed the faulty *Salvus* from Haddow, and heaved it into a nearby cloth sack, whereupon the Coatbridge Captain handed another set to him for checking. From that moment onwards, Park would personally inspect every single set of *Salvus* equipment that came into the West Mine. Only when he had satisfied himself that each set was in proper working order would it then be fitted onto the next miner on the rota. Incredibly, before the day was out, Park would have chucked a total of 27 faulty *Salvus* sets into that same sack.

At 5.35 p.m., the Whitehill Rescue Brigade duly arrived to collect the first group of hopeful evacuees. Their instructions to the three men were unashamedly bereft of social niceties.

'Get rid o' your chowin' tobacco. Moothpiece oan. Nose clips oan. Gas mask ower your heid. Nae talkin', no' a bloody word. Your *Salvus* will get warm, so don't panic. And don't ever take it aff. And don't fa' doon, or you'll be left lyin' there. Right boys, aff we go!'

And off they went.

5.18 p.m.

No sooner had the big claustrophobic *Salvus* gas mask been hauled over Tommy Currie's head, than the old fellow's breathing began to labour.

Undaunted and driven by sheer determination to escape from this hellhole, he continued marching along Lanemark until he could march no further. Less than 200 yards from the telephone station, his latest asthma attack was in full flow, and this time it was a belter.

As the Coatbridge team scrambled to release the poor man's nose clips and mouthpiece in an attempt to get him breathing normally again, Willie Jolly's Whitehill Brigade marched on ahead with 'Auld Whang' and Jim Haddow. Time was of the essence, and sentiment was the enemy. The words of the instructors were still ringing in Jolly's ears. *If any of the miners should collapse, absolutely nothing should be done to hinder the flow of the general rescue operation.*

And so, through no fault of his own, Tommy Currie was left behind in the West Mine. As he sat there wheezing desperately for breath, he wondered if another chance of escape would ever come along again. Not only had he just 'missed his ben' in the queue, but he now found himself wondering how he would ever be able to breathe normally under the suffocating oppressiveness of that bloody great mask, nostrils clamped shut and false teeth grinding for dear life on a hard rubber mouthpiece. The moment Currie began thinking the unthinkable, his wheezing accelerated in synch with his anguish.

As many asthma sufferers will know to their own cost, the condition is a distressing and potentially very dangerous one. When an attack strikes, the patient is still able to breathe in, but not out. The tubes in the lungs, called 'bronchi', have some muscle around them and are lined by 'mucous membrane'. During normal respiration, the bronchi naturally expand on inspiration and narrow a little on expiration. However, during an asthma attack, the trigger (for example, an allergen or simply a bad case of nerves) causes those same muscles to go into spasm in response, which has the effect of narrowing the tubes even more on exhalation, prompting the mucous membranes to swell up and produce a copious, sticky phlegm which narrows and blocks the bronchi, further impeding exhalation. The patient's lungs become full of air - 'fixed in inspiration', the medics call it - and he/she then tries desperately to blow the air back out, which results in the characteristic wheezing associated with the condition. The upshot is oxygen starvation and a build-up of carbon dioxide, which itself then leads to 'cyanosis', turning the skin an unnatural bluish colour. In extreme cases, asthma can actually be a killer ('status asthmaticus'), even when treatment is ready to hand.

This, then, was not a good situation, and the Coatbridge team's priority was now crystal clear. They simply had to start getting the other miners out without delay. Sadly, Tommy Currie would have to wait.

Meanwhile, the Whitehill Brigade had succeeded in marching the two other elderly conscripts, Carroceda and Haddow, down to the coal barrier. Only eleven minutes it had taken them, and largely incident-free into the bargain. No doubt about it, for each successive journey that the brigades were now making to and from the West Mine, they were gradually becoming more and more familiar with the walk-out route, and the duration of the journey was shortening too. They were getting good at this.

However for Carroceda and Haddow, it had already been the journey from hell, and the worst by far was still to come. Unlike their esteemed rescue brigade colleagues, both were wholly unaccustomed to having their lives depending on self-contained breathing apparatus. For each of them, it just felt so horribly claustrophobic under that awful black rubber mask, having to rely on one little valve controlling the inhalation of life-sustaining oxygen, while another directed the carbon dioxide exhalation into a tiny plastic bag. The constant in-out, in-out 'hissing' underneath their gas masks gradually became louder and louder as the racing of their heartbeats accelerated with the sheer effort of a gruelling trek through the guts of the colliery. Very soon, that same hissing began to sound like a force-ten gale assaulting their eardrums.

With oxygen supplies fast diminishing and absolutely no time to lose, the group immediately began crawling through the hole in the barrier. Two brigade men led the way, followed by Carroceda, then two others, and then Haddow, with the last pair of brigade men bringing up the rear. When several minutes later Captain Willie Jolly shoved back the screen cloth at the far side, they were all through into Bank Six, thumbs-ups being flashed all around.

Jimmy McCreadie was amazed at just how well everything had been going. Far too well in fact:

'All of a sudden, we heard somebody talking. And the thing is that you cannae talk at all when you've got a *Salvus* gas mask over your head! I turned round, and there was Auld Whang blethering away to us as if he was sitting in the pit canteen! Well, we all dived on top of him, trying to shove his mouthpiece back in. There must have been more brigade men on top of Auld Whang than you'd get in a bloody rugby scrum!'

Juan Carroceda may not have known it at the time, but the Whitehill team's swift actions had just saved his life. Another few minutes inhaling an atmosphere in which almost all of the oxygen content had been forced out by fifty percent methane, and the old man would surely have been well on the way to meeting his maker. Instead, he was now able to behold the wondrous sight of the seemingly never-ending 'human chain' of brigade men's cap-lamps that irradiated his path homewards like twinkling stars in a heavenly sky. It was a vision that Auld Whang described as reminding him of 'Blackpool Illuminations'.

Juan Carroceda and Jim Haddow reached the Advanced Fresh Air Base in Bank Number Six Mine at 5.43 p.m. precisely. They both knew they had made it the very moment that their *Salvus* masks were ripped off their grinning, sweating faces. It had taken the rescue team only eighteen minutes to walk the two elderly miners from the West Mine telephone station to safety, a truly remarkable achievement.

McCreadie himself was in no doubt about the dreadful ordeal that both men had endured:

'When the men came out through from the Knockshinnoch side into Bank Six, the tops of their heads would be burning, because of the gas and the sudden change in pressure and temperature. We knew we could get them out from the West Mine and through to the Advanced Fresh Air Base in about twenty minutes, but for them with their *Salvus* masks on, and in all that gas, it would be a gey long twenty minutes.'

Next, Carroceda and Haddow had to negotiate a further short trek to the main Fresh Air Base, their heads still 'nippin' like buggery' from the effects of the firedamp in the irrespirable zone that they had just come through. There followed a quick medical check-up for each of them from New Cumnock's own Doctor Fyfe, after which Carroceda was told to remain where he stood, his weary arms draped over a brigade man on either side, while Haddow was marched on ahead.

'Give him two!' the good doctor commanded John Wilson, Knockshinnoch's much revered 'senior first-aider', and the mask of a *Novox* respirator was shoved over his face.

'Two big deep breaths, Whang,' said Wilson, and a couple of blasts of clean oxygen filled his lungs.

'Would you like a wee nip, Whang?' Wilson then asked the old man, shoving a small glass of brandy into his fist. Carroceda, himself not a particularly keen drinker, necked it in an instant.

There was still the best part of a mile to go before Juan Carroceda and Jim Haddow would be able to wallow once more in the glorious spectacle of the New Cumnock daylight. Almost three days it had been, three long tortuous days buried alive in a stinking black tomb. Yes, the mile-long trek would be exhausting, especially on near-empty bellies, but they were on their way.

On their way home.

6.07 p.m.

At first, the massed ranks of onlookers standing on the Bank Auld Pit's grassy banking stared in bemusement.

They could just make out three figures emerging from the brick-built frontage of Bank Number Six dook, but no one had the faintest idea of their identity. The faces of all three were blackened by coal dust, a familiar sight for loved ones welcoming their menfolk back home from the pit after a hard day's toil. However, with only the whites of their eyes distinguishable from the muck disguising their facial features, it was impossible to tell who was who.

The only clue was the demeanour of the one in the middle. Wearing a heavy jacket, he looked stooped and elderly, and he appeared to be screwing up his eyes, almost as if he was staring straight into the midday sun. Not only that, but he was being oxtered out of the dook by two much younger-looking men wearing singlet vests. And the old fellow was smiling. Smiling the biggest smile that this little neck of the woods had seen in a very long time.

Someone in the crowd shouted.

'It's Whang! It's Auld Whang!'

All of a sudden the crowd started cheering. People began to surge forward towards the dook, bursting straight through the police cordon, the boys-in-blue only just managing to keep them from mobbing the three men. This really was the moment they all had been waiting for. Not only had another of the trapped miners now been rescued from the tomb that was Knockshinnoch, but Juan Carroceda was the oldest man in the whole pit and he had walked out. Bloody walked out!

'Look, there's another one!' came a shout from the midst of the crowd.

This time, the focus of attention was another elderly gent with his arms draped over two youthful muscular necks, his face unrecognisable beneath three days of sweaty grime. The cheering continued, only this time accompanied by tears. Tears of relief, tears of joy.

Now, surely, the rest will follow? Please, God, please!

Meanwhile, down in the West Mine, the telephone bell once more tried its best to attract human attention. Andy Houston lifted the receiver, heart in mouth. It was Halliday again.

'Auld Whang and Jim Haddow are out! Both safe and well, Andy! Eighteen minutes it took them to reach the Advanced Fresh Air Base. Only eighteen minutes!'

The Oversman turned once more to address his troops, the faintest grin betraying his customarily stoical expression.

'A wee bit of news, boys. Auld Whang's out!'

The men started whooping and hollering, handshakes all around. Houston raised the palm of his hand for silence, and got it immediately.

'Auld Whang made it through in eighteen minutes. So, boys, there's no reason why you lot can't make it in twenty!'

6.55 p.m.

As the big white ambulance screeched away from the Bank Auld Pit with its bell clanging and blue light flashing, the mood among the waiting crowds had shot up considerably.

Buoyed by the successful evacuation of both Juan Carroceda and Jim Haddow, every man, woman and child standing on the grassy slopes of the pit-head was now beginning to believe that they might – just might – see their beloved menfolk again. However, fear still hung heavily in the chilly autumnal air.

What if another big lump of Wilson's field should suddenly give way and send another huge 'tidal' wave of sludge surging further inbye, completely cutting off the rest of the trapped men from all hope of rescue? And what if the firedamp levels in the West Mine should continue to increase, leaving them hopelessly defenceless against a silent, malevolent killer? Or a roof fall, for heaven's sake, at any point along the mile and a half length of saturated, derelict old roadways in Bank Six? Good God, even a spark from a pit boot's metal stud, just one little innocent spark, could cause a catastrophe of Armageddon-like proportions in the gas-laden old mine.

Yes, hope was rising by the minute, but it was cautious hope laced with gut-wrenching trepidation.

The main rescue operation was now well and truly under way, as millions of captivated listeners all around the world found their ears welded to radio sets. Incredibly, by the time the assorted New Cumnock clocks had struck 'seven' on that most auspicious of Saturday evenings, 25 of the trapped miners had made it through to the safety of the Advanced Fresh Air Base in Bank Six, 11 of whom had since been taken up to the surface in the old mine's man-riding haulage. As each of them made his triumphant entrance from the blackness of the dook, whether on foot or by stretcher, screams of delight and cries of joy split the overcast heavens above.

Meanwhile, still down in the depths of Bank Six, Highhouse Colliery's George Harvey was still beavering away at his voluntary duties while his rescue brigade father, Willie, continued to perform the vital role of replenishing the spent *Salvus* sets to prepare them to be passed back along the line in the irrespirable zone, then through to the miners in Knockshinnoch:

'It was a very clever and well-thought-out plan,' George reflected, clearly proud of his father's and his own contribution. 'The brigade men, wearing *Proto*, escorted the miners, who wore *Salvus*, first through the hole in the coal barrier and then along the human chain of other brigade men in the gas-filled zone, until they reached the Advanced Fresh Air Base. The brigade men themselves were then relieved in rotation as their oxygen supplies diminished, with new men coming in to replace them. The volunteers like myself were only allowed to go as far as the Base, so we formed another chain back along the road to the foot of the dook. A very, very clever plan.'

Dan Park was another one of the many links in that same human chain:

'Our chain was two at a time, about a hundred yards apart, all along the one and a half mile long road back towards the main dook, and our job was to help the miners along the chain to the next pair of volunteers. Some of the men were out on their feet with pure exhaustion, and had to get a lift in the hutches to the pit-head. Mind you, some of them were too proud to hitch a lift, so they insisted on walking up the dook under their own steam!'

25 men out, and only another 91 to go. Surely it would all be plain sailing from hereon in?

7.00 p.m.

Just after seven o'clock, there was a loud knock on Jean McMurdo's big front door.

'It was Ian McKelvie from Ayr, but he had been staying with his mother-in-law in New Cumnock that weekend. In fact, the whole world seemed to be living in New Cumnock that weekend. All he said was, "Right Jean, come on and I'll take you up to the pit, because I don't think it will be long till John gets out". Up until then, I had resisted going to the pit-head, because I didn't want to get in the way of the emergency services. What good could I have done up there anyway?

My place was at home with the baby. When Ian came in, though, I realised that my place was now to be there when John came up, so my mother came over to look after the baby, and Ian drove me up to the pit-head.'

At roughly the same time, May Robertson sat staring out of the front window of her in-laws' house in the Leggate. They had advised her to stay put, rather than walk up to the pit-head, which they felt would be even more distressing for her:

> 'I watched as the ambulances went by, and I could see the men's faces at the windows. They were smiling, waving to the crowds lining the pavements. But no John, still no John. I had been fine up until then, but that was when I really started fretting. It was awful.'

Jessie Lopez, however, had other ideas, and two very good reasons for having them. Both her husband, Willie, and her father, Bill Lee, were among the trapped men, and Jessie felt that her place was to be at the Bank Auld Pit at the moment of their freedom:

> 'Nobody knew at the time exactly who had been trapped in the West Mine, and who had gone missing elsewhere,' recalled Jessie. 'However, I knew that Willie worked in the West Mine, and that my Dad had been working "up tae the daisies" in Number Five Heading, which was where the big crater now was. Both of them liked a wee smoke, so I took two packets of Capstan cigarettes with me up to the pit-head, one for Willie and the other for my Dad.'

And so, as a total of nineteen full rescue brigades and countless volunteers continued cajoling and dragging the miners all along the two-mile walk-out route from their Knockshinnoch tomb to the sanctity of the Bank dook, the womenfolk on the surface wrung their hands in pleading hope of their imminent return.

7.20 p.m.

A total of 29 of the trapped miners had now made it through safely to the Fresh Air Base in Bank Six, including the inimitable Jim 'Buffer' Carmichael. The 'ventriloquist's dummy', who had done so much to raise his neebors' morale, had escaped at last from the bowels of hell, but it would be some time yet before the 'ventriloquist' himself, Dave Jess, would be reunited with him.

All the while, messages were being relayed from Knockshinnoch's makeshift Headquarters on the surface down to the old rickety telephone below, which miraculously was still managing to receive them. Each call enabled Andy Houston to announce his latest 'news flash', as the remarkably resilient Oversman continued to fulfil his solemn promise and keep his men fully informed.

'Another news flash, boys! 7.20 p.m., and 29 men through to the Advanced Fresh Air Base, thirteen now on the surface!'

No cheering as such, only respectful, hopeful applause. Spirits rising by the minute, eyes closing in silent prayer, but air quality dropping in synch. Things were going well, but time was running out fast, and the men in the West Mine knew it. Tommy Currie just sat there, his eyes closed tightly in the dawning realisation that his chances of getting out alive were seriously haemorrhaging by the minute.

Meanwhile up above, Messrs McCardel, McDonald, Stewart, Dyer, Dick, Bone and Halliday could scarcely believe just how smoothly the main rescue operation was going. 29 men out already, including most of the elderly, and hardly one single incident of note. Thanks in huge part to the courage and dedication of the rescue brigades and volunteers, the eagle eyes of Dave Park, the calm leadership of Andy Houston, and of course the sheer guts and resilience of the trapped miners themselves. However, if long experience had taught General Manager David McCardel anything about life, then it was this.

When something looks too good to be true … it normally is.

8.10 p.m.

The rescue men from Coatbridge were now flagging badly, no doubt about it.

As they stood there fitting a seemingly never-ending supply of *Salvus* gas masks over the sweating foreheads of petrified miners lining up in the rapidly deteriorating atmospheric conditions of Knockshinnoch Colliery's West Mine, they cast an occasional glance at their own *Proto* devices lying discarded on the pit floor. Their own tickets back to the glorious fresh air of the surface, tickets rendered redundant by unshakeable professionalism and unconditional determination to get their own 'brothers' out first. As the firedamp levels continued to rise, time was now the fearsome enemy.

Meanwhile at the Advanced Fresh Air Base in Bank Six, 39 miners had now made it through, with 21 of them having then been hauled out onto the Bank Auld Pit hillside to the triumphant cheers and sobs of relief from waiting relatives, friends and neighbours. By ten past eight, Buffer Carmichael, Wull Gray, John Robertson and Sam Capstick – four of the men who had so hugely influenced the proceedings down below – had reached terra firma and were now in the arms of their loved ones, if only for a few seconds before being whisked off to nearby Ballochmyle Hospital in one of the ambulances in the waiting armada.

Mercifully, the 'roll-call log' at the underground base was growing by the minute, as was the list of names of the rescued men scrawled on the single piece of 'foolscap' paper that was pinned to the Bank Auld Pit office wall. The list was critically important and guarded very carefully. After all, the gaunt, deathly pale features of men exhausted from thirst, starvation and unimaginable stress were somewhat less familiar underneath umpteen layers of coal dust, in the slowly diminishing light of that chilly September evening.

The mood on the pit-head had changed dramatically. For some, faces which had been contorted in terror for almost three days were now smiling again. Smiling and laughing, the tears of hopelessness and anguish replaced by tears of joy and relief.

For the others, though, the nightmare continued. Time was running out fast, and they all knew it.

8.12 p.m.

Fireman Alex 'Eck' Clapperton's do-or-die journey along the walkout route was dominated by one continuous, overriding thought:

'Whoever suggested using the *Salvus* to get us out of there should have got a medal! It was a stroke of genius. The rescue brigades came in carrying the *Salvus* sets, and when it was your turn, a brigade man then fitted one onto you and gave you instructions on how to use it. I remember you had a mouthpiece, and a nose clip, and an oxygen cylinder. They told us, "Don't touch anything, leave everything as it is and it will last 30 minutes, just do your best". It was a completely new experience with the *Salvus* on. We were told that the older ones would be going first, then the younger ones. I was 28 at the time, so I was somewhere around the middle.'

Up until Clapperton's 'ben', the main rescue operation had being going remarkably smoothly. However, his own journey would turn out to be anything but smooth:

'I knew Waterhead Dook very well. It was fairly steep, about one-in-four as I recall. So there we were with our *Salvus* gas masks on, unable to speak to each other. Suddenly, the Brigade Captain turned down the wrong dook and signalled for us to follow him. Well, I knew every inch of the pit around that area, so I waved at them to come back up. Luckily they did, and we then managed to get back into the right dook and find our way down to the coal barrier.'

A very lucky break, then, the day only saved by the swift reactions of a young miner with judgement and experience well beyond his years:

'The hole in the coal barrier wasn't that bad, say about four feet square, the height of the bottom coal seam. We couldn't walk through, so we had to sort of crouch and scramble through. While we were going through the hole, one of the other boys suddenly lost his mouthpiece, and there was a wee bit of a stooshie. A brigade man quickly put him on his own airline, while another one managed to fit his mouthpiece back into place, and all was well again. The journey through the gas-contaminated area wasn't too bad really, because we knew we were on our way home. It was a fair walk, especially wearing the *Salvus*, but when we reached the Advanced Fresh Air Base and got our gas masks removed it was a tremendous relief. The first person I recognised was Doctor Fyfe, who gave me a quick medical check-up. I remember saying to him, "That's me, doctor, I'm going home now", but he replied, "Oh no you're not, you'll be going straight to Ballochmyle Hospital!"'

Alex Clapperton had made it through alive, and he was a very grateful young man. However, his lasting sentiment wasn't simply one of gratitude that his own neck had been saved, but one of great sorrow for those who would not enjoy that particular privilege:

> 'We had been told that two of the men working in Number Five Heading when the field caved in - John White and Sam Rowan – had swapped their shifts earlier in the day so that they could be on the backshift, rather than the dayshift. I don't think anything more needs to be said.'

Eck Clapperton's only thoughts were for his 'brothers'.

8.15 p.m.

Just as Eck Clapperton's group had departed from Knockshinnoch's West Mine, escorted by their allotted rescue brigade, yet another team was preparing to set off in the opposite direction to collect the next trio of hopeful miners.

This time it was the Kames Colliery team, from the nearby village of Muirkirk, and their brief was no different from those they had been handed on their earlier missions. Get the next group of miners fitted out in their *Salvus* gear and get their backsides out of that pit, post haste. Any questions? No? Right, get bloody well on with it.

However, once the Kames boys had descended the Bank Six dook and hiked their way along to the Fresh Air Base in preparation for their latest perilous sojourn into the guts of Knockshinnoch, their mission changed spectacularly. There they were met by New Cumnock's Doctor Fyfe, who immediately proceeded to set them a challenge for which even Willie Dick's legendary 'torture chamber' training could never have prepared them. The doctor addressed his question to the Brigade Captain.

'Who in your team knows most about first-aid and emergency medical procedures?'

'We've all had basic first-aid training, doctor.'

'That's not what I asked, Captain. I asked who in your team knows most.'

Blank stares, the Kames boys looking around at each other for inspiration. Finally, every pair of eyes had homed in on Douglas Hazell.

'That'll be Dougie, doctor,' the Captain announced, uncomfortably.

'Come over here a minute,' the doctor commanded Hazell. 'You too, Captain.'

Doctor Fyfe then proceeded to explain the latest development briefly, but very carefully. There was now a desperate situation on the other side of the coal barrier. One of the oldest miners, Tommy Currie, was an asthmatic. Twice the Coatbridge boys in the West Mine had put the *Salvus* on him, and twice the old guy had been overcome by an asthma attack. On the second occasion, he had made it as far as the coal barrier, only to collapse wheezing and gasping for dear life as soon as he started crawling through the hole. Now there was only one last hope for Currie, an intravenous injection of adrenaline, and if he didn't get the injection very soon, he would die.

'If I show you how to give the injection, will you do it, Mister Hazell?' the doctor pleaded, a big pair of earnest eyes staring expectantly at the brigade man in the dust-swirling beam of his cap-lamp.

'I'll try, doctor,' replied Hazell. 'I'll do my best.'

'That's all I ask, son,' Doctor Fyfe nodded. 'Well done.'

When the Kames Brigade men eventually scrambled down out of the hole in the barrier and into the Knockshinnoch side, Tommy Currie was sitting there on the pit floor, his head propped up against the coal wall behind him. His heavily strained face looked a ghoulish blue colour in the dim light, and he was still gasping for breath. The fact that he was even there at all was remarkable enough in itself, and due entirely to a truly magnanimous gesture from two of his neebors. Having missed his 'ben' because of an earlier asthma attack, Currie had already resigned himself to being among the last in the queue now, only for Jim Riddell and Matt Sanderson to step aside and let the old man go before them, an act of incredible courage.

Dougie Hazell didn't hang around exploring the social dynamics, though. He took the full syringe out of its plastic container, and rolled up Currie's sleeve. Their eyes met for an instant, and Hazell could tell immediately that the old man had all but had it.

'F - - - it,' he muttered under his breath. 'He's gonnae die anyway if I don't, so here goes.'

Following Doctor Fyfe's instructions to the letter, Hazell pierced Currie's exposed upper arm with the sterilised hypodermic needle and pressed the syringe. The old man was so far gone that the jab didn't even register. In went two-thirds of the syringe's contents, exactly as the doctor had ordained, and now all Hazell could do was wait.

Adrenaline, the 'fight or flight' hormone, has the effect of increasing the heart-rate and diverting blood from skin to muscle, causing the patient to go deathly pale, which Tommy Currie most certainly did immediately after Hazell's injection. It also mobilises glycogen from the liver to produce copious quantities of glucose, and this immediately generates energy. In the words of a medical colleague, 'it is fearsome stuff to use, and the patient perks up no end as the heart-rate increases, causing him to either start breathing normally again … or drop dead'.

Mercifully for Tommy Currie, it was the former, not the latter. A few minutes later, he was once more inside the hole in the coal barrier, this time being shoved and pulled on a stretcher, a procedure which had only recently been given special authorisation from on high. Suddenly, about half-way through the hole, and to the Brigade men's horror, the old man began wheezing again.

Lying there with at least fifteen feet still to negotiate of hauling Currie's frame through to the other side, Hazell's mind shot into overdrive. If the doctor wanted me to give Currie only two-thirds of the syringe's contents, then why the hell did he give me a full one? Again he muttered to himself, this time in the full and blinding knowledge that he was about to take the biggest calculated risk of his life. He fumbled for the plastic container, found it, and removed the syringe once more. He then pulled the old man's sleeve back up.

'Damn it, here goes again.'

In went the remainder of the adrenaline, and the Kames team resumed their lung-bursting manoeuvring of Currie through the hole. Once through the screen cloth and into the gassed-out area of Bank Six, he was no longer wheezing or gasping for breath. He's either fine or he's dead, thought Hazell, as he shone the beam of his cap-lamp into the old man's face. To Hazell's astonishment, the old fellow smiled and gave him an immediate thumbs-up.

It would be another 45 minutes before Tommy Currie would find himself being stretchered out into the glorious sweetness of the New Cumnock air and rushed into a waiting ambulance. By then, Dougie Hazell and the rest of his exhausted Kames Brigade neebors would have been declared unfit for further work, and stood down indefinitely.

For the rescue brigades, this was punishing stuff, but they were getting there. Slowly but surely, they were getting their 'brothers' out of that tomb.

8.22 p.m.

With 39 men now out and safely through to the Advanced Fresh Air Base, the telephone in the West Mine rang once again. Andy Houston answered it. This time it was the big chief himself, McCardel.

'Mister Houston, we now need you to come out,' he told his Oversman. 'We need you up here without delay.'

Houston began to protest, reminding the General Manager that he had given very careful consideration to the order of evacuation, and discussed it openly with the men. He was the Oversman after all, and as such he should be the last man out. The captain going down with his ship, and all that.

Houston's protestations fell on deaf ears. He was now needed on the surface, primarily because of his intimate knowledge of the layout in and around Number Five Heading. McCardel explained that the main rescue mission was going well, and that he wanted a number of the emergency services to start turning their attention to the crater in Wilson's field, underneath which a total of thirteen men were still 'missing'. In that regard, Houston's familiarity with the Number Five terrain would be invaluable, and as such he should come out of the West Mine with the very next group, leaving Dave Park in charge of the remainder of the evacuation operation.

Unsurprisingly, Park himself then accepted the GM's decision without demur, and reassured Houston that his place was now up on the surface helping the top brass to try to locate the missing miners.

Meanwhile, Matt Sanderson clocked a rather unsavoury incident, as the air quality in the West Mine continued to plummet:

> 'Well through the rescue operation, the name "Alex" was called. Alex was often deep in thought, and dreamy. There was a pause, and a man who was not Alex stepped forward. Our eyes met, and he dropped his. He accepted the mouthpiece and left. When Alex came forward the next time, the man with the names sheet said, "come on Alex, you lost your ben, you should have gone with the last team". But he should not have missed his turn. His name should have been shouted a second time, louder.'

Clearly, the conditions in the West Mine were now deteriorating very rapidly, and the men's anxiety levels rising exponentially. Indeed, so bad was the atmosphere by then that the Coatbridge Brigade found themselves with no alternative but to issue a rather sobering instruction to the remaining 77 trapped miners:

'The air quality was getting bad, really bad,' said Jock McMurdo. 'So we were told, "right boys, lie flat on the floor, where the air will be a wee bit better." It was then that we knew time was definitely running out.'

And it was running out fast.

9.02 p.m.

Just after nine o'clock on the Saturday evening, 55 men had now made it through to the Advanced Fresh Air Base, with 33 having reached the surface. A few minutes back, Alex 'Eck' Clapperton had taken his first gulp of the fresh New Cumnock air for almost three days. It tasted like nectar from heaven.

Now, Oversman Andy Houston was about to emerge from the Bank dook into the blinding spotlights illuminating the pit-head, thereafter to be whisked away from the cheering crowds into a waiting NCB van headed for Knockshinnoch's temporary HQ. For Houston, a trip to Ballochmyle Hospital would have to wait, because there was still work to be done. His lungs felt good inhaling the cool, clean air again, but his heart weighed heavily at the thought of the men he had left behind in the depths of Knockshinnoch.

At almost exactly the same moment down in the West Mine, another three miners' names were being bawled out by the hardy boys from Coatbridge. By that stage, the escaping miners were now facing the added burden of setting off on their perilous two-mile journey with their lungs already contaminated by deadly firedamp gas.

Sure, the oxygen flowing from the cylinders on their backs into their *Salvus* masks would do its best to keep them alive as their respiratory systems converted it into carbon dioxide, which itself would then be absorbed harmlessly by the chemicals in the breathing bags over their midriffs. However, as far as the methane itself was concerned, it would receive neither conversion nor absorption, and the damned stuff would continue coursing through the miners' lungs for the entire duration of their journey, wreaking havoc with their senses.

One of the names on the 'ben' this time around was that of Jock McMurdo, who was about to commence a truly nightmarish hour-long journey:

'By the time it was my turn to leave, the air was so bad that we were already lying flat on our backs on the pit floor. I will never forget the journey out wearing the *Salvus* mask. The air quality was so poor that I had a terrible headache from the strong smell of gas. I really thought the roof of my head was going to burst. It felt as if the journey would never end. It was eerie, but I managed to walk out by myself. Occasionally, you would pass the rescue team, only their lights showing in the darkness. There was a horn or bell on the equipment that you could use if you got into trouble. When I eventually got through to the Fresh Air Base, I was totally exhausted.'

To the throngs of anxious relatives and onlookers still standing on the grassy banking of the Bank Auld Pit, it seemed like an eternity since old Juan Carroceda had emerged triumphantly from the Bank dook as the first 'walking man'. It had been three hours now, three excruciatingly long hours.

Now, exactly half of the trapped men - 58 in total - had made it through to the safety of the Base, a fair number of whom still faced the long and arduous trek to the foot of the Bank dook, before being bundled into the rake's waiting hutches and hauled up to the pit-head to behold the laughter and tears of joyous reunion that awaited them. For the last few who had fought their way through the gassed-out roadways with increasing quantities of methane hindering their breathing, the journey had been a truly hellish one.

However, for the other 58 miners still down in the West Mine waiting anxiously for their names to be called out, the atmosphere they would breathe continued to deteriorate by the minute. Three hours it had taken so far, and another three it would still take to get all of the remaining men out of there. The big question was whether or not the air quality would hold up.

Again, absolutely nobody knew the answer to that one.

9.10 p.m.

'We had all been told that we would be wearing the *Salvus* gear,' said Willie Lopez. 'The brigade men gave us the low-down on how to use it. They told us, "If you feel it getting warm, don't panic, just keep going

275

and you'll be fine," and they assured us that a brigade man would be there with us every step of the way. You couldn't speak to one another or hear anything. We went down Waterhead Dook, and crawled through the hole into the higher workings of the Bank side, then into the gassed-out roadways of Bank Six. The feeling when I eventually made it to the Advanced Fresh Air Base and got my *Salvus* mask taken off was unbelievable. I had made it through!'

However, for Willie, the most emotional part of the journey was the reception he received at the Base, something he certainly hadn't expected:

'Doctor Fyfe was there waiting for us, and he gave us all a quick medical check-up. I'll always remember John Wilson, the pit's first-aid man. As soon as I got there, John walked up to me and gave me a great big cuddle. That was when it finally sunk in that I had made it. I was going home!'

Precisely twenty minutes later, another three men were being dragged by the rescue brigades into the Advanced Fresh Air Base, where their respective *Salvus* masks were immediately ripped off their coal dust-caked faces. As the threesome began gulping the stale air of Bank Six, the burly guy in the middle raised one hand to command attention.

'What is it, son?' John Wilson enquired, slightly concerned. 'Are you trying to say something? Take your time, son, just take your time.'

Eventually his respiration began to slow down, just sufficiently to allow him to stun everyone gathered at the Base by bursting into rather breathless song:

> The Bonnie Lass … the Bonnie, Bonnie Lass!
> The Bonnie Lass o' Ballochmyle!

The Master of Ceremonies had made it through. Dave Jess was on his way back home to Mattie and the weans.

10.03 p.m.

The longest hours of Jean McMurdo's life were the three she spent standing on the hillside waiting for her husband Jock to appear from the depths of Bank Six.

'I stood up at the Bank Pit for ages. It seemed like an eternity. All we had been told was that the older and younger ones were being brought out first. Since John was in the "middle" age group, I knew he would be towards the end, but I had no idea exactly where or when. His lamp number was 57, and for some reason that number was in my head, even although I thought it probably had nothing to do with the order of evacuation. I never actually saw John coming up in the hutches. It was a dark night and I was standing up the hill a bit. It would be just after ten o'clock when a Coal Board official came up to me and told me that John was out. The man then took me over to a big building, and there he was, standing all on his own. He looked completely washed out, and he didn't say much at all, other than something like, "Am I glad to see you!" They only gave us a few minutes together, before he was "wheeched" away to the hospital.'

Jessie Lopez's recollection of husband Willie's return some seven minutes later was of a moment of very mixed emotions. Jessie had turned up at the Bank Pit that evening with her two packets of Capstan cigarettes in her coat pocket. Happily, she was soon reunited with Willie on the pit-head, but tragically, she would never see her father Bill Lee again, since Bill was one of the thirteen 'missing men' who had been working in Number Five Heading. From that auspicious moment of reunion, Willie Lopez decreed that he would never smoke another cigarette for the rest of his life.

Ten minutes later, the gregarious Dave Jess was in the arms of his beloved Mattie, while another ten later still, locomotive driver Walls Walker was hugging his full-term pregnant wife, Jessie.

81 men had now reached the safety of the Advanced Fresh Air Base, with only 35 more to go. Yet still the Coal Board's top brass and their magnificent rescue services refused to count their chickens.

After all, with the firedamp level in Knockshinnoch's West Mine now at seven percent, they didn't even dare.

11.05 p.m.

Young Rab Cockburn was one of the tail-enders. Not of his own choosing, of course.

'I was in the last twenty or so to leave the West Mine, because there weren't many of us left by that stage. I really don't remember having felt hungry at any time. All I wanted was to get out, and I knew I would be one of the very last to leave. The brigade men fitted my *Salvus* gas mask over my head, and off we went, with a rescue worker leading the way and one at the back. The *Salvus* wasn't as heavy as I thought it would be. I remember going down the steep gradient of Waterhead Dook, and crawling through the hole in the barrier and into the 'no-go' area of the Bank mine. The brigade men just continued walking calmly, and we walked just as calmly beside them. All I could see in front of me was a long line of lights, about twenty or thirty yards apart. These were the cap-lamps of the brigade men, who were there to help you if you got into bother. The sight of those lights gave me a huge feeling of confidence.'

However, it was only when Rab arrived at the Fresh Air Base that he realised he had made it:

'We realised we still had another mile or so to go yet before we would be back on the surface, but when we reached the Advanced Fresh Air Base we knew we had done it. When my *Salvus* gas mask was removed, it was a great relief. There were several doctors there, and one of them gave me a check-up. I was still breathing very heavily, and he said to me, "Have you been running, son?" That comment made me laugh, and the doctor laughed too. Just at that, I spotted my own doctor, Doctor Fyfe. I looked over at him and said, "I've got an awfu' headache, doctor". He came straight over and handed me a bar of chocolate, then he turned to the others and said, "Look after this one, he's one of mine!" I never went up the Bank dook in any of the bogies, I just decided to walk up. When I reached the surface, I saw two men running over towards me. They were my brothers – Boncha and Gum, were their nicknames – and they oxtered me up the hill to where the ambulances were lining up to take us to hospital. There were an awful lot of folk on the pit-head, and they were clapping and cheering. I remember hearing one woman say, "Oh look, there's that wee boy we ken!" It was me they were talking about! It just felt great being out again.'

Exactly 100 men out, sixteen still to go.

11.25 p.m.

By the time it was Sam McCracken's turn to leave, the air in the West Mine was foul and stinking beyond description.

The remaining trapped miners still lay flat-out on the pit floor, in a desperate attempt to avoid inhaling the lighter methane gas as it swirled invisibly yet menacingly just above their heads. All the while, sheer guts and dogged determination kept the men of the 'permanent' Coatbridge Rescue Brigade darting around on their own weary pins, working their guts out in the same toxic atmosphere.

For Sam McCracken, the moment of highest drama came right at the very start of his make or break journey. It was his own *Salvus* apparatus. There was something wrong with it, and he told the brigade men exactly that. For the best part of five hours now, Dave Park had been checking and re-checking each and every set of *Salvus* apparatus, before permitting the Coatbridge boys to fit one onto each successive miner. True to his word, Park had already checked and approved the one that was now being pulled over Sam McCracken's head, making sure that there were no leaks that could have spelled disaster:

'The thing about my *Salvus* was that it felt really slack around my head. So I told the brigade man, and he set about adjusting it. When he handed it back to me, it felt slacker than ever. He then said "that's it", and off we went. I really didn't think the thing would work properly, and I was very nervous indeed. Mind you, it must have been fine. When we crawled through the hole in the coal barrier and into the contaminated workings of Bank Six, there must have been some kind of roof fall, because we had to clamber over some big piles of loose rock. I remember thinking how impressed I was that the rescue brigades had managed to haul those huge extractor fans all the way down from the surface over the piles of rock. It was then a good walk to the Advanced Fresh Air Base, and when we got there I couldn't get my *Salvus* mask off fast enough! Doctor Fyfe gave me a quick medical, then somebody handed me a wee glass of brandy. I had made it!'

Unlike his neebor, Rab Cockburn, Sam McCracken was then ushered straight into the man-riding haulage, to a clear instruction bawled out by the rake-runner.

'Keep your heids doon, for fear o' the condition o' the auld roofs!'

Sam's entrance into the cool, fresh New Cumnock air was a sensation that will live with him forever. Another quick medical examination, this time from Doctor Edgar, and he was then whisked into a waiting ambulance, en route to Ballochmyle Hospital.

Medical examinations, ambulances and hospitals; nothing but minor inconveniences after all he had been through. In a few hours' time, it would all be worth it.

Sam would be back home again.

11.33 p.m.

When the names of Knockshinnoch stalwarts Matt Sanderson and Andrew McDicken were eventually called out by Dave Park, only thirteen of the men on Thursday's ill-fated backshift were now left in the West Mine.

'We were bloody lucky,' Andrew insisted. 'We had being lying flat on our backs on the pit floor, because of the gas. Just before we got led away by the brigades, a Fireman tested the air again and we all realised that the firedamp level was now exceptionally high. We knew that there was next to no time left. The *Salvus* apparatus was all right, but it was heavy. A big black rubber gas mask over your head, and the breathing bag going out-and-in all the time. I never found it suffocating as such, because I knew we needed to get out of there, and fast. Matt Sanderson was in my group, but I can't remember anyone else. You couldn't speak or hear anything with the *Salvus* on, and that's what nearly cost us our lives!'

One part of the journey made Andrew's blood run cold:

'There was supposed to be somebody waiting for us along the road, but nobody was. The brigade man at the front just kept marching on, straight past the slope-road to the barrier. I couldn't believe my eyes, because I knew that area of the pit like the back of my hand. He would have led us into a road that was full of gas. So I just stopped walking and started waving my hands furiously, trying to tell the brigade men that they were going in the wrong direction. The Captain just signalled back, telling us to keep following him, so I just sat down and refused to budge. If we had followed him, we'd have lost our lives, no doubt about it. Eventually, he just gave up and followed me back up the dook, and I pointed down into the slope-road. We then got to the hole in the barrier in no time. There was plenty of room going through the hole, about two yards square, and we just had to scramble through into the old Bank Six workings.'

Matt Sanderson's take was remarkably, if frighteningly, similar:

'Andrew McDicken was in my group, although I forget who the third man was. What I do remember was a brigade man leading us beyond the slope-road that went to the hole. We carried on until Andrew made a noise through his mouthpiece to stop the brigade man, signalling that we had passed the slope-road. The brigade man insisted that we stayed with him and we set off again. After a short distance, Andrew refused to go another step, and got his point through that he worked in this area and was familiar with the layout. Andrew started back up the dook. The brigade men and the other two of us followed, and we were soon crawling through the hole at the barrier. Shortly afterwards, my head started to swim and I began to feel really ill. I realised that I needed to get my head down or I was going to faint. I stopped, and putting both hands on my knees, I lowered my head. I could not have been far from the Fresh Air Base. The brigade man came to my side. He did not ask any questions, but hit my mouthpiece and nose clip off, and putting his hand under my oxter he asked me to move. He propelled me forward at a smart pace, and then there were two lights ahead. I had made it through. The two lights I had seen ahead of me belonged to Doctor Andrew Fyfe, our local doctor, and John Wilson, Knockshinnoch's senior first-aid man. Doctor Fyfe asked, "How do you feel?" to which I replied that my head was pounding. He pointed to the floor and said, "Down there!" I lay down on the pavement, and the doctor said to John Wilson, "Give him three". John was kneeling at an oxygen cylinder. He gave me the mask, and I took three good intakes of oxygen. My head cleared immediately, and Doctor Fyfe said, "On your way". There was no tittle-tattle or wasted words, only essential first-aid. I would not be more than two minutes at the Fresh Air Base.'

Matt's reflections on his own personal drama could hardly have been more humble or self-critical:

'I do not know if it was personal weakness further up the walk, or if I was running out of oxygen. I don't know who the brigade man was, nor did I get time to thank him.'

Matt was then met by his brother George, himself also a Knockshinnoch miner, who walked him along to the foot of the main Bank dook, from where he hitched a lift in the rake. However, it was the reception on the pit-head which really surprised Matt:

'When we eventually reached the surface, I was a wee bit taken aback, when after walking unaided uphill to the man-riding station, someone then put a blanket over my shoulders and took my arm across to the baths. We were not allowed to wash at the baths, and we were sent to Ballochmyle Hospital as black as a lum!'

Less than two minutes later, also having trekked the full mile-and-a-half unaided from the Advanced Fresh Air Base to the Bank dook, and then up to the pit-head in the hutches, Andrew McDicken was similarly amused to find himself being wrapped up in a blanket, before being despatched to hospital. As the two old pals sat shivering in the ambulance, their cranial activity soon burst from involuntary hibernation into action once more.

For Matt, the words and whistles of Wallace Anderson's 'If I were a Blackbird' began ringing wonderfully in his ears.

For Andrew, there was only one thing that mattered. He leant forward and tapped the ambulance driver on the shoulder.

'How you doin', pal? I don't suppose you ken whae The Glens are playin' on Setturday, dae you?'

SUNDAY, 10 SEPTEMBER

12.05 a.m.

Having drawn the proverbial short straw, the last three trapped miners were eventually kitted out and sent on their way at 11.45p.m. on the Saturday evening.

Rab Anderson, Geordie Houston and Archie Crate were chaperoned on their perilous journey by the Coatbridge Rescue Brigade itself, a group of unbelievably courageous men who had overseen the entire rescue operation from start to finish, and whose job was now done. When, finally, the three miners had been passed along the human chain of brigade men invisible underneath their dazzling cap-lamps, before finding themselves stumbling into Bank Six's Advanced Fresh Air Base with bursting lungs, Saturday night had become Sunday morning.

The entombed miners were free, every last one of them. Soon they would all be home in the loving arms of the wives, children, parents and siblings that they thought they would never see again.

Up on the surface and having been given a thorough medical examination by Doctor Edgar, Oversman Andy Houston was now sitting in Knockshinnoch Castle's makeshift HQ, fighting off the leaden veils of sleep that were trying their best to drown out his consciousness. The men in the West Mine had been saved, all 116 of them, and now the focus had to switch to the awful plight of the thirteen 'missing' others who had been engulfed underneath the enormous inrush of muck when Wilson's field had suddenly collapsed into their workplace, the dreaded Number Five Heading.

The former war hero and proud professional that was Andy Houston would do his damnedest to help the big chiefs locate the missing men, but he just instinctively knew in his heart of hearts that they were hopelessly doomed, his own brother Jim included. Houston's eyelids felt like anvils as he wiped away the tears. Tonight in the village of New Cumnock, there would be much celebration for many families. For the others, the nightmare would continue.

Meanwhile down in Knockshinnoch's West Mine, silence ruled supreme. David Park was all alone now. Checking for the umpteenth time that every single name in Andy 'Doch' McKnight's little blue notebook had been scored off, he closed it and stuffed it into his jacket pocket. Another quick search of all the adjoining roadways in the vicinity of the West Mine telephone station, and Park's work was done. He wound the handle on the telephone. Halliday answered.

'Dave?'

'That's it, Willie. See you in about an hour.'

The Pit Manager pulled his watch from his waistcoat pocket, and noted that it was now 12.22 a.m.

The Depute Labour Director of the mighty National Coal Board took one long last look around. He could still hear the voices of his troubled neebors, as their long-gone echoes battled the deafening silence. He walked over to Walls Walker's diesel loco and switched off the lights.

David Park reached the surface at 1.18 p.m.

1.35 a.m.

With all the Knockshinnoch miners now safely on the surface, Kilmarnock Mines Rescue Station Superintendent Willie Dick had one final, but very important job still to do.

Get every last brigade man and volunteer out of Bank Number Six Mine, and right now. They had all performed a feat of gargantuan proportions, a miracle by any other name, but it was now time to get their backsides out of that gas-infested mine before a tiny spark from a solitary pit boot blew the whole damned place to hell and back.

The task of closing down the extractor fans and sealing off the pit bottom fell to the hard-pressed Whitehill Rescue Brigade. And that was when Brigade Captain Willie Jolly took his final call on the temporary telephone in Bank Six. It came from one of the Coal Board suits in the Bank Auld Pit office above.

'Captain Jolly, would you and your men now please go back through to the Knockshinnoch side and salvage as much equipment as possible? There will be unused stretchers, spare cap lamps and medical supplies lying around. Just gather up as much as you can.'

By this time, Jolly, a man of great discipline who always unfailingly respected orders from above and expected his own to be followed to the letter by those below, had now 'had it'. For a split second, he imagined the suit in the office above sharing a wee celebratory dram with the other Coal Board bigwigs, the very people whose inaction and ineptitude had caused the disaster in the first place.

Willie Jolly gave his response. It consisted of two short words, the second of which was 'off'.

EPILOGUE

Rescue Mission Complete

By half past three on the morning of Sunday 10 September, every single person had been evacuated from the depths of Knockshinnoch Castle Colliery's West Mine and Bank Number Six Mine. For almost three days, this incredible drama had held the world's attention in the palm of its hand. Now, the greatest mining rescue in history was complete.

The Long Drive Home

A great many heroes had emerged from modest obscurity during that auspicious weekend, a resounding tribute to the fortitude of working class communities in times of great need. Among them were five young Salvation Army officers from the Ayrshire coastal town of Saltcoats, who had performed a quite magnificent role on the Bank pit-head, ever since disaster struck right through to the joyous conclusion of the rescue operation. Standing there in their 'Army' uniforms in the lashing rain for days and hours on end, they had plied hundreds of rescue brigade men and volunteers with never-ending supplies of vital sustenance and compassionate encouragement. No one involved in the operation had anything other than the highest praise for those superb foot soldiers of the Salvation Army.

As the five exhausted youngsters headed homewards in their black Morris Minor motor car around four o'clock on the morning of Sunday 10 September, their excited conversations on a job well done had already succumbed to the heavy veils of richly-deserved sleep. Apart, of course, from Arthur Morris at the steering wheel, and his fiancée Iris Wyllie, to whom he would be married in a few months' time. As the two lovebirds chatted happily to each other, a pair of bright headlights appeared from around the bend. A moment later, the Morris Minor and the approaching lorry exploded head-on into one another. Arthur was killed instantly, and his beloved Iris would pass away in Kilmarnock Infirmary later that same day. Their three colleagues in the rear seats also suffered terrible injuries, one of whom, George Angus, would die in the same hospital six weeks later. Even today, the surviving witnesses of the Knockshinnoch disaster still mourn the tragic passing of those wonderful young people.

The Search for the 'Thirteen Missing Men'

At 7.00 a.m. on Sunday 10 September, General Manager David McCardel convened yet another meeting, this one attended by senior representatives of all relevant parties and authorities, to discuss the plight of the thirteen missing men in Number Five Heading. After a relatively short discussion, it was agreed that the men were now completely unreachable from both Knockshinnoch's main shaft and Bank Six Mine's 'escape route' through the coal barrier.

There was only one remaining possible way of reaching the thirteen miners, and even this was an outrageously long shot. In essence, it involved sending a party of experienced miners down into the crater itself, an exceptionally dangerous procedure. The thinking was that it might just be possible to get far enough down inside the crater to locate an open road on the 'rise' side of the heading, which could possibly provide access to the inbye workings of the South Boig District, from where a search could then be made for the men. It would be a procedure fraught with peril and extremely unlikely to succeed, but it was now the missing miners' very last hope.

At 7.00p.m. on the Sunday evening, two teams of courageous men, the first led by Knockshinnoch's Under-Manager Ben Kennedy, set out to descend the crater in Wilson's field, in the full knowledge that they might get sucked in by the still-advancing sludge, never again to return. Bound together by rope, the men began climbing down into the crater towards the black void of Number Five Heading, acutely aware that the heading's roof supports had been blasted away by the inrush. As they 'abseiled' down into the blackness, their pit boots slithered on the slippery sides of the crater, while the peat above them constantly cracked and crumbled in the pouring rain, great lumps of the stuff crashing down from the fields above into the chasm below before cascading uncontrollably down the vicious one-in-two slope of the heading itself. Almost unbelievably, Kennedy and his troops managed to descend to a depth of 800 feet down the vast crater, before hitting an impenetrable wall of sludge and being ordered to return to the surface.

George Sanderson vividly remembers the early morning of Monday 11 September. Standing there with a group of men in yet another torrential downpour, up to their knees in mud on the perimeter of the huge crater in Wilson's field, their instruction had been to dig out as many ditches as possible to divert the surface water away from the crater itself. Suddenly, there was an all-too-familiar shout, this time from one of the big chiefs of Wimpey Limited, the company who had been contracted to shore up the sides of the crater.

'Run, boys! Get out of there! Run for your bloody lives!'

Moments later, another massive section of Wilson's field cracked away and plummeted into the void beneath. That was the cue for David McCardle to reconvene all relevant parties to what would prove to be their final meeting. With great reluctance but very little option, everyone came to the same inescapable conclusion. Further efforts to reach the missing men by descending the crater were now unacceptably dangerous, and in any event futile, and should be abandoned immediately.

On the Monday evening, McCardle found himself with no option but to issue a completely unambiguous but utterly heart-breaking statement.

'We regret having to say that while exploration work will continue as rapidly as possible, no false hopes can now be entertained for the recovery of the thirteen men trapped in Knockshinnoch Castle Colliery. We unite in offering our deepest sympathy to the relatives of the men.'

For the rescue services, the search for the missing men was now over. However, for the men's own loved ones, their anguish would continue until all thirteen bodies had been recovered. Tragically, closure would be a very long time coming.

Messages From Around the World

Over the coming days, messages arrived thick and fast in the offices of the National Coal Board, while others plopped through many individuals' own letterboxes. Some expressed sincere condolence for the tragic loss of lives, while others were of congratulation for a brilliantly conceived and courageously executed rescue operation.

King George VI himself sent a formal telegram to the Coal Board, then followed it up with a much more personal letter of comfort for the bereaved families. Prime Minister Clement Attlee also sent his own personal letter, highlighting the skill and devotion of the rescue brigades. Telegrams were received from many other coalmining communities, including one from the Mayor of Barnsley and another from the West German Mining Congress in Essen. A telegram of condolence and support came all the way from the Mayor of Saint-Valery-en-Caux in the Normandy region of northern France, where the 51st Highland Division had been stationed for almost four years during the

Second World War, and whose community still felt a continuing strong bond with the Scots. David McCardel, the Coal Board's Area General Manager who had played such a prominent coordinating role on the pit-head during the rescue operation, wrote a personal letter to Charles Fleming, the Manager of New Cumnock's Commercial Bank, to thank him for the wonderful role he had performed in overseeing the huge telephone communications operation for almost 72 hours non-stop. Even one 'Mistress Maureen Ferguson from Stow on the Wold', a dear old lady with no apparent links to the village of New Cumnock, felt the need to write a letter of condolence to the bereaved families together with her generous donation of five pounds sterling.

Over the days and weeks ahead, the Coal Board, the New Cumnock community and the affected families would find themselves inundated by heartfelt messages of support from all over the country and much further afield. Perhaps this was hardly surprising, considering that the Knockshinnoch disaster had been covered continuously in great forensic detail by every television and radio station in the developed world, and by all respected newspapers across the globe, including the *New York Times* and the *Washington Post*.

The Knockshinnoch Colliery Disaster Fund was set up to provide financial support to the families of those who had perished, as well as some kind of modest recompense to those miners who had been rescued, many of whom would never again be able to force themselves to work underground. The local 'junior' football authorities got together to stage a fundraising exhibition match at the home ground of Ardeer Recreation in north Ayrshire. Even the Scotch Whisky Association got in on the act by donating 144 (one gross) bottles of whisky to the rescued miners and members of the rescue brigades, although folklore suggests that very few actually reached their rightful destination.

Public Recognition

Several individuals were publicly commended at national level for the role they had played during both the disaster and the ensuing rescue operation. They included the Coal Board's Depute Director of Labour, David Park, and Knockshinnoch Oversman, Andrew Houston, both of whom were awarded the George Cross, our country's highest civil decoration, granted in recognition of 'acts of the greatest heroism or of the most conspicuous courage in circumstances of extreme danger'. Andrew Cunningham, also known as 'Handy

Andy' and Knockshinnoch's modest Conveyor Shifter, was awarded the King's Commendation for 'brave conduct'.

A Holiday by the Sea

Just over a month after the disaster, every one of the 116 survivors received a rather pleasant surprise in the shape of an envelope arriving through their letterbox. It bore the name, 'Butlins Holiday Camp'. The letter was from none other than Billy Butlin himself, the South African-born entrepreneur who had built up an iconic nationwide chain of seaside holiday resorts across the length and breadth of Great Britain. And here he now was inviting all of the disaster survivors to enjoy a free holiday at the local Butlins camp, situated just outside the coastal resort of Ayr. Most of the miners jumped at the chance, since a holiday was a luxury that few could ever afford from their seven quid a week pay packets. Some however, did not. Willie Lopez, for example, felt that his place was with his wife Jessie, who was mourning the loss of her dad, Bill Lee, the poor man still buried somewhere beneath 'the daisies'.

And so in mid-October, it was the single guys who jumped onto Sanny McKechnie's double-decker bus and made their way to Butlins, for a few days and nights 'on the tiles'.

'It was great, it really was!' recalled Sam McCracken. 'We had a terrific time, and we got the whole thing for free. We really let our hair down that weekend!'

Next, went the married men with their wives and bairns, to occupy Butlins' famous wooden chalets and paint the 'town' red, helped considerably by a complementary babysitting service.

'That wee holiday was just what we needed,' May Robertson smiled. 'Just for us to get away together was great, and for John especially it was a huge relief.'

A man of few words, Jock McMurdo summed up the whole experience in his own inimitable style. 'I'll tell you this. We let off a lot of steam that weekend!'

And so a great time was had by all, except of course the distraught families and friends of the 'missing thirteen'. However, for those who had thoroughly enjoyed a well-earned blow-out on the shores of the Firth of Clyde, another huge challenge lay just around the corner. Just how would they cope with the aftermath of Knockshinnoch, and the pernicious psychological effect that their horrific experience would have on the rest of their lives?

The Clean-Up Operation

After an enforced lay-off of some two months, many of the survivors of the disaster ended up returning to Knockshinnoch, given the lack of alternative employment opportunities in the area. All who did were immediately deployed on the massive clean-up operation that would be required to shift the enormous quantities of sludge before coal production could resume. In the event, the clean-up would take the best part of a year to complete. As for the others, they simply found themselves physically and psychologically incapable of stepping back into a pit cage. Not now, and not ever again.

Matt Sanderson recalled the gruelling days of the salvage operation:

> 'I would be off work for about six or eight weeks. When I started back down Knockshinnoch, I was filling peat into hutches, getting the pit cleaned up for production. I started at the end of the roadway beyond the top of the North Rising Mine, where it dips down to the Black Band Mine. The sludge had reached to within 100 feet of this mine. This confirmed earlier views that there could be no open road beyond the North Rising Mine.'

Bob Dickson's job was even less appealing, since he was despatched to clear out the deep, narrow manholes at the sides of the main locomotive rail track that ran along the West Mine Turn. The manholes had been put in position to allow workers to jump down into safety whenever the giant loco came thundering along the track.

'I hated the pit cage,' said Bob, fighting off another dreadful fit of coughing brought about by the miners' curse, the horrific lung disease that is *pneumoconiosis*. 'Absolutely hated it. I just didn't like the idea of my life depending on a bloody rope. I was fine at the top, and fine at the pit bottom, but I hated that bloody cage. So it was very hard for me to go back down Knockshinnoch. One day during the salvage operation, I found something down one of the manholes that I'll never forget, It was a coo's heid! Now you don't expect to go to your work and find a coo's heid, do you?'

'Every time we got rid of some of the sludge, it just came seeping back in again,' said Sam McCracken. 'It was unbelievable how much of the stuff there was. Eventually we had to put up a big solid steel gate to stop it flooding the whole length of the West Mine.'

On his first day back, Rab Cockburn had made up his mind that he would have a go at getting himself back into the cage. However, during a brief interview with one of the new Coal Board bosses, Rab surprised even himself by completely losing the rag and shouting, 'I'm never going back doon there again!' By 'there', what Rab had been referring to was Knockshinnoch itself, because he simply could not face returning to his former tomb. However, since his father had earlier been killed in nearby Model Colliery, Rab knew he had no alternative but to continue working to support his mother, so he requested a transfer to the Bank Auld Pit where he would work until it closed many years later.

For those who could never again face the ordeal of going back underground, the search would go on for jobs on terra firma, any jobs at all. By way of example, Jock McMurdo found employment labouring on the railways for a while, this followed by a factory assembly-line job, before he eventually picked up a much more interesting position as a laboratory technician in the Coal Board's Lugar office, analysing samples of coal dust from the various pits and mines of the locale. Perhaps it was just as well he wasn't told at the time that his new job would eventually require him to go back underground to collect the samples for himself, a matter which was to cause him considerable anxiety every time he stepped into the man-riding haulage, or worse still, the dreaded cage.

Getting the Story Right

One morning in early November 1950, a message was sent for engineer Tom 'Toe' Melvin to come to the main office in Knockshinnoch's Colliery Square. There he was greeted by a middle-aged official dressed in a smart suit, who proceeded to take him to a waiting car. The official drove the engineer over the 12 undulating hilly miles to the Coal Board's Dunaskin offices, where he ushered him into a room on the ground floor. To Melvin's surprise, another five 'suits' were already sitting around the big table in the middle of the room.

'Take a seat, Mister Melvin!'

The invitation came from a rather rotund little man with an equally rotund little face. Melvin had no idea who his host was, nor indeed any of the others in the room for that matter. All he knew was that they were Coal Board 'high-heid-yins', and quickly clocked that this was a very strange situation indeed and that he'd better be on his guard.

The little man with the Alfred Hitchcock features continued.

'As you know, Mister Melvin, the Public Inquiry into the Knockshinnoch disaster starts next week and you, of course, have been called as one of the witnesses. So we just thought it would be a good idea for us to meet, so that we could all compare notes. Get our stories right, if you like. Do you understand, Mister Melvin?'

Toe Melvin took a sharp intake of breath. He looked around the table at each of the five men's faces. They all looked rather nervy and anxious. Melvin himself felt no nervousness or anxiety, only simmering rage.

'I'll no' be tellin' any bloody story!' he snapped. 'I'll be tellin' the truth. An' I'll be tellin' it the way it happened. I saw things for mysel' that mornin', and I telt them there was goin' tae be a serious accident doon that place. And that's whit I'll be sayin' at the inquiry. I'm no' for playin' any o' your wee bloody games. I'll be tellin' the truth!'

Five minutes later, Toe Melvin found himself standing at a bus stop in the pouring rain, having been shown the door and told to make his own way back to work. He looked at his pocket watch, and cursed that it was only 10.05 a.m. The next bus was the eleven o'clock single-decker service to New Cumnock, which would drop him off at Knockshinnoch just before noon, no doubt soaked to the backside.

'They'll probably dock three hours off my pay now,' Melvin muttered angrily under his breath.

It was three hours' pay that the engineer and his family could ill afford to lose, but at least he would be able to hold his head up high. A lot more than could be said for the odious cowards he had just left.

The Public Inquiry

The official report of the inquiry, which was conducted in public over several days (7 – 10 and 13 – 16 November, 1950) in Ayr County Council's Council Chambers, was published on 2 March 1951. Presented by the Right Honourable Philip Noel Baker MP, Minister of Fuel and Power, it was Sir Andrew Bryan, His Majesty's Chief Inspector of Mines who produced his *Report on the Causes of, and Circumstances Attending, the Accident which occurred at Knockshinnoch Castle Colliery, Ayrshire, on the 7th September, 1950.*

Bryan's report was published at two shillings and sixpence per copy. In my many interviews with surviving witnesses of the disaster, I was particularly struck by the fact that hardly a single household was without a copy of the little blue-covered report, even 65 years on. Without a question of a doubt, the New Cumnock community had been expecting justice from the inquiry. Whether they would ever receive that justice I will leave for you, the reader, to decide for yourself.

A total of 55 witnesses were summoned to the Public Inquiry, after which Bryan was able to draw a number of conclusions, and make several recommendations which would have an enormous influence on the safety of coalmining practices in the years ahead.

I would like to stress that the following is <u>my own personal interpretation</u> of the inquiry's main findings, nothing more and nothing less.

The cause of the Knockshinnoch Disaster was a massive inrush of both liquid and solid materials from the surface ('Wilson's field') into the face of Number Five Heading in the colliery's South Boig District. The heading had recently been driven to the bottom of a large hollow – or 'land basin' - which had been eroded away over many millions of years. This hollow was 44 feet deep, and consisted almost entirely of semi-liquid mud, resting on a shallow bed of boulder-sand and gravel, and covered by a twelve foot deep deposit of mainly waterlogged peat, the top two feet of which were fairly solid. It was Fireman Dan Strachan's now infamous 'shot' on 30 August 1950, fired into the breast coal in blissful innocence, that kick-started the catastrophic sequence of events which would lead to disaster. Firstly, the shot blew through the bed of sand and gravel at the foot of the land basin, causing surface water to start flowing down into the heading. Several days of extreme rainfall then had the effect of tripling the flow of surface water into the heading, which washed away the loose debris underneath a pair of wooden 'chocks' that had been put in place to support the roof. This water flow eventually caused the chocks to collapse, and resulted in a roof fall, slight at first, but quickly extending and weakening the coal face adjoining the base of the land basin. Finally, the bed of boulder-sand and gravel at the foot of the basin completely gave way, and the overhead lake of mud rushed down into the heading, followed by the top layers of waterlogged and solid peat. The inrush was absolutely colossal in volume and its unstoppable momentum as it rushed down the steep incline of the heading caused it to fill up many miles of underground roadways, resulting in the tragic loss of thirteen lives and the blocking-off of all possible means of escape for 116 others.

Two catastrophic human errors led to disaster. Firstly, senior managers should have been aware of the presence of either moss or peat in Wilson's field, the epicentre of the inrush. Secondly, they should have known that Number Five Heading had already been driven much closer to the surface (a mere 45 feet) than earlier forecasts had predicted (196 feet). Had those responsible realised the precarious nature of the conditions above and below ground, then Dan Strachan would surely have been instructed not to fire his fateful shot. Not only that, but the thirteen miners toiling away in the sodden squalor of Number Five Heading would almost certainly have been withdrawn from that area of the pit, and lived to tell the tale.

A large proportion of the inquiry's attention was focused on the definitions, characteristics and relationship between 'moss' and 'peat'. To fully comprehend the importance of this matter, I sought the professional advice of a leading national and international authority on 'hydrogeology', which includes the study of water resources and water pollution in coal mines. Please permit me to paraphrase from the advice I received.

The type of peat we have in Scotland is almost entirely formed by accumulation of 'sphagnum moss'. As such, moss is invariably found on top of actively accreting peat-bogs, which are of their very nature waterlogged. In my adviser's own words, 'moss and peat go together like fork and knife'. At the time of the Knockshinnoch disaster, there was a range of regulations in place governing 'working beneath accumulations of water', whether surface waters such as lakes and river beds, ground waters like peat bodies, and old flooded workings. In the case of peat, however, the problem is particularly insidious as it displays something called 'thixotropic behaviour'. This means that the peat appears solid until 'stressed', at which point it tends to liquefy and flow at about the rate and consistency of custard. Most significantly of all, breaking into a peat bog from below would certainly provide sufficient stress to liquefy it.

Therefore – and again this is my own personal interpretation – the surface moss should have been clearly visible to the naked eyes of planners and surveyors alike, indicating the near-certainty that the men in Number Five Heading were working underneath a peat-bog. And so when Strachan's shot kick-started the calamitous chain of events, the peat immediately stressed and liquefied, combining with the mud underneath to form the enormous inrush of 'sludge' which then collapsed down the heading, filling up mile-upon-mile of underground roadways.

So why, then, wasn't the presence of moss or peat in Wilson's field detected and reported? Well, for two reasons, basically.

Firstly, and most peculiarly, not one of the Coal Board's managers, planners or surveyors ever noticed the presence of moss on the surface of the field, despite the fact that at least two of them had considerable previous experience of working in such conditions. In short, at no time had a proper examination been made of the nature and constituency of the ground in the field. Secondly, and despite the fact that this peat deposit had been clearly marked by the appropriate 'symbol' on the master geological survey map of the area, that symbol had clearly been overlooked.

In the event, the inquiry drew two pretty damning conclusions. Firstly, there had been a contravention of 'Regulation 29 of the General Regulations, 1920 (Working under Moss, etc. – Precautions)', since Number Five Heading had been worked 'under a deposit of peat with a depth of cover of less than 60 feet or ten times the thickness of the seam, without taking the precautions required by the Regulation'. Secondly, there was 'a weakness in organisation in that insufficient arrangements were made to ensure that the planning engineers were kept adequately informed of the subsequent changes disclosed by the progress of the workings in the No. 5 Heading Section to enable them to check the accuracy of the forecasts in the development plan, made in April, 1950, for that district of the mine'.

To me, though, and as a former bureaucrat myself, one of Sir Andrew Bryan's most telling comments concerned the rapidly-changing nature of management in the coalmining industry, as the mighty National Coal Board continued to grow arms and legs. Referring to a set of recommendations spelled out by the 1938 Royal Commission on Safety in Coal Mines, he opined, 'Since these recommendations were made, the industry has been nationalised, and the number of officials between the owner and manager of a mine has been greatly increased. The precise definition of the duties of all these intermediaries is a matter of very great difficulty'.

Another of Bryan's most important conclusions was in relation to the decision of the rescue brigades to deploy *Salvus* breathing apparatus, and in the most trying of circumstances where the law did not make provision for its use. He readily acknowledged the awful dilemma that the decision-makers had faced, but concluded that their decision to deploy *Salvus* was 'not only triumphantly justified by the results, but it was right in principle.... There are many statutory requirements drawn in strict and absolute terms, full compliance with which in times of emergency would seriously hinder the saving of life…. The safety code is for the normal working operation of the mines, and it cannot be observed in all respects in these crises: risks are inevitable, and in some respects "necessity knows no law". In my opinion, it is best left at that.'

His Majesty's Chief Inspector of Mines had himself deployed a rare quality in coming to his conclusion that the use of *Salvus* had been the correct one, in that the end justified the means. That quality was common sense.

The Trial

In October 1951, more than a year after the disaster, the trials took place in Ayr Sheriff Court of four Coal Board officials. They were John Bone, Colliery Agent; William Carlyle Halliday, Manager of Knockshinnoch Colliery; Alexander Gardner, Sub-Area Planning Engineer; and Alexander McNab Stewart, Sub-Area Production Manager. In the event, all four were found not guilty of the charges against them, a verdict that was received with mixed emotions by the New Cumnock community. After all, surely someone had to pay the price of having allowed this catastrophe to occur in the first place, one in which thirteen miners had tragically perished? There again, the same four individuals had each played a huge part in the magnificent rescue mission which had saved the lives of 116 others.

The bottom line was that what had begun as a tragic disaster of epic proportions had rapidly metamorphosed into a brilliantly executed and highly successful rescue mission. In the view of many surviving witnesses, it was that which saved the bosses' bacon

Recovering the Bodies

It had taken four full months of the massive clean-up operation before the roadways of Knockshinnoch were finally safe enough for groups of experienced miners to begin their gruesome search for the thirteen missing men. Only when the bodies had been recovered and laid to rest in Afton Cemetery could the distraught families begin the grieving process and hope to find closure to this whole tragic affair.

The first three bodies were discovered on 20 January 1951, directly underneath the locus of the inrush, Wilson's field, where the men had almost certainly perished instantly. Bill Lee, Sam Rowan and John Smith would have stood absolutely no chance when the field caved in, none at all. As Bill himself had predicted, they had simply been far too close to 'the daisies'. The following day, John Taylor's body was found only a few yards away in the next 'stoop' to his three 'neebors'. Two days later, those of Willie McFarlane, Tom Houston and Jimmy Houston (Oversman Andy Houston's brother) were recovered yet another stoop further in.

Then on 29 January, the rescue parties were to make a particularly upsetting discovery. That was when the corpses of big Johnny Dalziel and his great pal, William 'Paley' Howat were found lying at the end of the South Boig District's Number 21 Heading. They had walked an incredible 2,100 feet away from their work locations, and both chins were sporting bushy beards. Clearly, they had survived for many days, and gone on a tragic walkabout in futile search of food, water and escape from their tomb, before finally succumbing to their inevitable demise.

Matt Sanderson was a member of the stretcher party sent in to recover their bodies:

'John Dalziel and William Howat had survived the inrush, but were cut off when the sludge burst through at the South Boig road-end. Messages written in chalk had been seen by the salvage parties [one member of which was Matt's own brother, George] at different locations, indicating that they had been alive for more than a week, and hoping for a friendly shout that never came. [One chalked message, dated Monday 11 September, read, 'more sludge movement, moving further inbye', while another on Friday 15 September simply read, 'still trying'. Eventually, the two great friends lay down together at Number 21 road-end in the South Boig.] We found them lying together with their boots off. That was a very sad day.'

It took almost another two months (30 March) for the salvage teams to recover the body of John McLatchie from where Number Five Heading's belt conveyor had been ripped apart by the inrush. Then on 2 July, Fireman Dan Strachan was discovered several yards inbye from the same belt conveyor, and nine days later Jock White was found lying a few yards still further away. The final body was recovered on 26 July, more than ten months after the disaster had struck. It was that of Jim Love, who was found lying almost directly underneath the crater, and ironically only a few yards away from where Sam Capstick and his exploration party had been forced to turn back from their heroic attempt to find an escape route in the aftermath of the inrush.

During all that time in the aftermath of the disaster, there was one man who would carry the burden of receiving and attending to the bleached-white corpses of those who had tragically perished. He was John Wilson, Knockshinnoch's senior first-aid officer, whose gruesome job it would be to identify the bodies by the serial numbers on their helmets, then scrub off all the bleach and clean up the corpses in order that they could be prepared for burial. On each gruesome occasion, a doctor would examine the corpses, declare them dead and calculate how long each had lived from the length of his beard. In Alex 'Eck' Clapperton's own words, 'John Wilson should have got a medal for the magnificent part he played.'

Whenever a miner's funeral took place at Afton Cemetery, the pit would be brought to a standstill, and all the men on the shift would walk across from the pit-head to the cemetery to pay their last respects.

May Robertson will always remember one funeral in particular, that of big Johnny Dalziel: 'Johnny's funeral was mobbed. My memory of the Salvation Army band playing "Sweeping through the Gates" will live with me forever. It was a very, very sad day.'

Eddie Smith, Captain of the Bank Pit Rescue Brigade, told me just before his sad passing, of the time that the enormity of whole thing finally hit him.

'It was about four months after the disaster, and I had to identify my dad's body. I'll never forget his funeral. The cortege left from our home in The Leggate, and there were hundreds of people lining the streets all the way up to the Afton Cemetery. The family went first, and the miners then fell in behind. That was the most emotional moment for me. All those people. Those wonderful, wonderful people.'

At long last, the 'missing thirteen' had all been laid to rest. For their families, the healing process could finally begin.

The Lessons Learned

The pulsating drama that was the Knockshinnoch disaster had gripped the world's attention for three full days. Now the drama was long gone, leaving behind a trail of shattered lives for some and cautious hope for others. However, the tragic disaster and the inspired rescue mission that followed also bequeathed an important legacy which would significantly improve the safety of coalmining practices in the future. Sir Andrew Bryan's recommendations were numerous and detailed.

Geological survey maps to be kept in the offices of <u>both</u> the pit manager and the surveying/planning department. Much stricter practices to be observed when working under moss or peat. Geologists to be consulted whenever mine workings approach 600 feet from the surface, and clear practices to be enforced including exploratory boring when these reach 150 feet. The width of headings close to the surface to be reduced dramatically. Sets of simple, lightweight self-contained breathing apparatus, requiring minimal instruction, to be kept at central Mines Rescue Stations across the land. Where possible, underground 'escape roadways' to be constructed, linking working areas to adjacent mines. The provision of robust, inrush-resistant telephone lines to be installed in underground working areas. And perhaps most tellingly of all: 'In the National Coal Board operation, the status and responsibility of all Planning Engineers, Planners and Surveyors at all levels should be clearly defined in relation to those of Colliery Agents and Managers'.

From that day onwards, it wouldn't only be necessary to know who was firing the shots, but who was calling them too. Never again in the coalmining industry would there be any hiding place for the men in suits.

And Life Goes On

In all my interviews with the surviving witnesses of the Knockshinnoch disaster, one question above all provided the most elusive answer, and that question was this. How did the disaster affect your life afterwards?

Perhaps not surprisingly, few of the miners would even admit that the experience had harmed them at all, either physically or mentally. Indeed, it was left to the women to talk about the 'softer' aspects of their menfolks' ordeals.

John Robertson would later concede that it took him the best part of a year to return to what he felt was 'normal' again, and insisted that the disaster did not really have any long-term effects on his outlook on life, probably on account of his strong religious faith. His widow May agreed, but added one significant observation.

'To be truthful, John didn't really change all that much after the disaster. However, there was one thing I did notice. Any sudden noise nearly made him jump out of his skin.'

Pit-boy Alex Walker, the youngest of the six 'Pup' Walker boys, wouldn't meet his future wife Isobel until well after the disaster, so she had no way of telling if it actually 'changed' him as such.

'I did notice one thing, though. Every year as the disaster's anniversary approached, Alex would become very withdrawn,' she told me. 'When I asked him what was wrong, he would just say, "Och, it's that time of the year again". He did once tell me that when he returned to the pit after the disaster, he was absolutely terrified to go back into the cage. Maybe that was the reason he later decided to become a rescue brigade man.'

Tragically, young Alex's brother, Archie – another disaster survivor - would be killed in Knockshinnoch a few years later, after being crushed by a falling girder.

Jean McMurdo's experience of life after the disaster proved to be very unsettling:

'The whole thing affected John badly. He became very withdrawn, and a bit "other-wordly" to be honest. He would get up out of bed in the middle of the night, saying "I need to go for a walk". He never spoke about it, and I never pushed him, because I just didn't want to know any more anyway. It was just too terrible. He was never the same again.'

Of the surviving miners themselves, Sam McCracken was the most forthcoming:

'The disaster affected me badly, so much so that I suffered a nervous breakdown. I was on anti-depressants and sleeping pills, and at times I would just sit mumbling away to myself. One day I was so far gone that I couldn't even hammer a nail through the felt on a garden shed roof. Eventually, I learned to live with it. I could tell when the next episode was about to start, and I would say to the wife, "that's it coming on now".'

Author's Footnote

The Knockshinnoch disaster caused the deaths of thirteen fit and healthy men, and I have no doubt that it left indelible mental scars on all 116 others. I will leave you with a direct quote from each of two of the survivors, which are as remarkably similar as they are eerily poignant.

It was Sam McCracken whose last words to me from his Afton Road armchair were, 'you never get over it,' while Rab Cockburn's from his back garden in Pathhead were, 'it never leaves you, son'. Personally, I will always remember the look of great sadness in their eyes when they said these things to me.

Not only did the Knockshinnoch disaster rob many families of a husband, brother, son, grandson or friend, but I am convinced that it also shattered the lives of each and every survivor and his immediate family. However, through the good days and bad days that lay ahead, everyone affected would always have one very formidable ally by their side.

The irrepressible spirit of the wonderful people of New Cumnock.

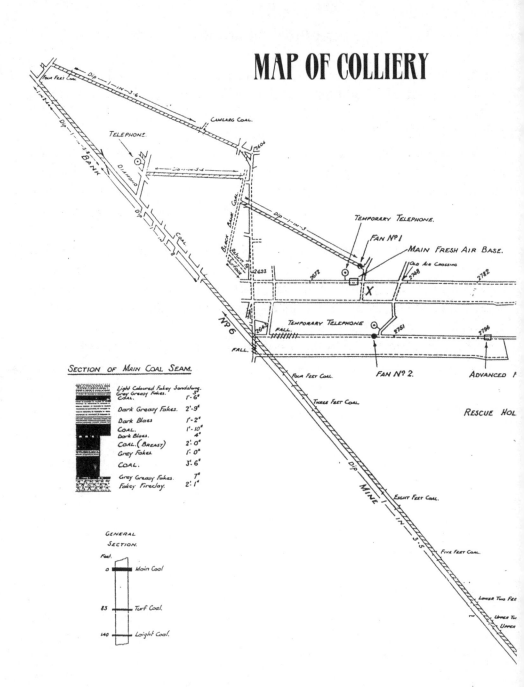

SECTION OF MAIN COAL SEAM.

Light Coloured Fakey Sandstorm.	
Grey Greasy Fakes.	3"
COAL.	1'-6"
Dark Greasy Fakes.	2'-9"
Dark Blaes	1'-2"
COAL.	1'-10"
Dark Blaes.	4"
COAL. (Breast)	2'0"
Grey Fakes	1'0"
COAL.	3'6"
Grey Greasy Fakes.	7"
Fakey Fireclay.	2'1"

GENERAL SECTION.

Feet.

0	Main Coal
83	Turf Coal.
140	Loight Coal.

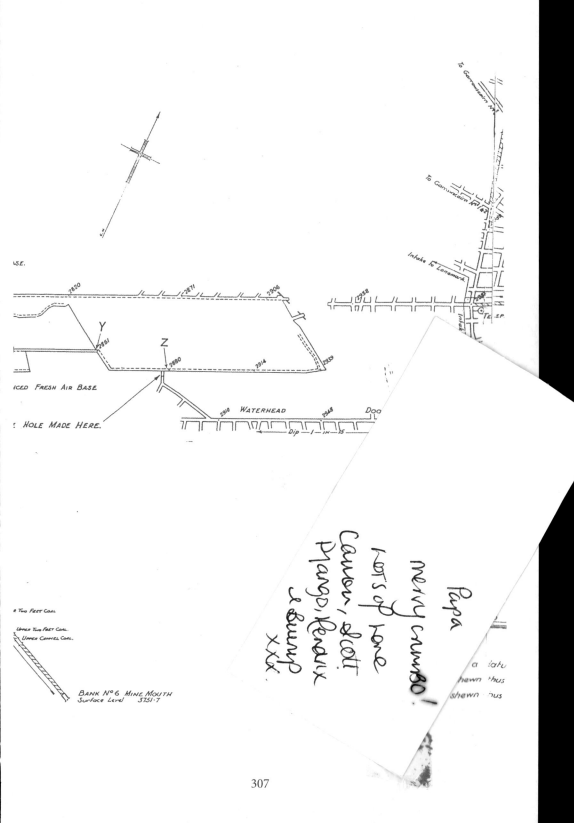

J. DALZIEL
W. HOWAT } 29-1-51

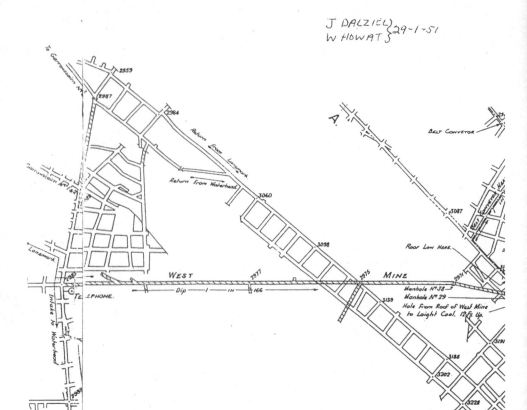

BORE

CASTLE & BANK COLLIERIES.

MAIN COAL WORKINGS.

Scale of Feet.

above a datum 3000 Ft below O.S. Datum.
ial shewn thus   3965 T.
ial shewn thus   3965 L.

308

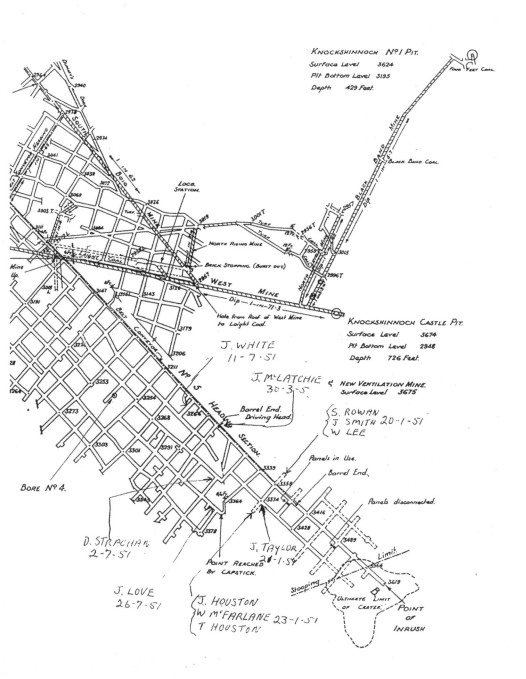

Knockshinnoch No.1 Pit.
Surface Level   3624
Pit Bottom Level 3195
Depth   429 Feet.

Four Feet Coal.

Black Band Coal.

Loco. Station.

North Rising Mine

Brick Stopping. (Burst out)

WEST MINE

Dip – 1–IN–71·3

Hole from Roof of West Mine to Laight Coal.

Knockshinnoch Castle Pit.
Surface Level   3674
Pit Bottom Level   2948
Depth   726 Feet.

J. WHITE
11·7·51

J. McLATCHIE
30·3·5.

New Ventilation Mine.
Surface Level   3675

Barrel End.
Driving Head.

S. ROWAN
J. SMITH 20·1·51
W. LEE

Panels in Use.

Barrel End.

Panels disconnected.

BORE No. 4.

D. STRACHAN
2·7·51

J. TAYLOR
20·1·51

Point Reached By Capstick.

Limit.

Stooping

J. LOVE
26·7·51

J. HOUSTON
W. McFARLANE 23·1·51
T. HOUSTON

Ultimate Limit of Crater.

Point of Inrush

309

THE
KNOCKSHINNOCH CASTLE COLLIERY
SURVIVORS

1. Joseph Adams
2. Robert Anderson
3. Wallace Anderson
4. William Andrews Junior
5. William Andrews Senior
6. William Armstrong
7. Sante Barrera
8. Robert Beattie
9. William Bickerton
10. David Breckenridge
11. Hugh Brown
12. T. Brown
13. Samuel Capstick
14. James (Buffer) Carmichael
15. Juan Carroceda
16. Alex Clapperton
17. Craig Clapperton
18. Robert Clapperton
19. William Clark
20. Robert Cockburn
21. Lachlan Conquhar
22. Robert Coyle
23. Archie Crate
24. Thomas Currie
25. Robert Daubney
26. David Dickson
27. Robert Dickson
28. William Edwards
29. James Ferguson
30. Joseph Ferrans
31. John Fulton
32. William Gray
33. Gibb Grozier
34. James Haddow
35. Charles Hall
36. Alex Hamilton
37. Alex Harrison
38. John Hodge
39. Sam Hood
40. John Horner
41. Andrew Houston
42. Charles Houston
43. James Houston
44. Robert Houston
45. William Hunter
46. William Inglis
47. David Jess
48. James Jess
49. James Jess Junior
50. John Jess
51. James Johnstone
52. Richard Keegans
53. James Kerr
54. Samuel Kilday
55. Archie Kilpatrick
56. James Kilpatrick
57. William Lopez
58. Patrick Loy
59. Robert Loy
60. Gibb McAughtrie
61. Robert McAughtrie
62. James McCann
63. David McColgan
64. Alex McCracken (Pum)
65. Alex McCracken (Nashie)
66. Samuel McCracken
67. Neil McCulloch
68. Andrew McDickens
69. Ronald McDonald
70. John McHarg
71. Andrew McKnight
72. William McKnight
73. Alex McLatchie
74. John McMurdo
75. Alex McNeish
76. Hugh Melvin
77. John Millar
78. George Milligan
79. Hugh Milligan
80. John Montgomery
81. James Montgomery
82. Hugh Munro
83. I. Murdoch
84. David Park
85. William Paton
86. Alex Patterson
87. W. Patterson

88. Robert Pollock
89. James (Speed) Riddell
90. Edward Robertson
91. John Robertson
92. James Robson
93. John Rollie
94. Matt Sanderson
95. Alex Scott
96. James Scott
97. Harrison Shearer

98. William Shearer
99. James C. Smith
100. Thomas Smith
101. Allan Stalker
102. Ian Stevenson
103. Thomas Stewart
104. John Strachan
105. Richard Telfer
106. Allan Thomson
107. Alex Thomson

108. Dan Thomson
109. Alex Walker
110. James (Pud) Walker
111. James Walker
112. Thomas (Pup) Walker
113. Walls Walker
114. James White
115. James Whiteside
116. Robert Wight

IN COMMEMORATION OF THE THIRTEEN MINERS
WHO WERE KILLED IN THE KNOCKSHINNOCH DISASTER

John Laine Dalziel, aged 50, Loader Attendant
James D. Houston, aged 46, Coal Miner
Thomas Goudie Houston, aged 40, Coal Miner
William Howat, aged 61, Switch Attendant
William Lee, aged 48, Coal Miner
James Martin Love, aged 48, Coal Miner
William McFarlane, aged 36, Coal Miner
John Park McLatchie, aged 48, Shotfirer
John Murray (also known as John Taylor), aged 33, Coal Miner
Samuel Wightman Rowan, aged 25, Coal Miner
John Smith, aged 55, Coal Miner
Daniel McFarlane Strachan, aged 38, Fireman
John Irvine White, aged 26, Coal Miner